PAUL GOODWIN is the co-founder of the Scottish Football Supporters Association (est. 2015), an organisation which aims to provide fan representation, support community ownership and lead campaigns and research to improve the state of Scottish football. Since 2010 he has been an authority on developing the concept of football clubs being owned by the community. Paul has featured on BBC *Sports*, *Sky Sports*, *A View from the Terrace*, and in *Nutmeg* and various other sports publications both in the UK and abroad. In his spare time he is the Manager of Kippen FC, a team that he resurrected after it ceased playing in 2018; he also coaches Balfron High School's senior football team.

# Our Game, Our Clubs

A Fans' Guide to Community Ownership

PAUL GOODWIN

**Luath** Press Limited
EDINBURGH
www.luath.co.uk

First published 2025

ISBN: 978-1-913025-71-7

The author's right to be identified as author of this book under the Copyright, Designs and Patents Act 1988 has been asserted.

This book is made of materials from well-managed, FSC®-certified forests and other controlled sources.

Printed and bound by
Ashford Colour Ltd., Gosport

Typeset in 11 point Sabon by
Main Point Books, Edinburgh

Images © Paul Goodwin unless otherwise indicated
Text © Paul Goodwin 2025

# Contents

| | | |
|---|---|---|
| | The Scottish Football Supporters Association | 7 |
| | Acknowledgements | 9 |
| | Foreword by Henry McLeish | 11 |
| | Introduction | 13 |
| 1 | Football's Community Ownership: Our Past is Our Future | 19 |
| 2 | The History of Club Ownership and Different Ownership Structures | 26 |
| 3 | Football Governance – Help or Hindrance? | 41 |
| 4 | Far From These Shores, From Great to Small | 53 |
| 5 | In England's Pleasant Land – the White Knights Come Calling | 73 |
| 6 | In Scotland – Armageddon and All That | 93 |
| 7 | Learning From Mistakes – Following Out of Love | 115 |
| 8 | Fans – 'Who are you?' | 138 |
| 9 | A Wake-up Call at Westminster and Holyrood – the Long and Winding Road | 158 |
| 10 | The Governance Conundrum and the European Super League | 177 |
| 11 | Community Ownership as a Viable Option | 198 |
| 12 | Community Ownership in Scotland – the Inside Story | 227 |
| 13 | Buying a Football Club for Your Community | 259 |
| | The Community Ownership Tool Kit – Things You Need to Win | 285 |
| | Appendix 1: Business Plan | 286 |
| | Appendix 2: Launching Your Campaign | 292 |
| | Appendix 3: Press Release | 296 |
| | Appendix 4: Funding | 298 |
| | Appendix 5: What a Fans' Organisation Needs | 300 |
| | Community Ownership Endnotes | 321 |
| | References | 323 |

# The Scottish Football Supporters Association

THE SFSA PROVIDES a platform for the ordinary Scottish Football Fan to have a say in the running of the game in Scotland. We are a voluntary organisation funded by donations from fans and other interested parties who believe that it is essential that the interests of the key stakeholders are represented and that football clubs and the football authorities are held accountable to those stakeholders. Our organisation is free to join for fans groups and for individuals who have a common aim of ensuring that Scottish football thrives for future generations to enjoy. Our membership is now over 82,000!

WHAT WE DO: We see our role as being split into four key areas which may expand depending on what our members wish us to do in the future.

### 1. Fan Representation
We believe that having a strong vibrant fans movement allows us to act as a focal point for any organisation to hear the views of Scottish football supporters, be it the media, the Scottish Government or national and international football authorities. Whilst we accept that fans views differ on a range of topics we do hope that we can bring a consensus opinion on the subjects that matter.

### 2. Supporting Community Ownership
We believe that our football clubs are best served by having the interests of their community at heart. This means the key stakeholders in the game – the fans – must have their views heard. We believe that the long-term future of our game is best served with football supporters playing an ever increasing role in the management and ownership of their clubs. We have a vast experience of the various models across Europe and we will work with any fans group in Scotland to further the democratic aims and ownership objectives they wish to achieve.

### 3. Campaigns
Orchestrated campaigns have been sadly lacking in Scotland for many years and the football authorities and many clubs have regularly ignored the will

of the paying public when it comes to the implementation of changes in our game. The very fact that there has been no one fans' organisation to unify the supporters has allowed the football authorities to treat the fans with disdain. It is our intention to campaign as a group on key issues that effect not only how the game is currently run but look to exert pressure to get the authorities to take our views into consideration when they make decisions.

## 4. Research

We believe that if we want to improve our game we need to constantly evaluate it and research ways it can improve. Who better to provide the answers than the fans of each of our football clubs. The knowledge, commitment and love that we have for the game has so much value and yet is often dismissed by clubs and those in authority at Hampden Park. Already we have proven our worth by consulting in a Parliamentary survey that looked at gathering fans views on community ownership and in the coming months and years we will ensure that all aspects our game are reviewed and analyse.

PARTNERSHIP OPPORTUNITIES: A truly unique partnership opportunity...

SFSA is a not-for-profit members' organisation that has been created to build long term success for Scottish football by enabling the involvement of thousands of ordinary Scottish football fans in its development. We need strong, committed partners to work with us in delivering the voice of the people – the fans of Scottish Football.

To join SFSA or to enquire about partnership opportunities, please visit https://scottishfsa.org

# Acknowledgements

WRITING ANY TYPE of book requires a team of people behind the person who leads the project who all contribute to making the venture a worthwhile exercise. In this case, the project has been several years in the making and much has changed in the football landscape since the first words were filed away back in 2019. Although I am the voice behind the story there are simply dozens of football fans from a multitude of clubs who have helped contribute to my shared experiences. They are the ordinary fans who have successfully done the heavy lifting to ensure that community ownership of football clubs in Scotland has grown to become a successful part of the football business in our country. I cannot list everyone here but I do hope that through the various chapters you will get an appreciation of just how much I value your contribution to changing Scottish football for the better. This really is your book. Thanks must go to my colleagues around the globe in making sure I got the facts right. For Argentina and Uruguay, Andrea Perilli, a Freelance Journalist; in Germany my friends Jacob Rösler and Dr Jochen Lammert; in Sweden, Urban Stoltz, ex Helsingborg IF player; in Turkey Necati Mete and in England former Portsmouth FC Director and fans' representative Colin Farmery. I also need to thank the notable Scottish Football historian, John Lister who really helped with much of the history and ensuring I got dates and facts correct.

Closer to home there are a few people that I do need to give very specific thanks to, not just for this book but also for having faith in me to help drive the fans' agenda forward. My Co-Founder of the Scottish Football Supporters Association (SFSA) is Simon Barrow who has been with me every step of the way since our launch in 2015 and this is a far better book as a result of his insights and his editing skills. I also need to thank our former First Minister, Henry McLeish, who inspired and mentored me when it felt the whole world was against me as I tried to set up a new fans' organisation. The reward is not just seeing this book in print but seeing the support of the Scottish Government for our Fans Bank, a concept I championed way back in 2015, but also in seeing Dundee University's School of Business Studies partner with the SFSA in 2024 to further develop research and development in football co-operatives. There is no doubt a consensus that community ownership and the opportunities that it brings can further enhance our game in the future.

Over the years there have been many colleagues who have contributed to the SFSA on our board and as volunteers. This has been a magnificent contribution and is a real testament to the positivity of fan power. I thank you all for having faith in me and not believing the narrative that opponents of fan power have disseminated since I started this journey.

I would also like to thank Gavin MacDougall and his team at Luath Press for their expertise and unwavering belief in this book. It is hugely appreciated. Last but certainly not least I have been fortunate enough to have the support of my wife Lynne, son Gregor and daughter Beth who have given me the opportunity to complete this book and to slip away to better weather in La Cala in Spain on a few occasions to get some writing done whilst they work hard at home.

I hope you enjoy the journey.

*Paul G*
*July, 2025*

# Foreword

CLUB OWNERSHIP WITHIN Scottish football has become an issue of outstanding importance, especially to those who are increasingly concerned about the commercialisation of the game and the fans who worry about the financial probity and stability of their clubs. This is at a time when financial transactions and ownership issues are often clouded in secrecy and valuable community and historic assets are at risk.

But now in a timely and authoritative book, Paul Goodwin, the driving force behind the Scottish Football Supporters Association, and an expert on club ownership, has produced a guide, to enable fans to have a greater say in how their clubs are run and to promote fan ownership. This is a must read for fans who might want to become club owners!

This is also a statement about the importance of fans in Scottish football and the opening of a new era, when clubs, representing community, culture and history, not just step forward and provide new opportunities to secure this remarkable heritage but offer fans a bigger part in the future of the game.

Scotland has a special place in the history of the game and a distinguished record of fan and community involvement, but fan ownership could take this to a different level. Clubs are community assets. In his new book the author builds on the idea of community and illustrates how real success can be achieved. Filled with interesting stories, knowledge and insights, this book is easily accessible to football fans, and to future football club owners!

Community ownership has been embraced throughout the world, including in Germany, Sweden and South America. Of particular significance, for a game cloaked in secrecy and obfuscation, is the prospect of supporters becoming stakeholders. A real opportunity for the game to be open, transparent, democratic and above all else, sustainable. Paul Goodwin is a pioneer of this new wave of community ownership with the experience and expertise to inspire those who wish to change our club game.

Having built this expertise in community ownership over the past decade, at home and abroad, the author has been involved with many Scottish clubs in their attempts to foster fan involvement. But this has been a challenge. Battling for the interests of fans has met fierce resistance from the football authorities opposed to giving fans and supporters a greater say in their clubs.

This is also a struggle about a clash of cultures between community and commerce. For far too long, fans and local communities have been locked out of the decisions that impact their clubs. This no longer makes any sense, if it ever did! Paul Goodwin's new book could help change all of this.

Acknowledging this world of accelerating change, the huge expansion of financial and investment interest in the game, the growing concerns of fans and supporters about the loss of cherished ideals and the relentless intrusion of often, 'secretive' financial transactions into who controls the game, this book provides an alternative to the way Scottish football clubs are currently owned and controlled.

*Henry McLeish*

# Introduction

## A Game Like No Other – The Football Community in Action

THIS BOOK IS about how being a football supporter is far from a passive experience, on and off the field. It is (or can be) about the transition from friendship, community, identity and tribal loyalty to a real interest in how your club is run, how the game as a whole is being managed and what difference you can make as an ordinary fan. In short, it is concerned with how you can be involved in 'community ownership' and other ways of shaping the game you and I love. It also looks to explore how the governance of the game needs to adapt to protect our clubs and the communities that they represent, even if that is uncomfortable for many who would prefer the status quo to remain intact.

## Football is in the Bloodstream

Let's start at the beginning. No matter where you travel in the world, there will always be a football connection waiting to be made to smooth your journey along the way. Whether you are on a beach holiday in Spain, safari in South Africa, or are promenading in Blackpool or Fife, you will find that a football blether allows many ordinary folk to communicate more easily. Football is a conversation starter which opens a door, enabling people to get to know one another incredibly quickly. This is because it's much more than a game. To those of us caught in its spell, it's an emotional aspect of your life that you can't hide. Football really does have the power to unite. It has more global followers than all the religions of the world combined. Through the beautiful game, complete strangers can become friends – and friendly rivals.

The fact that football is loved and revered worldwide means that you will rarely be more than ten feet away from another fan in any public space, no matter what you are doing or where you are visiting. With an estimated global audience of 3.5 billion viewers at the World Cup, as a football supporter you will have a lot in common with very many people on this planet through this unique love. What is guaranteed is that no matter where you are there will be someone in your orbit who cares about the game just as much as you do. So, not only is football a kick-starter for getting acquainted quickly, it is also a uniquely fast means for gleaning all kinds of information from your soon-to-be best pal!

Spotting a fellow fan is now easier than ever, with the football shirt a fashion item just as popular as body artwork. It allows other people a ready way to identify where you are from (unless it is one of those clubs with a significant worldwide reach) and it shows a deep love for the football tribe you belong to. In Scotland we know, of course, that even wearing a Celtic or Rangers shirt it is just as likely that these fans are from Falkirk, Dundee, Peterhead or somewhere even more far-flung, given the way that our supporter bases have evolved over the years.

The dominance of the big two clubs from Glasgow over many years has had, and continues to have, an identification not just with winning, but also with being part of a particular religious, political or cultural group. That can be the challenging side of the game. But, as we shall see, even negative energy can be turned into something much more positive.

In many other countries too, fans decide to follow big teams that win all the time, and which constitute exciting, glamorous brands. Seeing lads and lassies wearing Manchester City, Liverpool or Chelsea kits (among the most popular), can of course be deceptive. These clubs aspire to be global signifiers in their own right, often dissociated from a tangible experience of their community of origin. A new worldwide fanbase has been birthed through massive television and online audiences across all the continents of the globe. Indeed, it is now more than likely that English Premiership fans might be from Baltimore, Sydney, Accra or Tokyo, rather than from around the corner! That is the very reason why billionaires, Arab states and dubious business owners aspire to football club ownership – it is all about the brand and the audience it can attract. The power and reach of football can offer them something that no other business acquisition ever can.

## From Local Roots to Larger Horizons

Before the game sold much of its soul to broadcasting, Chelsea fans were from London and Liverpool fans were from Merseyside. Now, as a supporter, it's not that easy to recognise the visible local signs of community, and you would have to work so much harder to make a real connection in that sense. If anything, this book is about renewing those links. It is about how supporters and communities can regain control of a game that they helped bring into being, so that the huge market of football can serve the people who make

## INTRODUCTION

football what it is, rather than the other way around.

But what about me? Where am I coming from in writing about this extraordinary game and how do I see fans getting involved in reshaping it towards a better future? When someone hears my Glaswegian accent on a foreign trip, or even on a simple cross-border train journey, curious fellow supporters often ask what is for them the most obvious question. Are you a Celtic or Rangers supporter? With such limited exposure to the ins and outs of Scottish football, it is a reasonable starting point given the huge followings these clubs have. By some estimates, indeed, over half of those who support a team in Scotland back one of the Glasgow giants.

Just for the record, the answer I usually give varies according to the audience. The polite version veers towards the mantra adopted by my team, Partick Thistle. We are the great Glasgow alternative to the Old Firm. Of course, my own description makes Partick Thistle sound so much more bohemian and interesting than they really are. The important thing for me is that the Jags are part of my family. It's great to know that out there in the big wide world there are people who actually do know a little about my football club, even if it's just their rather exotic name. It is generally a knowledge limited by the level of exposure they have to the Scottish game. But just as I know that the Spireites are Chesterfield FC who play in blue and white stripes, there will be a collective knowledge out there that Thistle are the Jags, play in red and yellow, are the 'wee team' in Glasgow or more recently were trying to make supporter ownership way more complicated than it needed to be. A small piece of football knowledge becomes the starting point for passing time with a new acquaintance, or even finding a friend for life.

What we always discover through these encounters is that, as football supporters, there is ultimately far more that unites us than can ever divide us. Only the colour of our scarves makes us different on a match day. This is something that many outwith the game fail to understand, and which forms the basis for this book. Yes, we all support different teams, but in coming together as fans who love the game as a whole, we can find a common basis for re-asserting that the beautiful game really does belong to us, and that having true supporters and grassroots neighbourhoods involved in running our clubs is vital for its future flourishing, alongside the globalised, media-driven interest that the digital age offers.

So, the starting point on the long journey towards finding out how supporters can win with community ownership is recognising that the unique football tribe we belong to is central to our being, but also knit into a larger fabric (from the league we are in, right up to the overall national governing body). The beginning and end of the journey is always the team, though. This is the DNA that has been woven into the social environment which we have inherited from our family. Many esteemed anthropologists have explored the benefits and difficulties of fan culture and the importance to us of being part of a wider collective. That remains fundamental in all that follows.

## A New Energy for Community Ownership

We all know how a crowd can generate massive energy in the peak moments of a sporting event, driving the athletes or teams we have an emotional investment in to even greater achievement. What we now know is that the collective force which can motivate on-field performance, taking it to a new level, can also have a huge role in involving us in nurturing and shaping the destiny of the club in the widest sense. That means everything that happens off the pitch, as well as on it. The purpose of this book is to give the reader as much background knowledge on how community ownership in football has emerged, what it means, how it is changing the landscape of football forever and why that seismic change can only be good for the health of the game we love. Indeed, it is essential to its flourishing and provides the perfect antidote to the globalisation of the game.

In the chapters that follow, my aim is to take you on a journey. First, we will delve deeper into the unique world of the football community, exploring how the bonds that have been created through sporting experience and love of the game have become an energy that is changing the landscape for future generations. Through a bizarre range of circumstances, I have been involved in many of the purchases, or attempted purchases, by fans across Scotland. I have also been asked to speak about and share those experiences in Ireland, Turkey, Germany, Belgium, Spain and many other places – and of course at more than a few clubs too.

Strange though it may seem, involvement with community ownership has led to me being literally chased around a Premiership boardroom table by an irate club director, working closely with political parties and community organisations as they pushed for the rights of fans to buy clubs, having my identity stolen twice, presenting papers to the Scottish Government, co-founding what you could call a 'fans' union' (the Scottish Football Supporters Association – SFSA), and being told by some senior figures in the governing authorities of the Scottish game that they did not want to have anything to do with me and that they would freeze me out the game because 'clubs are against community ownership'.

It has not been a dull journey for me, and I guarantee that it won't be

## INTRODUCTION

for you either! But I am convinced that we will get there – that fan and community ownership and serious stakeholding will become an essential part of the future of football, enabling it to survive and thrive in ways which would otherwise not be possible. As a Jags fan, I remain, as you can probably tell, an eternal optimist – but one grounded in the hard experience of a battle that has now just come to an end, where three years after we were promised the club, we the fans are now in the driving seat to make that transition finally happen. Somehow it seems appropriate that what I anticipated to be the easiest of clubs to convert to community ownership became the most trying and professionally challenging for me. But more about that later.

My overall hope is that getting some of my own experiences and observations down on paper will not just entertain those who have been on the journey to community ownership, or who have witnessed at least part of it, but may also offer some useful insight for supporters interested in changing the dynamic at the club they love – wherever they live. This is part of a continuing conversation and learning experience. Every situation is different, and there is no single blueprint for success. But there are plenty of guidelines to draw on. You will see that throughout the book I do jump between Scotland and England a fair bit as the football history between the nations has always been closely linked. Of course, we have to recognise that now the gap between the nations grows with every passing day and that spells a new dimension to what the future will hold for clubs on either side of the border. It is not often that Scotland can claim to lead our football friends south of the border but when it comes to community ownership we can certainly justify that claim both in the size and scale of the clubs that have successfully adopted the model here in Caledonia.

I hope you enjoy reading this book and if you have questions or suggestions, do feel free to get in touch.

*Paul Goodwin, July 2025*
*paulgoodwin@scottishfsa.org*

CHAPTER I

# Football's Community Ownership: Our Past is Our Future

*You can have the greatest players in the world playing in the finest stadium but without the fans it means nothing*—Jock Stein

### In the Beginning Is... The Imagination

FOR MOST SUPPORTERS of football clubs there is an almost photographic album of memories that they carry with them throughout their lives. Stored away in the brain's memory banks is a potted history of the club he or she supports, its origins, the date of its formation and other key sepia-tinged historical necessities. These are all essential components of being a real supporter of your club. Such primal images are supplemented by key moments in the history of the club – the early mergers or name changes, the changes in club colours (how dare they!), the early grounds and other significant events. There will be that special time in a given year when European nights under floodlights were special, when a unique derby victory was achieved, when a climb up the divisions to unexpected heights took place, or when a cup triumph was secured against all odds. As Alexander Hope once said, 'Hope springs eternal in the human breast'.

The football gods have ensured that, no matter the size of your club, there will always be something that gives you hope for the forthcoming season. There will of course be a possibility that history can repeat itself, or at the very least that things will be better for you than the season recently ended. All these memories will be logged and noted somewhere, with the appropriate sounds, images and sensations that accompany them. If you are old enough to be from my generation, the smell of pipe smoke, stale beer and strong Bovril being stewed in industrial-sized urns is still within memory reach. More often than not, such collective memories are shared or learned from days gone by, being passed from generation to generation through word of mouth, preserved in a football eternity. These days that special history can be accompanied by a multitude of photos, blogs, vlogs and YouTube clips, immortalising various great moments in your club's history. I recently had the pleasure of being involved in the preservation of some of these beautiful football vignettes with the production of *Back o the Net* which was published in December 2023. If you love football you will enjoy this read: https://luath.co.uk/products/back-o-the-net?_pos=1&_psq=back&_ss=e&_v=1.0

## From Player Power to Committee Power

It would be unusual to find many football fans who have logged away with equal enthusiasm the memory of who has owned the club they love at key times in its history. Yet the ownership of our clubs has had, and continues to have, a major (often determining) say in how our other memories have been shaped, and how they will be shaped in the future.

One theme which we will return to many times in this book is the reality that most supporters tend only to be interested in what happens on the park from 3pm on a Saturday, or whatever time and day the television schedules now dictate. However, deep down most supporters now understand and accept that the health and well-being of their club is driven not just from the terraces, but as much or more by the action or inaction of those who inhabit the boardroom. It has only really been over the past 20 or 30 years that fans have felt the need to get to understand how the board at their club works or in many cases has failed to work. But the separation of those who play the game and those who administer it was not always so, just as the gap between players and spectators has not always been the unbridgeable chasm that we now see at the top of the football pyramid.

In their earliest days, football clubs emerged as small local entities created and run by the players of the beautiful game themselves. They were, in effect, small membership organisations, often with their origins in another larger sporting organisation (many were an athletic or cricket club that expanded), or else something that purposely sprang from the wider local community or the heavy industries of our towns and cities. More often than not it was just an escape from the toil and physical strains of that bleak workplace that created the platform for a club to start up. Football historians document clubs such as Woolwich Arsenal, or our own Third Lanark, emerging from the military ranks, just as the five original clubs in the Burgh of Partick emanated from the shipyards of the west side of the River Clyde. In essence, they were works teams, no different from giants in Germany that survive to this day in the form of Bayer Leverkusen and VW Wolfsburg. Most of the 19th-century clubs that emerged on these islands have a similar story of a working man's game developing from the heavy industries that surrounded each particular local landscape.

As clubs came and went and competed locally to be kings of their own domain, players soon realised that playing and running a football club was much more of a challenge than they had expected. This was particularly so following the transition from playing friendlies and the occasional cup competition, to having a national league fixture to fulfil. In the late 1800s, it was common for people in manufacturing to work nearly 100 hours per week: between ten and 16-hour shifts over six-day working weeks. With such a demanding work schedule and very little leisure time, the more successful clubs quickly started to allow people other than players to get involved in their organisation. Frequently, committees were formed, headed by a key player (usually a club captain, or an original founding player) to make sure everything was going in the right direction. In modern times, the role of club captain is about leadership on the park; in the early days of the game this was a far more significant role with the captain being one of the most important people at the football club, driving it off the park as well as on it. It was so much more than the symbolism of an armband and that early history is key to understanding just what an important leadership role the captaincy was in those early days.

Within a generation of lift-off, football's governing bodies were formed and the structures of clubs simplified to adapt to the new football landscape that was developing. Imagine the idea that the Football Association and the newly formed leagues were run by ordinary folk, dare we say, fans of the clubs! Committees remained in place, but the era of player power diminished to the extent that, within a few decades, future generations of players were virtual serfs to the club system as professionalism swept all before it. This dynamic stayed in place until Jimmy Hill (the former player, referee, coach, manager, players' union representative and TV pundit) inspired a revolution that started a process of re-asserting player recognition and far better financial rewards by ending the 'pay cap' for players. It is hard to believe that it took until the early 1960s for this to happen.

The new situation was one where players started to negotiate in an open market. This was just the beginning of a sequence of events that eventually led to the Bosman ruling in 1995. Driven by the European Union's commitment to freedom of movement, it resulted in seismic change across the football landscape. The reality was the situation arose through the bumblings of the French and Belgian football authorities, who ignored EU rules on freedom of movement in sticking with their archaic rule books. Before the Bosman ruling, a player could not leave at the end of their deal unless the club agreed to let him go on a free transfer, or received an agreed fee from the purchasing club. The joke in Scotland was that, in their heyday, Jim McLean at Dundee United had all his young, talented players on ten-year contracts with sweeties as an incentive, and the odd good behaviour bonus thrown in for good measure. Thanks to the efforts of a journeyman professional from Belgium, Jan Luc Bosman changed all that forever. The football landscape was transformed even in less wealthy countries like Scotland, where players now had control of their own destiny. At the top of the game, it opened the door to untold wealth and riches as it coincided with the significant growth in television revenues.

If we fast forward to the present day, there is much debate about Bosman eventually fuelling the wage bonanza that the superstars enjoy at the top of the game – which can create inflation and financial pressure for everyone else, as well as a crazy economic system at the top and the unbelievable earnings of football agents who syphon money out of the game. There is no doubt that freedom of movement has benefited players, of course. The better the player, the easier it is to add a zero or two onto the value of his contract. However, down the football food chain, this means clubs on the breadline can offer a one-year contract which is hardly helpful for a young professional with a partner, kids and a mortgage to pay.

Overall, the influx of money from the globalisation of television and digital interests has allowed the transfer market to expand to a level that looks completely unsustainable. Fair Play rules are wholly inadequate to deal with this situation. Will there ever be a level playing field? Will there ever be meaningful sanctions on clubs for breaking these rules? Think Rangers in Scotland who paid the ultimate price or the recent Manchester City and Everton charges. The opportunities for wealth creation through football have led to a chasm the size of the San Andreas Faultline between the elite clubs and leagues of world football and everyone else. Ordinary supporters have been side-lined. The European Super League saga is just the first of what is likely to be a concerted campaign by billionaire owners to further restructure the game in the interests of their wallets and sizeable egos. Post COVID-19 some sort of financial realignment is inevitable. But how and on whose terms? Can fan power assert itself positively, as it did in resistance to the so-called Super League concept in April 2021?

How do we build an alternative football economy which gives priority to fans, communities and the whole ecology of local football clubs – not just the branded corporations?

## The Arrival of the Men in Suits

If we think back to the earlier era I have described above, it is amazing that the game developed as well as it did. It is hard to appreciate now that senior clubs like Queen's Park, Partick Thistle and Rangers were competing in the FA Cup in England in an era where transport and technology were at their most basic. It is difficult to imagine how tough it must have been to get these cross-border fixtures to happen, never mind competing across the rest of Scotland. Now every amateur and professional team has its own WhatsApp group, website, Instagram, Facebook page and Twitter (X) feed for communication. Every member of the squad or committee can know much of what is going on in minutes. Late call-offs, player availability, changes to transport and postponements are all much easier to manage with that wonderful device, the mobile phone.

Back in the day, as membership of clubs grew, so did the importance of not just of helping the team on the park but also of building the football community and in the process forging the unique identity of a club. By the late 1880s, many clubs had memberships of several hundred and one of the first to organise itself was a club set up by a Scot from Perth who was instrumental in establishing the Football League in England. The Football League in England, the oldest league in the world, was founded by Aston Villa Football Club at the suggestion of Club Director William McGregor. His initiative was driven by the search for regular competitive football. After discussions with other club directors (of whom very few were initially interested) and after rejections from London area clubs, possibly under the influence of the Football Association, the Football League finally came into being in 1888. It had just 12 founder members.

McGregor not only takes credit for establishing the first league, but he was also the architect of the epoch-making restructuring at his own club. He developed what was to become the forerunner of the Football Board. He created a structure which allowed nine men (yes, men only!) elected by the clubs – 382 ordinary members altogether – to form the very first board. These elected members, or 'fans' as we can also call them, ran all aspects of the club. Similar structures emerged throughout the country. They were the earliest and purest form of community ownership, providing the foundations of governance for all the original clubs. Keeping members (supporters) happy was key to the success of any club, and McGregor proved to be just the man for that job.

Within the first 30 years after football's organised introduction, a pattern emerged across the country. This saw clubs merge and solidify their fan bases, as the popularity of the game continued to grow and competitive football took hold. Those who failed to keep pace or adapt quickly enough folded and became no more than a footnote in football history. The need and desire not only to be the best in the parish, but the best in the city (and of course the country), came with the introduction of league tables and knock-out cup competitions. The professional game as we know it started to emerge as competition on the park intensified. It was inevitable that the clubs with larger memberships would press ahead looking for dominance.

The first challenge for fledgling clubs was to find a ground they could call their own. This took decades for some to achieve. My own club, Partick Thistle, had four grounds around the Partick Burgh area before they eventually settled at Firhill in the northwest of the city in 1909. Others were more fortunate and found a special place they would call home pretty quickly, which allowed them to focus on the park without the constant searching for a home. The challenge all clubs faced was that to fund the purchase of a ground and then build facilities was not just time-consuming, but also very expensive. This was at a time when working men lived, at best, week-to-week and usually had a large family to support. Emerging clubs knew they had to raise money to finance these essential developments, and the natural way to do this was through offering members the opportunity to buy shares.

This was the first major breakaway from the original members' community ownership model which all our early clubs had developed. It is hard to imagine that it would be over 130 years before things would turn full circle, with some of our iconic football clubs moving back towards the earlier model of popular wider ownership. Over the next few chapters, we will explore the reasons why clubs have been listed on the stock market and why community ownership has made a comeback. But, in embarking on that journey, it is crucial to remember that this was the original state of affairs. It is not something 'new' or 'unusual', as opponents (overt and covert) of fans' power like to say. *It is the natural and founding dynamic of the People's Game.*

## Original Community Ownership in Scotland

In 1883 the Scottish Football Association (SFA) had its first review. It was noted that it had 133 live members registered. As such, it was the first record of community ownership of football clubs in Scotland. The situation then was: Aberdeen FC (30 members), Albion Rovers FC (30), Airdrieonians FC (100), Arbroath FC (50), Dumbarton FC (261), Dunfermline Athletic FC (220), East Stirlingshire FC (175), Falkirk FC (115), Hamilton Academicals

FC (100), Heart of Midlothian FC (220), Hibernian FC (200), Kilmarnock FC (100), Morton FC (90), Partick Thistle FC (80), Queen's Park FC (400), Rangers FC (180), Stenhousemuir FC (40) and St Mirren FC (300 members).

Could it be that 20 years from now the SFA will proudly be producing a list of all the clubs that are deemed to be community-owned, alongside the number of owner members each has? That is a future definitely worth working for. What's more, it is entirely possible and that is not something we would have imagined just ten years ago.

CHAPTER 2

# The History of Club Ownership and Different Ownership Structures

*Does football work without spectators? If the people can't come, there is no sense. We will do what we have to do, but I wouldn't like to do it without the people.*—Pep Guardiola talking about playing games behind closed doors during the Coronavirus (COVID-19) outbreak.

## The Early Years – Vested in the Community

AS CLUBS GREW, they needed finance and had to generate income, initially to purchase the land on which to create a home ground. Once they had the land, they needed to build dressing rooms and basic facilities for the increasing crowds. Income from the working man coming through the gate (or, more often than not, standing at a rope), was simply not enough to generate the level of investment required to take the club to the next level. It was a competition, not just on the park but off the park, too. The fortunate thing was that the popularity of the game was growing at a significant pace, so there was a solid economic platform to build on.

In the late 1880s, a significant number of Scottish players started to participate in English football as many of the larger English clubs began making payments to players. This had been made legal in England in 1885, and professional footballers were paid decent salaries for the time. This attracted many Scottish players to move down south to ply their trade. Famously, Sunderland won the league title with a team of Scots. Liverpool FC, founded in 1892, had 11 Scots. Preston North End, with its proximity to the border, was known as virtually being a 'Scotch team' (*sic*) in those early days. With bigger catchment areas and fast-growing fanbases, the early Scottish game was struggling to keep pace with the growth of the game south of the border, where better pay and facilities created an early talent drain from the north. That pipeline of football talent flowed continuously until it peaked in the 1970s. It is now down to a mere trickle, where we can probably name every *Anglo-Scot* plying their trade in the topflight of the game in England.

In Scotland, the game remained (in theory, at least) an amateur one until 1893. It was faced with local challenges for players and supporters and had to change in a way that would create the conditions for building on early successes. The most obvious route to delivering a modern ground, that was fit for purpose, was for the club to generate an income to supplement regular revenue from supporters. This saw the first major change in club structures, when members' clubs became private limited companies. Those from the higher social classes could afford to buy shares and they dominated the share lists of most clubs. Some of the 'ordinary folk' did join together to buy those early shares. This was the first and probably only time that many of their members would have been involved in such a grand business practice. In reality, by accepting the cash, clubs were turning their back on allowing members to have a say about how they were run. The wealthier professional classes gained the position, power and influence that such cash investment could afford them. The working person's influence and involvement in club ownership had peaked. Now he (and it was 'he') had to be content to confine his opinions to the side of the park on a Saturday afternoon.

This major development occurred across Scotland. The experiences of both Rangers and Celtic were fairly typical of the time and are worth referencing. Rangers formally became a limited company on 27 May 1899. The then match secretary, William Wilton, was also appointed the club's first manager. This enabled Ibrox Stadium to be constructed that same year. The club also appointed its first board of directors under the chairmanship of James Henderson. When you consider the club was only formed in 1872, this was quite speedy progress. The fact that they had played at two other grounds before finding the resources to buy and build at Ibrox was fairly typical of most clubs in this era. Finding a home was not an easy task, particularly for city clubs where land was always at a premium.

The origins of Celtic are rather different. It was established by Brother Walfrid, a Maris Brother (religious order) in 1887. It was a community charity for Irish immigrants. The plan was that the club would be based on the Hibernian FC model of community ownership. Such was the 'social enterprise' of the day, long before such terminology became fashionable. However, with the dawn of professionalism fast approaching, the club became a private limited company in 1897, and Willie Maley was appointed as the first 'secretary-manager'. He thus began what turned out to be a long, successful association with the club. Many other clubs were to follow the private limited company structure, of course, but in the first ten years of operation, the number actually decreased from 133 to just 19, as clubs folded, merged or decided to stay with their original sports affiliation.

A positive feature arising from this initial move towards the corporate world was that there was often a very wide spread of low-value shareholders. This meant that in the early years there was almost a democratic feeling about the restructuring that had taken place, and the opportunity to voice an opinion was always available at a club's Annual General Meeting (AGM). These were always very well attended, and they attracted considerable press attention. The private limited company structure served football well throughout the UK, and there were very few major casualties along the way – despite two world wars and the world's biggest financial meltdown to date in the 1930s. Football was far from perfect but it was wedded to the community from where it had sprung and delivered a vibrant, colourful escape for the passionate audience that continued to grow.

By the time we reached the Swinging Sixties there were a few lower league casualties, together with the loss of such iconic clubs as Accrington Stanley (partly seen as iconic by the fate of history and due to its interesting, pub-derived name). In 1962 Stanley were expelled from the league, owing significant sums of money to various creditors as well as to the tax authorities. In 1966, they folded altogether. However, as is often the case, a phoenix club eventually emerged, working its way back into the professional league through the pyramid structure several decades later. Closer to home, the sad demise of one of Glasgow's finest sides, Third Lanark, saw the private limited company structure fail to safeguard the club, known colloquially as 'the Hi-Hi'. Shortly after the first-ever international match between Scotland and England at the West of Scotland Cricket ground in Partick in 1872, several interested spectators from a then world record attendance of 4,000, decided to set up their own football team. The men in question were part of the Third Lanarkshire Rifle Volunteer Regiment. Some had already turned out for nearby Queen's Park earlier that year.

The dawn of 1873 saw the birth of the Scottish Football Association (SFA), with the recently formed Third Lanark becoming one of its founder members. They went on to have a rich and illustrious history, and when they finished third in the top division in 1961, no one could have foreseen that they would be heading for brutal extinction just six years later. It started with an unscrupulous benefactor beginning to buy up tranches of available shares. With an AGM some time away, there was no opportunity to allow minor shareholders to work together to stop the takeover. In fact, it was reported at the time that most of them did not even know what was happening. Instead, like many who would follow him, the new owner arrived and from day one set about maximising the club's assets for his own benefit. All the minority shareholders and board members could do was watch as this implosion happened right under supporters' noses. Even today, football fans from around the world often visit Cathkin Park. It remains a ghost-like symbol of a club betrayed by the greed of an unscrupulous owner, Bill Hiddleston. Like many other clubs that have imploded since, the Hi-Hi are now attempting to rise from the ashes after a long period out of the limelight. Unlike Accrington Stanley, they have started as an amateur team, so the climb to league status will take that much longer unless something dramatic or unexpected happens.

It is easy to focus on such failures (and there have been many) but the success derived from being a limited company far outweighed the negative eventualities. However, such success has not been achieved without some erosion of trust between the ordinary supporter and the club's boardroom. The average club runs financially on a season-by-season basis, and from the turn of the 20th century until recent times boardrooms have generally become a members-only institution, a clique within a club, a place where the only chance of ever getting on the board depended on how many shares you could scoop up, who you already knew, or how filthy rich you were. Football boards were never transparent and were accountable only to themselves, although, in theory, they had a fiduciary duty (enshrined in company law) to care for the business. As we will see later, this ability to operate behind a veil of secrecy led to the demise of some of our most important clubs, whilst we fans had to stand back and watch it happen.

## Keeping it in the Family

Aside from these high-profile cases, the private limited company structure has remained the key vehicle for the majority of Scottish clubs. As we saw from the Third Lanark example, if there is going to be a problem it is not down to the legal framework that surrounds the club. It has more to do with who owns the shares, what their objectives are and how they can use the system to their advantage. In many instances your club could well be in bother if it all boils down to ego, or turning a profit. More on that later!

For many small and middle-sized clubs, there is a huge list of shareholders who have a very small stake in the company. Some of these will date back to the origins of the club and can be traced through family inheritances, since these were traditionally passed from father to son in the days way before women were allowed to be interested in the game. Within these structures, there has also been the opportunity for individual families to take control of clubs – either through the purchase of shares, or through inheritance. This has created many famous dynasties over the years. Many of these have lasted over several generations, while others have been short-lived. The simple test in all of this for supporters is to ask whether the families involved have the energy and finances to support the club, and how they will work with (or ignore) supporters during their tenure. Sadly, more often than not in recent times, it has been far easier to ignore ordinary supporters than to engage with them. The final judgement on any football club board is this: did the owners leave the club in better shape than they found it?

At Clydebank, for example, local car dealers the Steedman brothers took control and they ran a very efficient club. For many a year, the model of rearing young local talent, signed from under the noses of the Old Firm, proved a huge success, as did creating the first all-seater stadium in Scotland. Sadly, the demise of the team as a senior club must be laid at their doorstep, too, because they sold the club and its assets to someone who had no interest in the football club or the community it served. In 2002 we watched on as a land deal saw a club of this stature die a slow and lingering death. It was a painful sight for lovers of football and was an early insight into the football authorities' failure of good governance as they stood by unable or maybe unwilling to do anything about it.

Probably one of the most interesting Scottish football family dynasties was the one to be found at Celtic Park, prior to the arrival of Fergus McCann as the man now lauded for having saved Celtic from the abyss. The mighty Celtic FC of the 1960s and 1970s was in serious turmoil by the 1980s, with no strategy, a board of directors with no new money and, as a result, no plan. Many a newspaper headline of the day had Celtic on a football life support machine. The future looked bleak for these giants, since the two families who held the club's ownership for almost a century had either run out of money or had decided not to invest what money they had in the club. Many commentators of the day described the two families, the Kellys and the Whites at the helm, as running things like a medieval dynasty. The press was not on side either, due to their treatment of the club's greatest-ever manager, Jock Stein, who had many allies in the press and beyond. Not only did the Whites and Kellys seem to run out of money, but they also ran out of goodwill from the fans, who saw no investment either on or off the park. The subsequent arrival of a new, seemingly financially superior plan at their biggest rivals, Rangers, and the hype that surrounded this, did not help either. History would of course correct that impression in the fullness of time.

Only through the dogged perseverance displayed by Fergus McCann, equipped with financial skills and the backing of a strong and united support, did Celtic rid itself of the old dynasty so that it could be restructured in a way that has led to its continued success both on and off the park ever since. It is a shame that McCann did not stay longer as he also made a huge impact in exposing some of the shocking governance standards at the SFA.

The thing about any dynasty is that it cannot live forever, and it will come to a natural end at some point. Another Glasgow institution, Partick Thistle, had four generations of the Reid family (well-known publicans and hoteliers) in charge – until eventually, without too much fanfare, the family sold to another Thistle family, the McMasters. However, even prior to this success story, there was a danger of things going in a very different direction when Ken Bates, then owner and chairman of Chelsea FC, was lined up to take the shareholding, only to be denied full control due to dual interest rules. (See reference to Hibernian and Bournemouth in Chapter 13 to bring this story up to date.) Given that Chelsea went bust just a few years later, the indications were that Partick Thistle had a very close escape at the time.

At the start of 2023, this family dynamic was being played out in Perth where the Brown family, custodians of St Johnstone for two generations, decided to exit the club. With over 30 years of service and the most successful period in the club's history achieved, the next move is crucial for the Brown family legacy. With the club for sale for over a year there was no interest from buyers in Scotland and American lawyer Adam Webb from Atlanta eventually took control. Could it lead to or maybe follow the model for clubs of a similar size such as St Mirren or Motherwell, where fans buy the club over a number of years? Word on the streets is that they have no faith in community ownership being an option.

## The Individual Benefactor

Within the private limited company structure there will always be scope for the sale of shares, or a rights issue which will allow for new shares to be acquired by whoever wants to buy them. When it comes to this scenario, the fate of clubs is so often in the lap of the gods. It really does depend on who turns up at your club with a plan, how badly those in power want to sell, or whether you already have a rich benefactor ready and willing to play ball. In Scotland, we have seen a multitude of these scenarios, some of which will be covered in more detail in subsequent chapters. A simple look at the good the bad and the ugly in recent years will now take us on a journey from the north of the county to the south, via our capital city.

## The Good – Ross County

There is no doubt that Roy MacGregor is Mr Ross County. He has followed the Staggies since 1966 and has used his considerable wealth to promote Dingwall and the Highlands, as well as his favourite team. Since he got involved with the club during the 1991/92 season, he has taken them on a remarkable journey from the lower regions of the Highland League to a cup victory at Hampden Park. He sees part of his role as being wider than just Ross County. The youth academy has not only produced Scotland players, such as Gary Mackay-Steven and Don Cowie, but also feeds a lot of talent to the Highland League teams too. This helps to improve the level of football in the area as a whole. In a recent interview, MacGregor said:

> I need to leave the legacy that I started. This is a Highland club for Highland people. I don't want a millionaire from abroad coming in and destroying the club's fabric. I want what I built to be kept. I can see myself being here in five years' time if that's what is needed.

Those of us who have been privileged to have met him know this to be true. His financial backing keeps the club at the elite level, but without it you would expect the club to be more likely to bounce between Division One and the Championship at best. The question however remains as to the longer-term sustainability of Ross County post-Roy MacGregor.

It has been interesting to see that the now relegated Staggies have continued to outspend even some of the teams in the Premiership as they attempt to bounce back in season 25/26. There is no obvious sign that MacGregor is changing his strategy of strong investment in the playing staff.

## The Bad – Gretna FC

Maybe it was not all bad, but the tenure of Brooks Mileson at Gretna was certainly not dull. A self-made millionaire who took Gretna from the Northern League in England to the Scottish Premier League and a Scottish Cup Final too, he ruffled a lot of feathers on the way. Mileson was the English owner of the now-dissolved professional football club Gretna FC, as well as being something of a philanthropist. He made his money in the world of construction and then in the sale of a specialist insurance business. He only stepped in to buy Gretna when a bid to purchase his local team, Carlisle United, had fallen through. Quite bizarrely, he was an advocate for grassroots football and had already helped over 70 fans' groups and supporters' trusts with donations, prior to taking on the challenge at Gretna.

Why Gretna FC was ever elected to the Scottish league structure in the first place says more about poor judgement and dubious governance in the game at that time than anything else. Brooks Mileson was never conventional, nor was he a typical owner. The success he bought meant he had few allies in the game. He chain-smoked, wore a ponytail and had a fashion sense usually seen in *Miami Vice*. His dislike for wearing a tie did not make him very welcome in many of the blazer-wearing boardrooms across Scotland. If refused entry on those grounds, he was known to just watch games with the travelling support. Usually, he was the one leaving games with a smile, as his team romped through the divisions, defeating all before them while being fuelled by his ambition and, of course, his money.

Gretna's demise was sadly just as swift as its rise, with the maverick benefactor dying suddenly. It left a wee club that was never sustainable, bereft, with no funding and no sugar daddy. The good news is that from the ashes a community-owned club called Gretna 2008 arose. They now play in the Lowland League, which is probably a level at which a club of their size would expect to be able to operate with relative success.

## The Ugly – Hearts Under Romanov

Vladimir Romanov, a Russian-born Lithuanian businessman and former submariner, initially acquired a 19.6 per cent stake at Hearts during the 2004/05 season. After Romanov made financial guarantees around an agreement to stay at Tynecastle, his stake increased to 29.9 per cent, which was welcomed by fan representatives at the time. Romanov eventually increased his majority share in Hearts to 82 per cent by leveraging his Lithuanian bank, Ūkio Bankas, and investment company, UBIG, to fund the purchase. When the global banking and financial crisis hit, his businesses in Lithuania became insolvent. His shares were held by the liquidators of UBIG and were eventually purchased by the Foundation of Hearts thanks to the generosity of Ann Budge. An arrest warrant was issued in his name, requiring him to answer to a number of irregularities in the accounts of both Ūkio Bankas and UBIG.

There are not many positives to take from the Romanov era. From a fans' perspective, winning the Scottish Cup is always nice, and ensuring the club would stay in Gorgie was what they wanted. He also arrived at a time when the rather unpopular concept of a merger with Hibs was one of the alternatives being discussed. Nobody could see the car crash that was to eventually follow. Desperate to survive, Romanov orchestrated a final share offer that took £1 million from fans, weeks before the demise of the club. Alas, he stayed on board to go down with his ship (submarine?) until the subsequent liquidation event. The painful memories for supporters during this period will forever be woven into the history of a club that has now emerged as Scotland and the UK's largest community-owned club.

## 'We Are a Really Big Club' – The PLC Listing Phenomenon

When people think about the major transformation at Tottenham Hotspur, they automatically seem to think of 'Mr Amstrad', *The Apprentice* star, Sir Alan Sugar. However, Sugar was very much a bystander in the process that took Spurs on a significantly different ownership journey. The man who would put Tottenham Hotspur on the map in global financial markets was Irving Scholar, a property tycoon who came to Tottenham with the intention of leasing a box in the West Stand of White Hart Lane, which was due to be rebuilt by 1982. However, Scholar became convinced that the club would get into financial trouble over the rebuilding of the stand and, as a fan with a keen interest in its fortune, he started buying up shares from various shareholders in order to get into the boardroom. As is often the case, there was a rift in the boardroom, and it allowed the astute Scholar to buy up 25 per cent of the club for just £600,000. Together with the help of Paul Bobroff, who had bought 15 per cent of shares from the family of a previous chairman, he ousted the families who had been major shareholders for many years.

In 1984, with Scholar in the chair, he inherited a club in debt to the tune of nearly £5 million. This was the largest debt in English football at the time, but a rights issue following his takeover brought in millions of pounds to clear the decks and, of course, to make him a mighty fortune in the process. As chairman of Spurs, Scholar worked to build a strong business model, as well as floating the club on the London Stock Exchange. In fact, in doing so, Spurs became the first sports club in the world to float on any stock exchange. Scholar played a significant role in the commercialisation of English football clubs, and his activities in these areas would later see him branded a visionary in a 2001 BBC TV documentary called *The Men Who Changed Football*. His next trip along the football road took him to Nottingham Forest, where he failed to have the same impact that he had had at Spurs.

What Scholar had seen in Tottenham was the chance to take a large club and float it on the stock market in a lucrative way. He began a trend that clubs such as Manchester United soon began to follow, having seen the opportunities as a result of the lack of sports stock available in the City. In Scotland, only Rangers and Celtic would have the resources and brand appeal to follow suit.

The ongoing commercialisation of the topflight in England would also lead to the formation of the Premier League, with Scholar one of the prime movers pushing for its formation. Within almost the blink of an eye, the opening up of this valuable market would lead to a completely new type of owner. Being a fan of the club was more often than not incidental to the plan that followed. Now it was all about following the money and a new wave of investors were waiting to pounce.

## The Arrival of the Billionaires

In the initial stages of market floatation, many shares were bought by ordinary fans of the clubs involved. Among other things, supporters were keen on having a share certificate that they could hang on the wall. The share prospectus tended to sell the opportunity to be part of a new future for a club, which would of course rise to new heights and use its newfound wealth to enhance sporting achievement. But to achieve that, clubs needed an endless supply of wealth on tap, rather than a one-off share issue, even if they had to sell their soul to get it. The West End of London was the perfect example.

Founded in 1905, Chelsea was bought in 2003 by Russian billionaire Roman Abramovich, (now disgraced thanks to his relationship to his close friend Vladimir Putin) ushering in the club's current phase of success. He paid Ken Bates £140 million for a club that Bates had bought out of administration for just £1. Manager José Mourinho then led them to two league titles, an FA Cup win and two League Cup wins in three seasons, using the buying power that the new owner brought to the table.

Abramovich is a Russian-Israeli billionaire businessman, investor and political influencer, and having a multimillion-pound pad just around from Stamford Bridge seemed the perfect excuse for a vanity project like Chelsea. At the time, he was the primary owner of the private investment company Millhouse LLC. According to Forbes, Abramovich's net worth was US$12.9 billion in 2019, making him the richest person in Israel, where he lived, the 11th richest in Russia and the 120th richest in the world.

Maybe you can start to see the attraction of owning a football club. Having a few Ferraris or a million-pound yacht is one thing, but owning a topflight soccer club gives your brand or ego massive impact globally every Saturday, and many European midweeks too. Abramovich's arrival seemed to kick-start a stampede of billionaires attracted to the growing worldwide reach of the English Premier League, where games are broadcast globally. The Premier League, working in partnership with independent research agency Nielsen Sports, has compiled and collated broadcast and audience information data from individual markets and the figures are staggering. Research has established that cumulative audiences for live Premier League programming rose 11 per cent to 1.35 billion in season 2018/19, as Manchester City and Liverpool contested a thrilling title race. There was a cumulative global audience of 3.2 billion for all programming between August 2018 and May 2019, an increase of 6 per cent on the previous season. These figures are only for standard in-home viewing and exclude out-of-home and mobile device viewing. By the time the game bounced out of the Covid years the Premier League was the most-watched sports league in the world, broadcast in 212 territories to 643 million homes, with a potential TV audience of 4.7 billion people in 2022.

Growth was driven by new free-to-air coverage in several countries, notably Brazil and South Africa, while there was also a continued increase in live audiences in the UK. The Premier League was shown in a total of 188 of the world's 193 countries recognised by the United Nations. With these figures in mind, it is now not surprising to find that the Premier League has mostly billionaire owners all wanting to showcase what they offer. What that also means is that they have a seat at the top table, one that controls what should be the fans' game. The question is, are they the right people to be involved in football governance? I think we all know the answer to that rhetorical question following the attempt to create a European Super League.

## Billionaire Club Owners Within the English Premier League

PlanetFootball.com have ranked every Premier League owner in terms of their wealth. This really should be a league table of how the Premier League looks at the end of season 2023/24, but as we know money is no guarantee of success as there are many other variables involved to dictate the outcome of competition. If you have five minutes to spare, it is worth reading about some of the wealthiest clubs on the planet and dreaming about what it might be like if big money were to come to your club.

1. Newcastle United FC – Saudi Public Investment Fund, RB Sports & Media, PCP Capital Partners, Saudi Arabia
   Net worth: £489 billion

# THE HISTORY OF CLUB OWNERSHIP & DIFFERENT OWNERSHIP STRUCTURES

2. Manchester City FC – Abu Dhabi United Group, Silver Lake, Abu Dhabi
   Net worth: £17.37 billion
3. Chelsea FC – Todd Boehly, Hansjorg Wyss, Mark Walter
   Net worth: £12.47 billion
4. Arsenal FC – Stan Kroenke
   Net worth: £10.18 billion
5. Aston Villa FC – Wes Edens, Nassef Sawiris
   Net worth: £9.39 billion
6. Liverpool FC – John W Henry, Tom Werner
   Net worth: £7.74 billion
7. Fulham FC – Shahid Khan
   Net worth: £6.24 billion
8. Everton FC – Freidken Group
   Net worth: £6.2 billion
9. West Ham United FC – David Sullivan, Daniel Kretinsky
   Net worth: £5.76 billion
10. Wolverhampton Wanderers FC – Guo Guangchang, Liang Xinjun, Wang Qunbin
    Net worth: £5.45 billion
11. Tottenham Hotspur FC – Joe Lewis, Daniel Levy
    Net worth: £4.58 billion
12. Crystal Palace FC – John Textor, David Blitzer, Josh Harris, Steve Parish
    Net worth: £4.34 billion
13. Manchester United FC – Glazer Family, Sir Jim Ratcliffe
    Net worth: £22.01 billion
14. AFC Bournemouth – William P Foley
    Net worth: £1.26 billion
15. Brighton & Hove Albion FC – Tony Bloom
    Net worth: £1.03 billion
16. Nottingham Forest FC – Evangelos Marinakis
    Net worth: £489 million
17. Brentford FC – Matthew Benham
    Net worth: £220 million
18. Sheffield United FC – Abdullah bin Mosaad Al Saud
    Net worth: £158 million
19. Burnley FC – Alan Pace ALK Capital, Velocity Sports Partners (VSP)
    Net worth: Unknown; estimated £200–300 million
20. Luton Town FC – Luton Town Football Club 2020 Limited
    Net worth: Unknown

This exercise has not been updated since 23/24 season but the ownership and wealth of the two promoted clubs at the 24/25 season has been well quoted in the media. Leeds United – The 49ers Group, net worth £5.2 billion, would be in 10th place in the rich table; and Sunderland – Kyril Louis-Dreyfus, net worth £2 billion, which would put the Black Cats in around 13th place in the table.

In Scotland we do not have 'the billionaire problem', although we do have a few millionaires *in situ* and a growing interest from *investors* from the USA, which is an interesting development. In the recent past, Paul Conway and Chien Lee were joint owners at Barnsley FC as well as having interest in (they owned or part-owned) FC Thun, KV Oostende, AS Nancy Lorraine, Esbjerg fB, FC Den Bosch and FC Kaiserslautern. They were also looking to find a club in Scotland which could be purchased at a very low cost. Partick Thistle were first up before the timely intervention of Lottery Millionaire Colin Weir, but they also looked at Livingston and Dundee before being put off by the SFA rules around multiple ownership that would restrict their holding to under 10 per cent. In 2024 that particular rule was to be amended by the SFA, giving the green light to Bill Foley, owner at AFC Bournemouth, investing in Hibs. It remains to be seen if this rule change has a significant impact on the opportunity for community ownership in Scotland as boards scamper to find investment funds that might take them higher up the league table. What might happen is hard to see as the Scottish Football Association is charged with the health of all football across the nation. In practice, the SFA is held in check by the vested interests of individual clubs and through the influence of the Scottish Professional Football League (SPFL) on its board. This means it is hardly independent or focused on the common good.

Nobody in the early days of football could ever have imagined just how complex the world of governing the sport might eventually become. What we will explore elsewhere is how fixated these organisations have become with the conventional model of having wealthy benefactors running clubs, despite the obvious fact that very few of these *investors* have the integrity of a Roy MacGregor. In fact, this point is very much to the fore in England where the investment from 'foreign' investors throughout the pyramid is something that fans want the Football Regulator for. Recently in parliament Plymouth Argyle's former overseas owners were labelled 'vultures' as the financial crisis that almost drove the club to extinction 14 years ago was highlighted to MPs – just as the Pilgrims court foreign investors once more. It is a story that will continue to run and run.

## Money for Nothing – Calling for the SFA to Have a Debate About Financial Rule Changes

It was recently announced (leaked to the press) that the billionaire owner of AFC Bournemouth, Bill Foley, was interested in buying up to 25 per cent of Hibernian. To do so would require a change of the SFA rules, which currently prohibit multiple ownerships of football clubs. The current limit would see a new owner being restricted to 9.9 per cent, as we saw when Mike Ashley, then of Newcastle United, held that amount of shares. I am not sure many people would have wanted him in Scottish football given his reputation in the northeast of England.

This announcement raises many questions that the SFA need to consider. It is of course no surprise to anyone that there has been no proper debate or scrutiny around this. We have seen it before with the influx of the betting companies and of course the questionable wisdom of continuing with sponsorship from the alcohol industry that has seen us have Glen's Vodka and the recently announced Carling deal. The cash is needed *but* our clubs are excluded from having meaningful discussions about the sense in these deals. As I have found, even trying to debate these concerns sees you vilified by the powers that be.

Is changing a rule that has served Scottish football well in the past worth considering and if so, how will it benefit the wider game? If we use Partick Thistle as an example, the infamous Ken Bates tried to buy the club when he owned Chelsea. Due to the dual interest rules he was unable to buy the Jags, which was a huge escape as within six months Chelsea went into administration. If we fast forward to 2019 when Chien Lee and Paul Conway of Barnsley (and owners of a selection of other clubs) also tried to buy Thistle, once again the dual interest rules stopped it from happening. At that time Jags fans were in regular contact with Tykes fans, who were warning us that they felt no benefits from being part of the wider group of clubs and that the owners were overseas and had no interest in the fans. On the field, Barnsley continued to bounce between the divisions and the *Moneyball* business strategy they were sold produced very little return for the club. With the dual interest route blocked for this investment group, it of course allowed for a path to open up for Partick Thistle fans to buy the club for the community.

So, the existing rules have been proven to be a safeguard for at least two of our clubs in the past and there may have been more given that so many of these types of deals are done in secret. Of course, when it comes to the Bill Foley 'investment' there are more questions than answers.

The obvious question is in changing the ruling regarding dual ownership, what the benefits would be for Scottish football. From a Hibs perspective they might argue that it would give them access to better loan deals from other clubs and with further investment they might be able to challenge more at the top six of the league. The Romanov Lithuanian experiment is a salutary reminder that this model has been tried and tested and dumped before. Opening up the market might help fuel another race to nowhere given that the top of the game is a duopoly.

Will the SFA look at the bigger picture? Will all the clubs be able to contribute to the debate? Of course, we know that is unlikely. The Scottish Football Association is charged with the health of all football across the nation. In practice, the SFA is held in check by the vested interests of individual clubs and through the influence of the Scottish Professional Football League (SPFL) on its board. This means it is hardly independent or focused on the common good. It will come down to what the key clubs want.

Given what we are seeing in England with the problems with Financial Fair Play, what impact will allowing our clubs to be part of debt-ridden clusters of clubs have? Does this move help the financial sustainability of our clubs? Remember, being in the English Premier League you are allowed to have up to £120m in debt…

The reality is a very different scenario to asking Taylor Swift for a few bob and is essentially stepping into the unknown, with few obvious tangible benefits. In opening up this multi-club pathway, what impact will it have on governance at a local level? Another key question for the SFA to address is that with fewer and fewer Scottish players in our top teams, do they want this new investment to bring in even more foreign players? Should this change in the rules not be debated throughout the game?

CHAPTER 3

# Football Governance – Help or Hindrance?

*Football has its holy trinity: the players, manager and supporters. Nothing else matters. Directors don't come into it. They are only there to sign the cheques.*—Bill Shankly

JUST THE VERY mention of the word governance will probably have most fans ready to turn to the next chapter in the book. Yet good governance is critical to the overall health and well-being of the game, both at club and national level. Ignorance is certainly not bliss when it comes to what goes on in boardrooms at grounds around the country. Likewise, at the national level, much more scrutiny in recent years has meant that both the FA in England and the SFA in Scotland have been forced to try and modernise, with mixed results. You would be hard-pressed to find any fans who think these organisations are fit for the 21st century. What fans would like is openness, transparency and accountability at a basic level from organisations that have little semblance of acceptance of any wider democratic need.

## A Question of Balance

Throughout this book we will try and give an overview of the football landscape that has led to the continued development of community ownership primarily in Scotland. In many of the conversations that I have had with fans' groups over the years, there is no doubt that the democratic deficit is noted right across the game. This backdrop is very much part of the desire to move to a community ownership structure to try and redress the balance and to get some sort of democratic process into the clubs that we love. We might not be able to change FIFA, UEFA, the FA or the SFA but there is certainly now a route to get Local Club FC safe, stable and sustainable and to give its fans a voice that leads towards the top table. Getting there is of course a completely different story.

You start to see a picture emerging when a submission to Parliament from the Sports Minister at Westminster says, 'Over the decades the structures of the game have failed to govern fairly or effectively or modernise accordingly'. The structures have been stuck in the unique history of members' organisational malaise and the wider game has suffered as a consequence. There is no doubt that taking a snapshot of the wider football business has given the supporters the desire to see change. Whilst changing structures in the corridors of power in Zurich or Geneva will be virtually impossible, for most ordinary folk attaining the chance to make their own club better for future generations is something that can be done. In looking upwards it is important to see how these structures allowed the game to drift towards corruption and self-interest. If it can happen at FIFA, then it can also happen in Dumbarton or Bury. It is essential that we all learn lessons and be on our guard.

## On the World Stage

Traditionally the FA and SFA were the giants of the game and had significant privileged positions in the FIFA corridors of power that by far outweighed where they were in the world game. Until 1930, and the first World Cup, FIFA was virtually a meaningless organisation, which is why the English, quickly followed by the other home nations, resigned over the interpretation of "amateur" in the Olympic football tournament, which was sub-contracted to FIFA. The first three World Cups were poorly subscribed, and after the Second World War FIFA was penniless. It was bailed out by the proceeds of the GB v Europe match at Hampden in May 1947, which attracted a six-figure crowd, and the agreement of the home nations that the FIFA levy on all international matches would subsequently be applied to the Home International matches, which were hugely attended. The countries in the British Isles have had a rollercoaster ride when it comes to their relationship with the world governing body. Much of this was wrapped around the historical origins of the game and, in the British Isles, we still had to be convinced of the merits of a body more powerful than the home nations – who after all created the game. It is always a challenge when the big boy takes your ball in the playground and you suddenly realise that you will never get it back again.

Until the outbreak of the Second World War, seeing themselves as the original pioneers of the game was leading the home nations into a cul-de-sac and they often went into battle with the strength that FIFA was mustering as a world governing body. British football had to prove itself continually on the field as 'the masters of the game' against an ever-wider range of former pupils, given the continued growth in football's popularity. Having taken the beautiful game to the Empire and beyond, there was still an air of superiority about British football which was, to a certain extent, like the people and the press, still believing that our football was a cut above anything else on offer. Much of this can be seen in the early intransigence that the home nations had to the World Cup in its infancy. There is no doubt that this was fuelled by a critical press that assumed national primacy. The very thought that we couldn't learn anything from Johnny Foreigner on the football field was partly due to arrogance and in some way was exacerbated by the fact that England and Scotland were still very much top sides in this era – as their results against many upstarts clearly indicated.

The British Football Association's seemingly independent global role outside of FIFA, most notably by continued control over the laws of their game through the International Football Association Board (IFAB), allowed it to play a major role without really engaging with the wider football world. Falling out of love with FIFA was a regular occurrence for both the FA and the SFA. It was noted at the conference to celebrate 100 years of FIFA in 2004 that the FA had in fact only been a part of FIFA for 75 years of that time.

After the war years and the decline of the British Empire, the role that the home nations' associations would play in leading football would further diminish, as the world governing body developed a more strategic role in the development of the worldwide game. By the late 1950s the emergence of the World Cup as the dominant football tournament on the planet was giving FIFA the authority to flex its growing reputation. By the time the World Cup was held in Mexico in 1970, the emergence of coloured television and the ability to transmit live to all corners of the globe, via satellite, made the growing commercialisation a powerful drug. This new Technicolor phase was creating an empire and the game was giving FIFA the financial rewards that would allow continued growth. Tucked away in Switzerland it was doing what it did best: creating structures and rules that were devoid of proper scrutiny and would allow the likes of Havelange and Blatter to rule by fear and favour for the decades to come. Power and money became dangerous bedfellows for the beautiful game and nobody could do anything about it.

## Federation of International Football Associations (FIFA)

Many of the recent scandals at FIFA were laid very firmly at the door of Sepp Blatter, the Swiss banker turned football administrator who ran FIFA for many years. However, once the investigations started to unravel, the finger was very much pointed at João de Havelange who preceded Blatter. Havelange was a Brazilian lawyer, businessman and former athlete who served as the seventh President of FIFA from 1974 to 1998. His tenure as President is the second longest in FIFA's history, behind only that of the revered Jules Rimet. He received the title of Honorary President when leaving office but resigned in April 2013 as the web of deceit he created started to unravel. Havelange had succeeded the English gentleman Sir Stanley Rous and was then himself succeeded by Sepp Blatter. He was the longest serving active member upon his resignation. In July 2012 a Swiss prosecutor's report revealed that, during his tenure on FIFA's Executive Committee, he and his son-in-law Ricardo Teixeira took more than $41 million in bribes in connection with the award of World Cup marketing rights. This was not a mere $1 million found down the back of the Swiss sofa, this was industrial-scale money laundering. Both men were found to have received those massive payments as 'commissions', stated explicitly to be bribes, by the marketing company International Sports Media and Marketing, known as ISL.

Havelange, then the President of FIFA, in December 1997 granted ISL FIFA's exclusive marketing rights and, in May 1998, sold ISL exclusive TV and radio rights to the 2002 and 2006 World Cups. ISL paid FIFA €166 million for the marketing rights and €1.14bn for the TV rights. Ironically, commercial bribes of this nature were not ordinarily governed by Swiss law at the time. Havelange was of course succeeded by Blatter who had been his loyal deputy. It was alleged that he was aware of the bribes but it seems that at best he turned a blind eye, at worst he saw an ongoing opportunity to eventually take office.

In 2015 the Justice Department in the USA cited deals between FIFA, sports marketing groups and broadcast corporations for the television rights to air the World Cup and other international soccer tournaments. Dating back to 1991, the indictment alleges those involved conspired to receive bribes from marketing firms in exchange for exclusive television contracts – to the cumulative tune of more than $150 million. As Attorney General Loretta Lynch stated, 'It spans at least two generations of soccer officials who, as alleged, have abused their positions of trust to acquire millions of dollars in bribes and kickbacks.'

Blatter was also arrested in Switzerland and was sacked at the age of 79 by FIFA's ethics committee, terminating his fifth stint as president. He of course would not go quietly. Sadly for lovers of the beautiful game, one of the stars of the 1980s, Michel Platini, was also implicated in a deal with Blatter that would see both of them serve five-year football bans. Not only had significant sums of money changed hands but the awarding of the ultimate tournament, the World Cup, also came under scrutiny. In 2010, FIFA awarded the 2018 World Cup to Russia and the 2022 World Cup to Qatar, which led to reports of vote buying. Nothing has ever emerged that has changed any of the outcomes. So far, we have heard precious little from the Swiss authorities who were said to be still investigating this. It has to be said that without the groundbreaking work by journalist Andrew Jennings most of this information would not be in the public domain. I would encourage you to read more about it. https://pressgazette.co.uk/news/andrew-jennings-maverick-reporter-who-brought-down-fifa/

### How Did FIFA Get This Corrupt?

Some would argue that the mess created all comes down to how FIFA is organised as much as it is about the people who were allowed to be in charge. Each of the 209 member nations gets a single vote when it comes to electing a Federation President and executive committee. That means that Angola, Bermuda, or San Marino have, in theory, the same say in federation decisions as Argentina, Germany, or Spain. The smaller countries, and the men who run their countries' federations, also receive an equal cut of FIFA's revenues – which means there is little incentive for them to change any of the structure to the voting process. A further complication is that FIFA has no real influence on how the governance procedures are addressed or how each of the member countries conducts themselves. As a result, the next corrupt Jack Warner could still be sitting at the top table very soon.

### Will Any of This Actually Lead to Change Within FIFA?

What this whole shambles established was that the governance at the top of the game was not fit for purpose and that individuals had found a way to use the power and influence that football provided for their own needs and desires. Strides have been made over the past five years to distance FIFA now from the previous generations, and knowing that legislators and foreign powers will act where they see corruption should see continued reform. Gianni Infantino made the move from UEFA in October 2016, having served as Secretary General of UEFA since October 2009. During his time there, UEFA introduced Financial Fair Play and improved commercial support to smaller national associations and the expansion of UEFA Euro 2016 to 24 teams deemed him to be a reformer. Sadly, he too seems to come with financial skeletons in his cupboard.

## Union of European Football Associations (UEFA)

On 20 June 2019, the French football legend Michel Platini, who led European football's governing body from 2007 to 2015, was held by French anti-corruption police investigating alleged corruption in the 2010 vote to award the competition to the gas-rich Gulf state.

He denied wrongdoing and a statement from his representatives said the facts of the case were 'unknown to him'. Platini said he had been released without charge, adding that there has been 'a lot of fuss over nothing'.

It used to be said that if America sneezes then the whole world catches a cold. In football parlance, when FIFA went down with bronchitis, UEFA by association caught an immediate case of influenza. It has direct links to the scandal that brought down Blatter through popular President Platini and the issue of his bonus payments and of course the accusations of vote rigging. The Panama Papers leak in 2016 seemed to raise questions about the role FIFA's president, Gianni Infantino, played in deals that were concluded when he was Director of Legal Services at UEFA, European football's governing body. The papers claimed UEFA concluded offshore deals with one of the indicted figures at the heart of an alleged 'World Cup of fraud', despite previously insisting it had no dealings with any of them. Infantino seems to have escaped without any further investigation. The current president is Aleksander Čeferin, a former Football Association of Slovenia president, who was elected as UEFA's seventh president at the 12th Extraordinary UEFA Congress in Athens in September 2016 and automatically became a Vice President of the world body FIFA. He came into the job as a reformer and so far, has had a scandal-free presidency.

What seems certain is that football has had to learn some very difficult lessons as to how it conducts its affairs. This is, of course, being done against the backdrop of billionaires and Arab states now owning prestigious football clubs in Europe. None of these wealthy new owners will be shrinking violets. So, we can expect that the financial muscle that they have along with the influences they exert in their own domestic leagues will have a direct influence on UEFA's direction of travel. As ordinary fans, all we can do is watch with interest and, as we saw with the European Super League proposal, we need to shout loudly when we get the chance.

## The Football Association (FA)

In February 2017, not for the first time, the UK Parliament had a debate about FA governance, with the motion running:

> This House has no confidence in the ability of the Football Association (FA) to comply fully with its duties as a governing body, as the current governance structures of the FA make it impossible for the organisation to reform itself; and calls on the Government to bring forward legislative proposals to reform the governance of the FA.

For those working in football this was pretty compelling stuff. What followed was that a motion of 'no confidence' in the Football Association was indeed passed by MPs debating the organisation's ability to reform itself. This was the latest stage of a saga that began in December 2010 when the Culture, Media and Sport Select Committee announced it was to launch an inquiry into domestic football governance. In February 2011 the former FA Chairman Lord Triesman told the committee he found it 'impossible' to make the changes he wanted while in the role. By July 2011 the inquiry's first report recommended substantial reform and asked the Government to consider legislation to make it happen. Given that football governance is rather one-paced, it was no surprise that by July 2012 a Select Committee launched a follow-up inquiry after being disappointed with the response from football's governing bodies.

At the FA, then chief David Bernstein stepped down and was replaced by Greg Dyke. He later describes the FA as incapable of reforming itself, which surprises no one. The old chestnut that the football authorities in England and Scotland use, that FIFA don't look kindly on Government interference in football, is brought to the table, but now that FIFA's credibility is tarnished with its own scandals that are in the full public glare, the claim carries no weight. In early 2016, Greg Dyke who went into the job as a reformer did not seek re-election when his term ended, citing his struggle to push through reforms. The then Sports Minister Tracey Crouch said the FA may lose funding if it does not press ahead with reforms. £30 million is a considerable amount of cash for even the FA. When nothing emerged from Wembley Stadium, the Select Committee launched a new inquiry into football governance. When it met in February 2017 the no confidence motion was passed and MPs warned that legislation would be brought in if changes were not made.

## There Are Two Sides to Every Story

It came to pass that with significant pressure from the Government, the FA finally voted to change its governance structures. It proudly announced this great achievement on its website:

> On Thursday afternoon, FA Shareholders ratified the new corporate governance proposals, which had previously received unanimous approval from the FA Board and Council. The majority of the approved governance reforms will come into effect from Thursday 27 July 2017.

Push came to shove and a range of reforms were approved by the FA to allow it to modernise. To most observers these were too little too late, and the FA has little influence now that it is dominated by the billionaires of the Premier League! This followed a six-month review period and a comprehensive consultation with a range of shareholders and stakeholders including representatives of the National Game, the Professional Game, supporter groups, the Professional Footballers' Association, the League Managers Association, Government and Sport England.

On Monday 3 April, the Council unanimously agreed the reform proposals and on Thursday 18 May they were officially ratified after a shareholder vote at the FA's AGM, held at Wembley Stadium. So, political pressure finally changed the course of football governance in England. It only took six years and three different Sports Ministers to get change, but change did happen. However, as the doyen of football governance David Conn reported in the *Guardian*,

> The Football Association has ratified the modest reforms proposed to its governing council and board, so mercifully drawing to a finish a torturous and long-winded saga of internal reordering. The immediate consequence is that the FA's structure and makeup of its board, which will have three women and seven men by next year, complies with the – also modest – requirements of the new official code for sports governance.

Conn and many other observers were far from impressed at just how long it took to deliver these reforms and just how little impact the reforms were likely to have. What it did do was take away the threat of impending legislation and release the £30 million of grassroots football support that the FA received via National Lottery funding. An important point to note is that, during the work of the Select Committee, the views of football supporters in England were taken on board by having the Football Supporters' Federation (now known as the Football Supporters' Association) sitting at the table.

Of course, even in the world of football governance, things can and do change. Thanks to the rise of the European Super League concept, the reform agenda was given a massive boost and the fan-led review of the game made many suggestions for meaningful reform. The most significant of these was the need for an independent football regulator. However, with a pandemic, a major cost of living crisis and the UK changing Prime Ministers more regularly than Manchester United's kit, the desire for change has most recently been put on the back burner. What we do know is that legislation for Reform of the Game and the introduction of an Independent Regulator was passed in the King's Speech in 2023 with implementation in 2024. The exciting news for football fans is that with universal support across all the political parties, something will happen soon! Despite the change in government at Westminster in 2024, this legislation remains on track and is scheduled to have its third reading at Westminster in autumn with implementation in early 2026.

## The Scottish Football Association (SFA)

In Scotland, sport is a matter devolved to the Scottish Parliament under the constitutional devolution settlement. Many football observers, although committed to our Parliament, sometimes wish it wasn't. At Westminster, we can see how various Sports Ministers have taken the football reform debate to new levels while here in Scotland the SFA, our governing body, have been left to their own devices. Given that the creation of this members organisation has its roots going back to the 1870s, even those within football knew that the multitude of archaic committees and voting structures were not fit for purpose for the 20th century, never mind the fast approaching 21st century. With no Government threats or prodding, it was left to the SFA to write its own terms of reference. In fairness to George Peat, at least he saw the need for change. Maybe not reform as was being demanded in England but change nevertheless. George Peat rose to the position of President having been the SFA Treasurer and an accountant by profession. He spent 22 years on the board at Airdrieonians before finding a home at Stenhousemuir just before his hometown club went into liquidation, which seemed to escape the attention of those voting for him. However, hats off to him as the McLeish Report that he authorised as Scottish FA President didn't miss the mark. Peat was quoted as saying:

It was my original intention to sanction a report that was wide-ranging in its investigation of Scottish football and uncompromising in its recommendations. I have not been disappointed by Henry's work. The Scottish FA have shown a willingness to embrace change and there is a determination within the board and the organisation as a whole to provide a world-class service to Scottish football. This report includes many sobering realities for us and the game in general but will not shy away from our responsibilities. We are committed to change, and we believe now is the time to act for the same of game at all levels, from grassroots to elite performance.

McLeish himself said:

The review is intended to provide a comprehensive assessment of the problems, challenges and opportunities facing football. My report goes far beyond the obvious manifestation of underachievement and under performance. It asks searching questions about the mindset of the game in Scotland and the structures, mission, ethos and organisation of Scottish football. Our institutions are amongst the oldest in the world. The burden of history influences what we do and there has been, for far too long, a reluctance to embrace modernisation and make the game effective and efficient in the 21st century.

A key part of the report was to modernise the game and to set realistic but achievable targets for the organisation to reach. It did so through its 2020 vision programme which it aspired to achieve. It is sad to report that McLeish, now a director of the Scottish Football Supporters Association, when he should have been brought in to make the changes happen, was asked instead to review the progress of the SFA's '2020 Vision' document. Our thanks to the BBC and to Henry for allowing us to quote from his interview.

## Decades Behind and Needing Much More Ambition

'There have been some minor successes, but we really haven't achieved the goals that were set out,' said McLeish. 'It's a question of attitude and I come back to this point I've constantly stressed: the SFA structure is still old-fashioned. It's decades behind and if you look at some of the more promising countries of the world, they're going massively forward and it's all about investment in elite talent.'

'On the national side I don't think there's much progress been made at all,' added McLeish.

'The SFA have not built on the success of Scotland's women.'

He says, unless there is a dramatic overhaul, Scotland will continue to struggle to qualify for major competitions in the future, with the buck stopping with the SFA board.

'I feel very let down,' McLeish explained. 'I thought the review would produce a great deal more than it did but it's now up to those who occupy the seats of power at Hampden to take a think and actually realise if we're going to move forward, they have to completely change attitude, change the institution, change the vision and have a much, much bigger ambition.'

## A Proper Structure at the SFA and How Scottish Rugby Acted

When the Scottish Rugby Union (SRU) faced financial meltdown around 2003, with unmanageable spiralling debt and the move to professionalism, it knew that it needed significant changes to safeguard its future prosperity. It appointed former player, administrator and sheriff Bill Dunlop to come up with the solution that Scottish Rugby desperately needed. The changes led the way towards better governance as the Dunlop report of 2005 set a vision and structure for Scottish Rugby ahead of its time. It was reported in the press at the time that,

> The nub of the issue was whether ultimate responsibility for running the organisation sat with the elected President or with the paid Chief Executive. After eight weeks of deliberation and five meetings, Dunlop and his Working Party recommended that a newly constituted SRU Board be given the 'autonomy and discretion' to run the affairs of the SRU, so long as it remains 'accountable', 'responsive' and 'transparent' to the stakeholders (principally the clubs). Dunlop stressed that 'all stakeholders should be represented when decisions are taken', which was facilitated through the election of four Council members (elected stakeholders) to the board.

Dunlop's recommendations were adopted with an overwhelming majority at a second Special General Meeting (SGM) and until recently the structure created was held up as a template for good corporate governance of a national sporting body. 'It isn't complicated,' says Dunlop.

The purpose of the board is to run the SRU as a commercial company. The purpose of the Council is to monitor and oversee how the SRU runs all its functions, including the rugby side of it. The way in which the rugby is run should be distinct from the commercial, and they [the Council] should be getting involved in that, but they're not.

Few would argue that Scottish Rugby is not in a better position than it was 15 years ago. It has seen significant change with improvements in operational, financial and professional performance. The growing professionalism of the modern game has seen two significant club sides emerge to support the national team. It has also seen record international attendance and significant growth of the women's game.

The difference between the Dunlop Report and the McLeish Report is that significant changes were adopted by rugby, whereas the McLeish Report was only partially implemented and got stuck in inertia. Yes, many boxes were ticked but the more meaningful reforms never happened. In retrospect, the problem with McLeish's report was that it was simply not radical enough. If the SFA had adopted the same governance structure as the SRU it could have had the benefit of a significant talent pool of highly capable executives running football like a business, rather than the vested interests of the club and the SPFL leaving it devoid of ambition.

What the future holds we don't know but one of the reasons that Henry McLeish joined the board of the SFSA is to ensure that we continue to work to get the type of reforms that Scottish football supporters deserve. He said,

> Governance is a key part of the game, and it is essential that all the stakeholders are represnted in its processes and strategies. Much good work has been done but further reforms are required to ensure that there is openness, transparency and accountability. Only then will our game be brave enough to look at itself in the mirror and recognise what it sees and what it does not see.

Following this assessment in 2020, McLeish and his colleagues at the SFSA created the Scottish Football Alliance to follow the lead of the FSA in England in developing a fans-led independent review of the game in Scotland. Its findings were published in 2023 and the calls for significant changes in the way Scottish football is governed was debated at Holyrood in 2024. The Sports Minister has now organised a series of Round Table discussions looking at governance of the game in Scotland. As you would expect, the SFA have insisted there is no need for reform here in Scotland as everything is fine!

CHAPTER 4

# Far From These Shores, From Great to Small

*In Argentina our self-esteem is linked to our football.*—Mauricio Macri, President of Argentina from 2015 to 2019

IN THIS CHAPTER we have recruited some local experts to take a look at how community ownership looks in some other territories.

The early international pioneers brought the rules of the game they played from UK shores and adopted the membership models that were commonplace in cities like Glasgow and Sheffield. They started with a blank sheet of paper where the only rules were those that you created yourself. There were no templates to follow, players and officials had to learn from each other in what was a new adventure. The early organisation within these new clubs on foreign shores was somewhat fluid. It is not that who owned the club didn't matter, it did, it was just that no obvious alternative to the initial community ownership was considered viable at that time. With no real economic value attached to the entity, actual ownership was not an issue for those early adopters who just wanted to play football. There were neither vultures nor philanthropic local businessmen waiting in the wings to take on club ownership – that dynamic would be a long time away.

Much of the infrastructure that was put in place came about with the arrival of more formal organisation as the national associations came into being. The lawmakers had arrived and with them there were rules and requirements that ensured that best practice was being followed. Clubs suddenly had guidelines that they had to follow if they wanted to be part of organised football. These changes in themselves helped fuel the clubs' growth to become more organised, as the early football structures were more co-operative than competitive off the park. From this standing start, it was a slow organic process for the new football community as it set about organising itself in an orderly fashion.

At club level much of what became normal just evolved with different jobs emerging from the tasks in hand of putting on a game. As the popularity of the game and the individual teams grew, it quickly changed from putting on a game with your mates to a public event that had to be managed accordingly. Someone had to take care of the kit: buying it, cleaning it, preparing it for match days. Someone had to look after the park and then eventually the stadium. Someone had to organise the fixtures and talk to the opposition, so quite quickly the role of match secretary followed. In fact, the earlier roles that the clubs established are all tasks that are still followed today. At the larger clubs by paid employers and at smaller clubs by volunteers doing what needs to be done to get a match on. A fantastic depiction of these early days has recently been portrayed in the Netflix drama, *The English Game*, where these early stages of the development have been very well documented.

In many of the countries who followed Scotland and England's early football development, the origins of the clubs gave an indication of how the ownership structure might follow. In South America most of the early clubs that were formed had their origins in works teams, being recreational vehicles of British expatriates who brought the passion for the new game with them. Often, they started life as subsets of cricket or athletics clubs or as an offshoot of other sports or general recreational clubs. What is interesting for those of us who have an interest in community ownership is that democratic processes that were put in place in those early days have stood the test of time and have evolved to suit modern times in many football nations.

In this chapter we will look at how the ownership of clubs has evolved differently from what we have seen in the United Kingdom. We know that there are many who do not support community ownership and would rather that the success in South America, Sweden, Germany and Spain were dismissed as being irrelevant or simply not capable of working here in the UK. However, whilst the overall league and association structures will never be able to be replicated *en masse* there is no valid reason that we can't appreciate and celebrate the successes.

## Argentina: The Fan Powerhouse of South America

It is said that the Welsh took rugby to Argentina and the Scots gave them football. In fact, the truth is somewhat more complicated than that. There is no doubt that those early engineers, miners, steelworkers and industrialists did indeed start the love affair that Argentina has for the beautiful game. Quite quickly they were joined by Italian immigrants who brought their own passion for the game to provide a unique cosmopolitan formula that has endured to this day. What surprises football fans in the UK is that all association football clubs in Argentina are owned by their members. Every club is organised as a not-for-profit organisation according to Argentinian law (*asociación civil sin fines de lucro*). In the country where football and politics have always been uneasy but intertwined bedfellows, the ownership of the clubs has survived the military junta, war and dictatorships. It is a testament to the strength of their private members' organisation origins that they endured the changing landscape to remain run by members who are elected by the *socios* (fans' groups). What we know from history is that has not always been easy.

Of course, with democracy often being touted as one of the most important aspects of community ownership, when your county is ruled by a dictator or a military junta then you can be assured that there will be major issues around who is running the football clubs. It was claimed that during the Perón dictatorship there were many ways that the *socios* were used to infiltrate clubs and to use 'an army of fans' to ensure that the important messages were conveyed to the people. When football plays such an important role in society there is always a danger that it will be used as a way to influence the wider public.

Following the political unrest that accompanied the Juan Perón dictatorship there was a claim that this infiltration and coercion of the clubs should be investigated by FIFA. Of course, FIFA was not the huge commercial beast that we now recognise so it had far less power or influence and was less likely to get involved. If an investigation ever did occur, you will be hard pressed to find any information about it in the archives. The use of football as a political tool was downplayed, not because FIFA were concerned about political interference but because football became a bystander to the Argentine coup d'état which was a right-wing coup that overthrew Isabel Perón as President of Argentina on 24 March 1976. A military junta was installed to replace her; this was headed by Lieutenant General Jorge Rafael Videla, Admiral Emilio Eduardo Massera and Brigadier General Orlando Ramón Agosti. The political process initiated on 24 March 1976 took the official name of 'National Reorganization Process', and the junta, although not with its original members, remained in power until the return to the democratic process on 10 December 1983. It was during that period that an observer noted that football in Argentina was the only place that you could still actually have a vote that mattered. No democracy in the streets but democracy on the terraces via the *socios*. What a powerful statement for community ownership of football clubs that is!

Unlike the UK where community ownership has tended to be an alternative governance model after failure of conventional ownership, in Argentina it is all they have ever known – there has never been a viable alternative. Some of the most famous clubs in South America have not only survived turbulent upheaval off the park, they have also avoided the purge seen in British football with its catalogue of administrations and liquidations. However, one of the arguments used against the power of the *socios* has been the violence on the terraces that has so often blighted South American football. It is of course not related directly to ownership but with the fans being so well organised and powerful it did offer an easier backdrop for these problems to manifest themselves.

If there was ever a testament to how powerful community ownership can be then this Argentinian example is right up there alongside Germany as a different way to run a club. From the smallest community clubs to the club that categorises its members as their 12th man, it is a fantastic example of how a structure has adapted and adjusted over the years without selling its soul. Step forward Boca Juniors – the pride of Buenos Aires. Boca are a South American club powerhouse and a case study in fan power working to maintain the spirit of the club. Founded by five young Italian immigrants in the blue-collar neighbourhood of La Boca in 1905 and still 100 per cent supporter-owned today, 'Los Xeneizes' are deeply connected with a working-class identity and the sentimental choice of fans across Latin America as a second team.

They consider themselves the favourite club of '*la mitad más uno*' or 'half plus one' of the Argentinian population and surveys suggest that this is only a slight exaggeration. They are seen by many commentators as the Barcelona of South America with a wide eclectic fan base and have produced many famous world-known players such as Maradona. At Boca, 'the 12th man' is not just a catchphrase, but a nearly century-old pillar of club tradition as well as the name of the team's main supporters' group, La 12, a passionate crew often linked to hooliganism as well as a powerful voice in the inner workings of club management. They were Ultras before the expression was even defined. The other clubs in the league structure might not be as vociferous but they follow the same structures. Every fan group has an election process that gives the members the opportunity to vote in elections, to be elected to club committees and to step forward to the board that runs the club. It highlights that even in a country where democracy has had its challenges in the past, the concept of one member one vote has survived the test of time.

## The Faroe Islands

From the vast regions of the Argentinian Pampas to the 18 rocky islands that identify themselves as the Faroe Islands, community ownership of football clubs still survives today. Supposedly the home of Thor the Viking God, it took a world war to kick-start the tiny island's love of the beautiful game into a proper league structure. With a population of around 50,000 it is everything that Argentina is not. With the club TB (Tvøroyrar Bóltfelag) being established in 1892, the love of the game was adopted early on these tiny islands. It was only with the large number of British troops based there during the Second World War that the foundations were laid to establish a league structure in 1942. All the clubs playing in the four tiers of Faroes football are owned and run by the community that they represent. The clubs are in essence small community enterprises – local co-operative companies that run all aspects of the game in the country. There have been several cases of clubs being in trouble over the years, but all have survived to tell the tale and continue to thrive.

## The German Way: Perfect Football Engineering

To get a better understanding of just how this works in Germany I spoke to Jacob Rossler who until recently was the Fans' Representative for Union Berlin FC and Dr Jochen Lammert a Cologne FC supporter and a leading football academic and researcher from Fan Q.

Jacob explained:

> In simple terms, all German football clubs are 'fan-owned'. The whole concept is so ingrained into supporter culture that those who are – with a few loathsome exceptions (almost exclusively in the topflight, the most 'honourable mentions' being Leipzig, Hoffenheim, and to a lesser degree, Leverkusen, Dortmund, Frankfurt and Wolfsburg among some smaller clubs) – are deemed to be outwith this.
>
> Fan ownership here maybe differs in meaning from what you understand. The German word '*Verein*', which for 99+ per cent of all German clubs from the lower to the upper leagues (exceptions have been mentioned) is the basic legal form, would be something like a 'union', an 'assembly' or a 'registered association' – if any of those make sense to you. The idea is very German and comes from earlier times, when mainly males formed *Vereine* in order to pursue

their leisure activities, sports, shooting, hunting, collecting stamps – you name it. Basically, those *Vereine* are non-profit organisations. But over time the old idea that says 'engaging in sports' is the main purpose of a *Vereine* does in fact contradict the non-profit idea. This means that even Bayern Munich is an *eingetragener Verein*, 'e.V.', a legal form they share with, for example, a pigeon breeding club. The difference in revenue is probably not the only thing differing here.

In every club, all members (Vereinsmitglieder), have a say in the best sense of representative democracy. Each year, each club has to hold a general assembly and according to the respective constitution of the club, every three to five years there are elections. I'll explain an example using my club, FC Union Berlin. We've just been promoted to the First Division and as a newcomer have a yearly revenue/turnover of 75+ Mio €, which in my understanding would place the club second in the SPL. This multimillion-euro enterprise is, on the membership level, run like an 1880s gymnastics club in Hannover. Once a year the club president and the board of directors have to tell the members how the year went, and they need to be 'cleared', meaning that the members vote if they did their job alright. Every five years, the members of the directors' board face elections, which happen in the general assembly. The elected board of directors then elects the president and two vice presidents. They run the club in general but, of course, appoint people for the business jobs. In my club, the elected people are not paid at all, in some cases they receive some representation allowance. And if they screw up, any of them, the membership can gather votes for a quorum (in many clubs 10 per cent of the membership) and an additional general assembly can be held, where the members decide upon dismissal of the persons in questions.

Dr Jochen Lammert explained:

The biggest issue in the discussions here is the DFL, the German Football League. In order to be allowed to play in one of the first two leagues, the *Verein* may only 'sell' shares as long as they hold 50 per cent plus one vote. And since the club is the members, this means that no external sponsor can theoretically outvote the members. This system is highly appreciated by almost all German football fans, but of course not by all deciders on the club level. This has been a tour de force through German football. And for everything I said, there are usually 'buts' and exceptions, but the basic picture stands.

When we think of German engineering we can't but help think of the quality of BMW, the style of Audi and the reliability of VW. Why? Because we as consumers know that it is true that these products live up to the promise of the offer they give to the consumer. Of course, outwith the car industry there are dozens of other global brands such as Bosch, Siemens, Adidas, etc, proving that our friends in Germany tend to deliver well thought through quality products time after time.

The German way is always under review and being evaluated. This is of course the complete opposite of how football here in the UK is managed where unless prompted by Government the preference is to just plod on regardless, don't change anything and avoid confrontation.

I was reminded of this in the excellent David Conn article in the *Guardian* that I would recommend anybody with an interest in community ownership to read. Conn has watched and admired the 'German way' off the park for years and in this article firmly nails his colours to the mast with regards to what he prefers when it comes to the English Premier League (EPL) against clubs working with the 50 plus one community ownership model. Rather than restricting the development of the game in Germany, it seems that at all levels the so-called lack of finance compared to the perceived 'commercial strength' of the EPL has produced the right results for fans. Fast forward to the hammering that the mighty La Liga giants had in the first leg of the Champions League semi-finals a few years back and you have to say that what they are doing in Germany seems to be working.

Germany is of course a large country, with passionate fans and a world leading economy, so it has a great starting point. What it also has are clubs that are deeply embedded in their communities, right from the top of the Bundesliga down to the local village team. It is that pride and passion that is the lifeblood of football in Germany and today they seem to have captured a special essence of football that is just so efficient on and off the park. Indeed it is so Germanic. It's a bit like those aforementioned cars. They just have a feel to them that says quality, reliability and it will not let you down. So too with their football. They have quietly and effectively built a marketing platform that has allowed for democracy that brings fans/customers with them, which is easier when you have local talent prevalent, a safe standing, an integrated travel policy and a pricing policy that allows access to even the larger clubs at a price that is affordable no matter where you sit in the socio-economic ladder.

What is also needed is recognising that where the German model works it recognises that fans are the most important stakeholders in the game and, if you work with them, they will likely spend more money with you and encourage more people to join the club – success breeds success. There is certainly scope for better fan engagement and there is a platform in place through the development of Fans' Charters where clubs align the rights and responsibilities of the fans within their own democratic structure. It is of course a cultural thing, and it means that it helps define the attitude at the top of the game.

Christian Seifert, the Bundesliga Chief Executive since 2005, is at pains in a long interview with the *Observer* to ensure the fans are top of his list of priorities. 'We value the fan culture we have,' Seifert emphasises.

> We are the last of the big leagues with standing areas and nobody wants to touch these standing areas. The clubs are committed to having many cheap tickets because it is considered very important in Germany that people who do not have very much money are able to come to the stadium. Here, football is one of the last activities which really brings people together, across all ages and all classes of income.Most chairmen and chief executives have been very much involved with football, they have been supporters and players. They see from a pure business perspective they could raise prices and make more money. But they have decided to take less money and enable people whose families have supported the club for generations, and young people, to keep coming. We want to have our whole society as part of our football, in our stadiums.

From the terraces to the boardroom is a pathway that is not uncommon. 'This is our German football culture: to have standing, and cheap tickets, and the clubs controlled by their members,' Chief Executive Hans-Joachim Watzke told the *Guardian* in 2012.

> We want everybody to feel it is their club and that is really important. I was a supporter standing for 20 years, I know what it is to stand there, the feeling, the discussions you have there. In Germany, we are a little bit romantic.

## Defending the Rights

As we have seen in Germany a majority control by a single entity (person, or company) is not permitted by the Deutsche Fußball Liga and is the law for clubs. The law suggests a registered club should have a minimum of seven members. The league requires that either a club, or a limited company which is controlled by a club with 50 per cent plus one vote, can get a licence to participate in the German first or second league. In the lower leagues, it is required to be a club rather than having a company structure.

An exception to the 50 plus one rule allows a company or individual investor that has substantially funded a club for at least 20 years to gain a controlling stake in that club. This exception most notably applies to Bayer Leverkusen and VfL Wolfsburg. Both were founded as sports clubs for employees of major corporations (respectively Bayer and Volkswagen) long before the 50 plus one rule was established. However, in season 2019/2020, multimillion-euro-valued technology giants SAP co-founder Dietmar Hopp counted significant controversy that has led to the worldwide coverage of the fans' unrest. Having gained control of 1899 Hoffenheim – where he had been a youth player – he successfully funded the club's rise from the lowest reaches of German football to the Bundesliga. He has become a universal figure of ridicule to the fans of other clubs who have staged protests at stadiums across Germany aimed mostly at the football authorities for allowing him to go unchecked.

The other club that has been targeted is RB Leipzig who have been accused of bypassing the law through legal loopholes; essentially not being fan-owned and undermining the system. The battle to retain the original German model continues to evolve with supporters of clubs throughout the country concerned for the outcome.

## Italy: The Azzurri Fans' Passion Ignited

Italy is in some ways similar to the UK in that clubs started as members' clubs owned by the individuals but in the fullness of time evolved to become private limited companies. At many of the larger clubs they saw an increased influence/dependence on significant business figures that gradually took the ownership, but not the club, further away from the supporters. There have been many trials, tribulations and a few scandals too, as Italian football has wrestled with everything from money laundering, match fixing and of course violence at grounds. The pathway to looking at the possibility of community ownership has been inspired by what fans have seen in other countries. Like many countries without a national fans' organisation to guide it progress was impossible.

Fortunately, Supporters in Campo the national fans' association which was established in 2013 is now on hand to help fans. One of its primary objectives was to lobby for supporter ownership in Italy. The Supporters in Campo (SinC) collective was born from the cooperation between supporters' groups that promote the sustainable ownership and management models for sporting clubs. They were inspired by the growing fans movement in the UK and the successes of fan-owned clubs.

The cooperation was aimed at developing the involvement of supporters in the decision-making processes and ownership of football clubs, therefore empowering and enhancing the positive contribution that fans and supporters represent in football. On the one hand, it was a response from the supporters who, after experiencing pain and agony with their club, now want to have a voice and control over the club management and avoid new dangers for their beloved team. With figures very similar to the UK there were about 150 professional clubs lost in the 15 years prior and it was time to give the fans the responsibility of these clubs. Italian football has not been without its controversies but in many ways the growth of a new organisation for fans was not unexpected given that it was a form of opposition to the mass commercialisation of football and its constant removal from the community. The organisation believed that if it were to be successful it had to recover its social value and a new approach must be taken to establish a relationship between club and fanbase that was strong and positive.

As we have here in Scotland with the Scottish Football Supporters Association and the Football Supporters' Association in England and Wales, the activities of SinC have developed into a form of dialogue and discussion with the official institutions and with the main professional leagues of Italian football and building a fan collective.

At a recent Football Supporters Europe Conference SinC council member, Stefano Pagnozzi, described their activities in depth:

> SinC is a young movement that still has a lot to learn. We help
> fan groups form, and we support them in all phases. The network
> is a meeting place to exchange experiences and learn from each
> other's mistakes! We have developed a handbook that demonstrates
> our principles, while helping new fans organise themselves
> democratically to fight for a voice in their club.
>
> Italian football has many problems. The entire sector needs

substantial reform and stricter rules to address certain needs. Resources are lacking, many of which are concentrated in Serie A between a few clubs. Equal opportunity mechanisms that benefit the entire system are missing. This leads us to the constant disappearance of a dozen clubs every summer.

The economic crisis has certainly had a decisive influence on our sporting culture, specifically for small and medium-sized local businesses. These clubs have been the most affected in the last ten years by economic difficulties. In terms of participation, there are a few clubs that have managed to open up to their community. Usually, the fan is seen as a problem, not as a necessity to help grow and protect the club.

From a community ownership perspective the value of the clubs means they are pretty untouchable for the ordinary fans of the larger clubs.

In Italy the concept of one member one vote is growing from the bottom up and the practices that are put in place will stand the test of time, however, it will be a long hard climb to get community ownership established at the top level.

## Spain – *Socios* at the Heart of the Country

There is a very interesting dynamic in La Liga where they have, in effect, a mixed economy with some clubs now owned by individuals or large corporations and some retaining a member ownership structure. Spain has a rich member ownership history and fan ownership models were the norm throughout the first 80 years of football in Spain. Indeed they inspired many of the member organisations that sprang up in South America. They were in essence protected from any change during the period of dictatorship by General Franco who thought it wise not to interfere in football.

However, when democracy did emerge, change did come. In 1992 the Spanish Government passed a law that caused the end of most fan ownerships over football clubs. Ley 10/1990 del Deporte, through its Article 19.1 made it mandatory for professional football clubs to become privately owned PLCs from June 1992 for the 1992/93 season of Primera División, and subsequent seasons onward. This was a response to corruption and the economic failure at some clubs and a reaching out to try to modernise football. At the time it seemed like the obvious thing to do but for community-owned purists it was a shocking act of vandalism on a structure that was not to blame for the failings at some individual clubs. La Liga is now hugely successful, but we will never know if these changes helped make it so.

That law also made four exceptions. A club would be allowed to maintain its existing legal organisational structure if it could be shown that it was turning a profit for the previous five years (starting from 1985/86 season), in audits performed by LPF (Liga Profesional de Fútbol) and operations as member-owned non-profit sports associations. As a result of this exception, the four clubs were allowed to keep their differing legal organisational structure. In addition to this, Real Madrid, Barcelona and Athletic Club Bilbao were also given recognition due to the ethnic groups that form an integral part of the clubs' culture, traditions and support base.

## Real Madrid

The members of Real Madrid are called *socios*, and the club is owned entirely by them. This is evident from the fact that the board of directors was elected and decided even before the founding of the club in 1902. It was founded as Madrid Football Club in 1902 but changed its name to Real Madrid after the grant of royal patronage by King Alfonso XIII in 1920. It was decided before the formation of the club that business decisions, as well as the ownership of the club, would be in the hands of its members. Naturally, any decisions that require the voting of more than 90,000 people would be a cumbersome process. Thus, the *socios* hold an election to form a Member Assembly, which comprises of around 2,000 members elected by the *socios* for four-year terms. This is not dissimilar to how many of the larger clubs in South America operate. The Member Assembly's main responsibilities revolve around the financial facets of the club, such as framing and approving the club's budget for the season. The Member Assembly also has certain other powers such as the ability to discipline the club president, as well as authorising the club to borrow money to suit its needs as and when needed.

### How the Club President is Elected

The president is elected as the head of an electoral group that also includes the board of directors. The Real Madrid Statutes (the documents that govern the functioning of the club) state that the president must be Spanish (at the time of election) and a member of the club for ten or more consecutive years.

To be eligible to run for election, the candidate must give a substantial bank guarantee. A bank guarantee is a promise from a bank or other lending institution that if a particular borrower defaults on a loan, the bank will cover the loss. When Florentino Perez ran (and subsequently won) in 2009, the bank guarantee he had given amounted to about €57 million.

## Athletic Club Bilbao

A true outlier in world football since 1898. It has more than 33,000 members who are eligible to vote in regular elections for club leadership positions – and their most important policy is a sacred pillar of both Athletic's identity and that of the Basque region they call home: the *'Cantera'* philosophy, which requires that only players of Basque heritage may appear in their iconic red-and-white striped kits. The policy limits the available talent pool but creates a powerful collective identity. In fact, the Basque club is one of a select few which have never been relegated from La Liga, Spain's topflight. And pride in the *Cantera* ethos is so strong that fans have repeatedly expressed that they would prefer relegation to abandonment of their home-grown ways. There is no doubt that this is a club that can defiantly claim to be part of the fabric of the city and the region, standing out as more than just a football club. The club's website says it best: 'Athletic Club as an institution, along with its supporters, are characterized by their desire to defend values which are becoming increasingly uncommon in football and in sports overall in the 21st century.'

## FC Barcelona

They're far wealthier and more widely supported than their Basque counterparts. But as the de facto national team for the Catalan region, the Blaugrana occupy just as central a place in their local community – they just happen to have exported the alluring magic of 'The Barça Way' worldwide. As in Bilbao, FCB are owned by over 200,000 individual members, or *socios*, who vote in club elections and help fill the 98,787-capacity Camp Nou stadium, one of the game's true cathedrals. The team is also powered by its *penyes*, or supporters' clubs, which number some 1,200 and can be found around the world, earning Barça the tag '*Més que un club*' (More than a club). *Penyes* fuelled Camp Nou's original construction and helped the club survive during the dark days following the Spanish Civil War, when military dictator Francisco Franco – a staunch fan of hated rivals Real Madrid – made life difficult for FCB and Catalonia as a whole. Fans building a club literally brick by brick was the Barça way and in more recent times we have seen this model adopted by Union Berlin who got their fans to build the stadium as well as creating one of the best fan dynamics and cultures in doing so.

## Swedish Football: Scandinavian Passion Is All About the Fans

Many football fans are aware of the high level of fan involvement in German football and the much vaunted '50 plus one' rule that is in place ensuring that clubs are majority owned by their members, with a handful of exceptions. Such an approach to club governance is also in place further north in Europe, in Sweden. In Swedish football, club ownership follows a similar 50 plus one rule to that of the German Bundesliga. As is the case with Germany, this approach to governance is entrenched in history and tradition and is not without its opponents. Originally multi-sports organisations, in the mid-90s Swedish clubs were given the right to separate their football sections into limited companies. During this process however, Sweden's Sports Confederation – Riksidrottsförbundet, or RF – also inserted a 50 plus one rule in order to ensure that the football clubs remained majority owned by their members.

In 2012, the Swedish elite football association noticed that Allsvenskan was weak in comparison with other premier divisions, and they set up a goal to be the best league in Scandinavia by 2017. By looking at the last few years we can see great progress. In comparison to other Scandinavian leagues, the Swedish teams are on top when it comes to attendance. The report by Deloitte regarding the economy of Allsvenskan and the clubs is showing that the clubs need to become even more professional than they are today, and marketing should focus more on digital and new media. Another aspect of the report shows that the Swedish clubs are developing their facilities with more hospitality programs just like teams in the bigger European leagues are doing.

The rule regarding minimum 51 per cent ownership of a football club by members has always been important in Sweden but is blocking external investments that could enable big revenue streams and help attract greater players. Despite this, the Swedish elite football clubs have turned more and more into the commercialised structure within the organisations. However, much more needs to be done continuously to both keep up the revenue stream and to survive and compete at the top whilst retaining the supporter culture. There is a balance to be had and there has been a fear in recent times about losing the special community status.

There is however some flexibility in that the Swedish Sports Confederation allows clubs to create limited companies together with investors as long as the club controls a majority of the votes. The Swedish Sports Confederation (RF) is the umbrella organisation of the Swedish sports movement. Through its member organisations, it has three million members in 22,000 clubs. The Confederation was formed on 31 May 1903 to help regulate sport in Sweden.

The idea is that there is a pan-sport board of directors that can speak on behalf of the united sports movement in contact with politicians, the Government and other institutions/organisations. In some respects, they are the equivalent of Sport Scotland or Sport England as well as providing service in areas where these cannot or don't want to build up their own competence. Across Scandinavia other sports such as alpine events, handball, basketball etc have significant influence and there is very much a meeting of minds and the ability to coordinate the sports movement in fields like research and development. In certain areas it acts in place of the Government through managing and distributing governmental grants to sports.

Unlike in Germany, where 14 of the 20 Bundesliga clubs are structured as limited companies in some form, the take-up has been less enthusiastic in Sweden. Partly because there's less capital available (smaller country), partly because the members wouldn't have it and partly because the cases where clubs have set up limited companies (examples being Hammarby, AIK, Djurgårdens) have not exactly benefited from doing so.

Just as we have seen in Germany, this model of ownership and approach to football club governance has come under threat in recent years. Surprisingly, the Swedish FA (Swedish: Svenska Fotbollförbundet, SvFF) themselves backed a proposal to remove the '50 plus one' rule and allow clubs to engage in other forms of club ownership; fortunately, the Svenska Fotbollssupporterunionen (SFSU), the umbrella organisation for democratic, not-for-profit supporters' groups in Sweden, organised a campaign to counter such a proposal and were successful in ensuring that '50 plus one' survived in Swedish football as well as in other sports.

From football's perspective, the campaign's key moment was when groups from eight major clubs coordinated the passing of motions at their club AGMs, which stated unequivocally that 50 plus one should be retained and that moves at a national level to remove the rule should not be supported by those running the clubs on the members' behalf. This in turn led to the SvFF altering its position, and set in motion the chain of events that has led to the preservation of member ownership in Sweden. Such a successful campaign is a prime example of the influence and power that supporters can hold at their respective clubs and the part they can play in deciding how football is governed in their country. The taste of success has forced all the sporting organisations to evolve into corporate businesses with professional competencies, especially with the players, but also in finance and marketing to compete with the best.

## Malmö FF: A Great Example

How do Malmö do it? Well, they want to make every member a meaningful shareholder by all having a single vote at AGMs where resolutions are debated and passed.

Malmö FF made the transition from an amateur club to fully professional in the late 1970s under the leadership of Club Chairman Eric Persson. The club is an open member association, and the AGM is the highest policymaking body where each member has one vote, therefore no shares are issued. The meeting approves the accounts, votes to elect the chairman and the board, and decides on incoming motions. During the successful 2010s era, Håkan Jeppsson was the chairman after taking over from Bengt Madsen in 2010, prior to his sudden death in 2018. The club's legal status means that any interest claims are made to the club and not to the board of directors or club members. Daily operations are run by a managing director who liaises with the chairman.

With an equity of 497 million SEK the club is the richest football club in Sweden as of 2019. The turnover for 2018 was 343 million SEK. The highest transfer fee received by Malmö FF for a player was 86.2 million SEK (€8.7 million at that time) for Zlatan Ibrahimović who was sold to Ajax in 2001. At the time, this was the highest transfer fee ever paid to a Swedish football club.

## Turkey: A Changing Landscape

Almost all sports clubs in Turkey are owned by their members. The sports clubs that were created in the early 1900s were primarily created by British workers and followed a similar pattern as we saw in South America where they eventually became members' organisations. Our guide in Turkey is Necati Mete, a fans' representative for Fenerbahçe FC who talked us through it.

In Turkish Laws, clubs are defined as legal entity. In Turkey, in accordance with the law, clubs may have two kinds of structures:

1) A club may be established as a public association which is committed to law of associations. In Turkish law of associations, an association must have at least seven members to be legally established. This association must be a non-profit organisation. Associations may obtain profits yet there's no aim of sharing this profit among members. The aim is to use this profit for sportive purposes.

To this extent, we can clearly state that all the clubs in Turkey are founded as public benefit associations. Clubs have members and they vote for their president/board at the ordinary general meeting. General meetings are arranged every 3–4 years depending on the club's charter. In order to be a member, one should pay an entrance fee and yearly contribution defined by the club. This is the only massive interaction between the fans and club. Apart from these, other interactions are in demonstrating that you are an ordinary regular fan.

2) The second option: sports clubs may organise as companies, and they may be open to the stock market. In Turkey, some of the clubs are incorporated in terms of their football branches such as Fenerbahçe SK, Galatasaray SK, Beşiktaş JK, Trabzonspor etc.

In this option, only the football branch is allowed to be incorporated. The other branches like basketball, volleyball, table tennis etc still belong to the association, and they are not open to the stock market.

In these clubs above, members still vote for clubs' presidents and boards. But the football branch has a specific board, voted by the investors. Yet again, the club's president is also the president of the football branch. To sum up, in the second option, clubs are still public benefit associations but the incorporated branch, which is football, has specific statutory rights as a 'company' and they have investors (not an owner). Is this system under the threat of globalisation? Definitely yes. It's basically because of the financial difficulties as the clubs need more money every day and global interest is always a glamorous option. In the near future, it's been said that someday, with the legal arrangements, Turkish clubs may be bought by a foreigner, which did not happen until today. After COVID-19, we'll see what's going to come out. Local Turkish politics try to assist clubs financially, as especially the four big clubs above have millions of fans all around Turkey and Europe and authorities don't want fans upsetting. Yet again, in the near future, no one can be

## Uruguay: Small but Perfectly Formed

sure what will be the outcome of financial difficulties.

It is a well-known fact that capital cities in most countries are more likely to have more football teams representing them than other metropolitans, and Montevideo, the capital of Uruguay is the perfect representation of that. But what's odd about Montevideo is that it has almost all the teams that play in Uruguay's top division and they are the country's most prominent footballing city and one of South America's most respected.

Uruguayan teams tend to be owned by their members, although in recent years we have seen management groups acquiring those teams with financial issues or as prospects to develop young players (such is the case of the City Group).

### *Uruguayan Football: Decan*

There is probably little surprise to read that football club ownership in Uruguay has followed a similar trajectory as those other members' clubs that were established in South America. All the major clubs in Uruguay are member-owned with similar member structures.

Surrounded by the prowess of two of world football's giants, Brazil and Argentina, Uruguay, despite having a relatively low population of just under three-and-a-half million people is a phenomenal footballing country and Montevideo has played a pivotal role in its success. Uruguay is known for *la garra* (literally 'claw', the supposedly characteristic combination of toughness and streetwiseness), the stamina of the Maracanazo.

One single, charismatic individual provided the impetus for turning kickabouts into regular, professional competition. Anglo-Scot, William Leslie Poole, considered the 'Father of Uruguayan Football' was a schoolteacher and founder of the English High School of Montevideo. Pupils of his school created the 'Albion Football Club', Uruguay's first football club, in 1891. Community ownership has thrived to this day in the country, maybe because of its size which has limited commercial opportunities for clubs. There is no doubt that many in the country look across to Europe and wonder what might be if the structures were different. Part of the strength of each club is how many *socios* that they can retain as members, so they have to work hard at being a football community. There are three other sources of income that fuel the football clubs in the country, distribution of cash from the national association based on the performance of the national team, commercial deals done by the league and individual clubs and of course the sale of talent which at the top income level is to Europe and at the lower level to its fellow South American clubs. Shortfalls have to be made up from wealthier fans who might contribute – given that they are also club *socios*. In any one year there is an average of 400 Uruguayan players signed for clubs abroad which shows us how reliant the clubs are on exporting their talent to survive.

### What Does Voting Look Like for Members?

Our friend in Uruguay, Andrea Perilli, Freelance Journalist and Community Manager talks us through the process.

> Many of the *socio* groups have small local subgroups which have the objective of making sure that there is a constant dialogue between the fans and the club. It also acts as the perfect place to develop talented individuals who can go on to work in the various club positions. There are generally quarterly meetings where information is shared and cascaded from the club. At election time if you are a fully paid-up member you can apply to get on a committee.
> 
> The election process is open and transparent and tends to happen at the weekend of a match where hustings take place and tables are assembled outside the ground to invite members to get information and decide on who they are voting for. Proof of identity is essential to cast your vote to the *socio* officials who manage the process. Voting is a key part of the democratic process and is encouraged by registered votes allowing discount on the club's services and facilities and in some cases from future match tickets.

### A World in View

British football has been slow to look at the ownership possibilities that exist elsewhere and has consistently focused on the here and now and the vested interests of individual clubs. There has been an over-dependence on benefactors, some rich, some less rich and many have driven clubs to bankruptcy and used the clubs to enhance their ego. What we can see is in the wider world there are other ways to look after the clubs that we love. There is proof that there can be success on and off the park when clubs have a shared ownership that brings openness, transparency and accountability to those who deserve it most – the football supporters.

*Contributors:*
Germany Dr Jochen Lammert & Jacob Rossler
Sweden Urban Stoltz ex Helsingborg IF
Turkey Necati Mete
Argentina & Uruguay Andrea Perilli

CHAPTER 5

# In England's Pleasant Land – the White Knights Come Calling

*Football is not merely a small business, it's also a bad one. Anyone who spends any time inside football soon discovers that just as oil is part of the oil business, stupidity is part of the football business.—*
Simon Kuper

THE FA AND the SFA have developed 'fit and proper tests' for anyone wanting to be involved in football, yet over the past 40 years there have been over 150 insolvency events or administrations at football clubs in the United Kingdom. It really is a staggering figure that those in football authorities should be ashamed of. The fact that the fit and proper tests have failed seems to be of little concern to the football authorities who shrug their shoulders and seem happy enough to continue to look the other way.

In so many instances over the years the scrutiny of *who* is running our clubs and *how* they are running the clubs has been virtually unchecked. The fit and proper test has hardly been worth the paper it is written on, and the financial scrutiny of clubs seems to have been deliberately ignored. Another obvious error is that once a share certificate has been acquired the football authorities feel they can no longer interfere in the workings of a limited company and step back. To say it is a light touch towards the governance of members is a bit of an understatement. It means that the only 'real' scrutiny is through the initial fit and proper test. If you pass that then you have a home run as there is no ongoing evaluation, monitoring, benchmarking or real support for new owners. As the business guru Peter Drucker says, 'If you don't evaluate it, you will never improve it'.

The ongoing difficulty for football has been that when clubs are in a major crisis the most obvious route to survival has been galvanising the supporter base. Getting the damsel in distress to signal for any white knights out there willing to rescue the club from the impending disaster is key. Sadly, spotting a genuine white knight is very often a fruitless task. Time pressures and the reluctance of sensible businesspeople from taking on a distressed business that is usually being hounded by players wanting wages, or HMRC, very often means that the damsel is more likely to lure in a villain instead. Sorting the wheat from the chaff is not something that football has ever done effectively. In fact, some might say that it is a challenge that the football authorities find beyond them. Sometimes it works when a Roy MacGregor at Ross County, or a Matthew Benham at Brentford arrives on the scene but more often than not we have seen many in the mould of Craig Whyte at Rangers.

There is no doubt that many of these administration events could have been avoided had better protocols been in place at the League and the Football Associations. If you think of club failures, cases such as Rangers, Hearts, Portsmouth and Leeds United come to mind, but below these very high-profile cases many others have gone under the radar as they have been at smaller clubs and have attracted less attention from the mainstream media. In the pre-social media age there was little scrutiny or publicity when these disasters happened and, more often than not, they were deemed to be local news stories. Now in the full glare of the open digital age the whole world knows a lot more of the details and can debate about the dramas that subsequently unfold in real time.

In writing this book I turned to a very close friend of the Scottish Football Supporters Association, Bryan Jackson, to have a chat about why clubs end up in administration. Many of you will know him as the administrator who was involved in driving clubs such as Dundee, Dunfermline Athletic and Heart of Midlothian out of administration towards community ownership. This is not intended to be a book or indeed a chapter of lists but a roll of honour of some of the administration or insolvency events within the UK football industry seems a good place to start. Looking through the carcasses of these clubs in distress should in theory prevent some of these nightmares from re-emerging in the future. However, the reality is as long as human beings find clubs attractive then problems will persist. We know football is not just about the sport and often it can be the platform that allows the worst excesses of ego, power and money to show its face.

## The Reasons Why Clubs Fail: Football Groundhog Day

If you were looking for a huge list of different reasons why clubs fail, then you will be disappointed to hear that there are not that many. In fact, most of the stories from the clubs listed below have a remarkable similarity about them, which makes the fact that it keeps happening all the more scandalous.

In simple terms, clubs go into administration or liquidation when they get to the point that they run out of money. It is not really any different from you or me going bankrupt. The real learning is in making sure that the people who run the club do not fall into the traps that football sets for them season after season.

Having looked at many of the most prominent club failures there are common reasons why they end up calling in the receivers. The strangest thing about this is that it really is not rocket science and it is quite startling that clubs keep collapsing time after time.

So much of the turmoil that has been described has been driven by the personalities involved and the dangerous combination of power, money and egos at play. Maybe in the future football clubs will be run by Artificial Intelligence and they will stop making the same mistakes in some sort of *Groundhog Day* routine.

You have to ask why any successful businessperson would ever get involved in owning a football club. There are maybe a few options that we can consider before looking at how the best laid plans of mice and men often go awry. More often than not there could be a combination of more than one of these factors driving them to step into the spotlight.

- Owner has a huge ego
- Owner is a philanthropist who cares about club/community
- Owner is a benevolent benefactor with the club at heart
- Owner sees a business opportunity (profit motive)
- Owner is the continuity solution who inherited the situation

One of the biggest lessons that is rarely heeded is by people who have been successful in business thinking that they have transferable skills that can guarantee football success. Very often success in one field brings not only money but the trappings of wealth and ego. This anonymous saying often used in business training courses sums it up, 'There is a thin line between confidence and arrogance... it's called humility. Confidence smiles and arrogance smirks'.

More often than not the offer to get involved comes when the club is struggling. Normally investors would run a mile from speculating in a failed company yet are happy to overlook the failings just because the business has the letters FC after its name. As we will see in more detail in Chapter Seven where we look at the few failures of community ownership, the mountain new owners face is more often than not debt from previous regimes or financial instability due to the failed plans of those who were the previous leaders. If you buy a structure that is unstable it can be quite a challenge in the weekly sequence of win, lose or draw to build a successful plan that can quickly change things.

## What Are the Traps?

Through this book we refer to the fact that lessons from failure are very rarely learned in the world of football. In some respects it is because those in charge don't see the traps, don't recognise that the traps exist, think they have a special gift to overcome the obstacles or simply take on a task that is too large or too fast for them. Usually it is a combination of the traps that leaves those with limited resources in trouble. Many new owners will have recognised the scenarios described below at some time or another and often it is only the ones with enough collateral and resources that can escape to live another day.

### An Impossible Challenge – 'Ain't No Mountain High Enough'

The success rate of Mount Everest climbers is pretty low at only 29 per cent of those attempting managing to scale its heights. Despite the 71 per cent failure rate, hundreds of people still seek permission to climb Mount Everest every year. In recent years, attempts have been made to minimise the chance of death on the mountain. You could call it the equivalent of football's fit and proper person test. The scrutiny of those attempting the challenge has increased significantly to ensure those putting themselves forward have the right level of experience, knowledge and resources to succeed. Yet despite that, the odds are stacked against them being successful even though most of those attempting the challenge are experienced climbers and technically capable. Not too dissimilar to taking over your local team and getting them promoted. Theoretically speaking, if you buy Scunthorpe United and the pyramid system is in operation, with the right investment you could get them to the Champions League. However, as the excellent book *Money and Football* by Stefan Szymanski explains, the chances of doing so are so remote that it will never happen. In football terms, the danger is that the mountain you have taken on is almost certainly too high to climb.

## The Pace of the Business – 'The on-field performance has a role to play'

The game offers little respite for any new market entrants. Football is a business like no other where the weekly turnaround is fast and furious. Most clubs are run as seven-day-a-week businesses with activity starting in the morning and running right into the evening with academy and community football filling the schedules. There is simply no other business like it. It is an unforgiving environment and many of the white knights who do step forward find the lack of control and the constant hamster wheel of football a difficult challenge to master. The reality of the situation is that there is so little control that can be exerted by an owner that can impact the on-field performances which drive the success of the club. They are so remote from the actual football side of the business that the only thing that can be done is to help fix problems with financial support. It is not like taking over a failing restaurant where you can change the menu, change the décor and change the chef, throw out some PR and get a new audience. Football is nothing more than a results business that moves so fast that there is little that new owners can do to make a guaranteed impact. Changing managers and then players takes time and no matter how much money you throw at it there is no guarantee of success. What is likely to happen as you wrestle with these problems is that crowds will go down, further reducing your revenue and the crowd that stays to support you will get restless and start baying for your head. Every Saturday evening up to 50 per cent of clubs and their supporters can be depressed, disappointed and desperate as they have failed to win – again.

## Chasing the Dream – 'The Jordan scenario'

There is no doubt as we look through the archives that this is the most obvious reason for clubs to fail. It is the simple premise that if you spend more than the income you are generating you are heading for trouble. In football terms, what you have today is not what you have tomorrow and so much of this changes every Saturday at 4.45pm when you are either going up or down. So much of the business model is based on the vagaries of lady luck rather than any business decisions. The simple premise that many failed to grasp is that what goes up has to come down. Relegation from a higher division can happen to even the most glamorous of football clubs, just as it does for models (no matter how famous or beautiful you might be). More often than not there is a period of instability at the club that has led to on-field failures or at the very least a decline in sporting fortunes. However, this is not always the case; sometimes the clubs have just overstretched in the desire to follow the dream of obtaining promotion. Going down the pyramid when you have the infrastructure and costs of the league above can quite quickly exacerbate the inevitable crash.

## Why Do Clubs Go into Administration?

Every one of these statistics has a story behind it and a group of fans who never asked for their team to be taken to the brink of oblivion. Here are just a few of these stories as it is important to understand just what can go wrong.

### The demise of Leeds United and their rebirth in 2019

Leeds United are historically one of the largest clubs in England and won the league in 1992, the season before the formation of the Premier League. In the following years, Leeds continued to be relatively successful, never finishing outside the top five in the league and reaching the semi-finals of the 2001 Champions League. However, during this period, Leeds were spending money which they didn't have. Under Chairman Peter Ridsdale, the club took out massive loans to finance their excessive spending, with the expectation of gaining extra revenue from cup runs in Europe and competing for the Premier League. But after failing to qualify for the Champions League in successive seasons, the club struggled to keep up with repayments. With concern for the club growing, Ridsdale infamously said, 'we lived the dream'. That dream turned into a nightmare for the fans.

Desperate attempts to raise funds began which involved the selling of any players of value at the club, including Rio Ferdinand to Manchester United for £30m. These player sales caused a high turnover in managers, adding to the turmoil at the club. Leeds narrowly avoided relegation in the 2002/3 season but eventually went down in 2003/4. A consortium of local businessmen took over the club, inheriting debts in excess of £100m. Another overhaul of players followed in an attempt to reduce the wage bill and the club sold off their training ground and stadium. Despite these efforts, the loss in TV revenue that came with missing out on the Premier League meant the club still struggled to pay off their debts.

In May 2007, the club was relegated to the third tier for the first time in their history and were placed into administration.

The club was put up for sale at the start of the new season and former Chelsea owner Ken Bates became the successful bidder. The club played in the third tier for the next three seasons before being promoted back to the second tier, where they remain to this day. With new Italian owner Andrea Radrizzani and a charismatic world-class manager in Marcelo Bielsa, the drama continued to unfold and can be followed in the excellent Amazon Prime series *Take Us Home*. Leeds United are now once again trying to get at long last back where they belong in the Premier League having recently been relegated again.

### Portsmouth FC: The bell tolls for Pompey

The Portsmouth story from 1998 to 2020 is probably the most interesting for us neutral observers as it covers a period of many highs for Pompey as well as a period where the benefits of the conventional 'benefactor' model ownership structure were called into question. The rollercoaster started in what should have been a season of celebration in the club's centenary season. Season 1998/99 saw a serious financial crisis hit the club and in December 1998, Chairman Martin Gregory quit his post after being the target of abuse from Portsmouth fans which gave him no choice but to sell his 97 per cent ownership of the club. In February 1999 Portsmouth went into receivership. They avoided relegation again that season and were then saved from closure by new chairman Milan Mandarić, a Serbian-born American IT guru from Silicon Valley. He had previously dabbled in football in the USA and had owned Nice which he sold in 1998.

After struggling for a number of years in the second tier of English football (now the EFL Championship), Portsmouth won promotion as champions to the Premier League in the 2002/3 season. This was due in large part to Mandarić's appointment of the experienced manager Harry Redknapp and a heavy investment in playing staff. In January 2006, Mandarić sold a 50 per cent stake in the club to French-Israeli businessman Alexandre Gaydamak. This really was the start of the downfall of this once proud club and led to a story so bizarre that it is hard now looking back to believe that it actually did happen. Fasten your seatbelts if you are ready to read a summary of what was probably the worst series of events to hit any club in the UK in history.

After the club's survival that season, Mandarić sold his remaining share of Portsmouth to Gaydamak, but stayed on as a figurehead in his role as non-executive chairman. Despite the lack of infrastructure investment in the much loved but decaying Fratton Park and having one of the smallest supporter bases in the league, Pompey thrived for a remarkable seven-year period. The icing on the cake came in season 2008/09 when they were surprise winners of the FA Cup, inspired by their African talisman Kanu. During this time it is hard to imagine many fans having too many concerns about the direction of travel for the club. With the growing wealth of the Premier League fuelled by larger and larger TV deals and an owner with business interests in places such as Luxembourg and the British Virgin Islands, openness and transparency were in short supply.

This successful period was sustained by excessive spending that their 20,000 attendances could not justify. The wage player bill for the 2007/08 season exceeded £55m, which was central to a £17m operating loss for that season, taking their debts to over £60m. The club was funded by taking out loans, which were guaranteed by Gaydamak, illustrating the heavy reliance on the owner in the single benefactor model. This reliance can also be viewed as fragility, and this was realised during the 2008 financial crisis in which creditors began to seek repayment of loans. Gaydamak was forced to pay off the banks and it became to him that the club owned money. As a result, he decided that he could no longer fund the club and looked to sell his shares.

Sulaiman Al-Fahim then bought the club in 2009 for £1, dominating headlines, and pledged to inject £5m in an attempt to pay off the club's debt. This rushed sale to new owner Al-Fahim resulted in failures from both Gaydamak and the FA to carry out proper due diligence. It was clear that the sale and its hasty nature were motivated by the interests of Gaydamak and not the best interests of the club, another big disadvantage of the single benefactor model. It quickly became apparent that Al-Fahim didn't have access to sufficient funds to operate a loss-making and debt-riddled Premier League club. Wages were left unpaid by the club and the Premier League forced Al-Fahim to sell after only 43 days in charge. This resulted in yet another rushed sale of the club. In 2018 it was alleged that Al-Fahim stole £5 million from his wife to fund the purchase of Portsmouth Football Club and was sentenced in his absence by Dubai's first instance court to five years in jail.

On 4 October 2009 it was reported by Reuters that the Portsmouth FC owner Al-Fahim was to sell the majority shareholding in the Premier League club to Ali al-Faraj. At the time, Al-Fahim's advisors described al-Faraj as being of 'moderate wealth' which proved to be far from sufficient. Al-Faraj never once set foot in the city of Portsmouth and is known fittingly by supporters to this day as 'Ali al-Mirage' with many even questioning his existence. His finances proved just as elusive, and the club was soon placed into administration.

This was the first time that an existing Premier League club had to announce administration after a High Court ruling. They were £70m in debt and were docked nine points which practically assured relegation in 2010. Creditors were few and far between and Pompey lacked legitimate creditors to pay off their debt. Having been FA Cup winners against Manchester United, a juggernaut of English football in 2008, with a squad led by Harry Redknapp, falling into administration during the summer of 2009 was big news for football fans. By 2010, the club had entered administration for the third time in 20 years, highlighting a real lack of leadership and authority within the football club that had become driven by a profit motive and egos.

By the summer of 2009, when Portsmouth had gone through four owners, Chief Executive Peter Storrie said he would continue to attempt to guide the club in the right direction.

The change of hands between a multitude of 'businessmen' during the summer of 2009 highlights just how inept the control of who runs clubs is and how inept the football authorities are in dealing with anyone who claims to have the funds to buy and run a club. How quickly things can turn in football when our clubs are not in the right hands.

The Pompey Supporters Trust was founded in 2009, initially to try and gain some influence in the club to prevent the continuation of the trend of disastrous owners one after the other. However, in 2012, with the club in another administration and no bids that the supporters deemed suitable, they decided to attempt a takeover of their own. Two thousand three hundred members raised over £2.5m and bought over 51 per cent of the club. The trust had a mission to deliver ownership for the people who love it most. The objectives were simple: *to have a club that is run sustainably, transparently and in the proper manner*. The club paid off the last of its remaining debts in 2014. The tenure of the fans at what was the UK's biggest fan-owned club didn't last long and after a four-year period they readopted the benefactor model when the American billionaire Michael Eisner and his investment company Tornante offered £5.67m to buy 100 per cent of the club. In Chapter 8 we will explore just what has happened to the Pompey since then. If this plot and sub-plots sound like it would make a film, then you are not going to be disappointed as Amazon Prime have now produced a fantastic documentary called *Our Club* that tells the story in detail.

### *York City 2002: No salvation for the Minster Men*

In December 2001, chairman at the time Douglas Craig put the club up for sale for £4.5m. The club's longest serving chairman stated that if a buyer for the club and the ground was not found by the end of the season, they would resign from the Football League. It was a huge threat that left the club under real duress. An unlikely saviour appeared at Bootham Crescent with the arrival of a retired Motor GP driver John Batchelor who did a deal and took over the club in March 2002. Sadly, all was not well in York and the underlying structural issues and lack of liquidity meant that by December 2002 the club was placed in administration. The York City Supporters' Trust were the only bidders and bought the club for £100,000. As part of the deal there was a payment plan for the £160,000 that was owed in tax to the authorities. In the end, he failed to pay off any of the tax owed and went back on his promise to have elected supporters on the club board, deteriorating his relationship with the York City Supporters' Trust. With virtually no on-field investment of a level that was needed for a club of its size, the Minstermen didn't win any games in their last 20 in the 2003/4 season. They were relegated from the football conference ending a 75-year stay in the Football League. The truth is that the club has failed to recover ever since, and the downward spiral has continued to this day.

### Notts County 2000 and 2019: An age-old problem

Proving that history is no barrier to off-the-field troubles, a truly iconic club that has suffered along the way is Notts County. The oldest team in the Football League were not alone in suffering the full effects of the collapse of ITV Digital in 2000. ITV Digital was a new TV company that had an unsustainable business model. They had rightly predicted there would be a major boom in the football TV marketplace but sadly for ITV Digital and for so many league clubs, they had the wrong model at the wrong time being run by a business that was under resourced. It was very interesting that several years later when BT launched their own platform, they spent a considerable amount of time dissecting what ITV Digital did and didn't do to ensure that the same mistakes would not be made again. There was cataclysmic impact felt in the English Football League and in particular at the lower levels when ITV Digital could not pay £178m of the £350m owed to the Football League. Many of the clubs had budgeted on income that was not going to materialise and it resulted in some clubs unable to pay wage bills and more importantly VAT and HMRC liabilities.

It all started to go wrong for County. In November 2000, a sale agreement had been made between DCP Holdings Ltd – a company owned by Pavis and his wife, Vivien – and Notts Holdings Ltd, ultimately possessed by American businessman Albert Scardino. The agreed balances due were not paid and the consequences were severe. The club was placed into administration in June 2002 with debts of around £6 million, partially built up by inflated player wages in a gamble to gain a promotion which failed to materialise. After a failed takeover by two-man partnership Raj Bhatia and Frank Strang, the club's future looked 'bleak' and 'devastating' in the words of administrator Paul Finnity. The cost of running a wage bill and operations meant Notts County quickly went into administration. Narrowly avoiding relegation in 2000, they then lost the well-known Scottish manager Jocky Scott and his coaching staff. Having failed in its attempt to renegotiate its debt, Notts County were placed into administration in order to protect its limited assets. County, founded in 1862 and original members of the Football League, went into administration in June 2002, for longer than any other club in league history. The club were given an ultimatum that if they did not come out of administration by 27 May 2003 they would be expelled from the league. There was a real feeling that the situation that was emerging was unique, and some other clubs did feel that exceptional efforts were being made just because of the historical links that football had to the club. That argument was well used when it emerged that the deadline for coming out of administration was extended three times. In doing so they created another record as on 12 August the club had been in administration for an unprecedented 421 days, surpassing the record previously held by Queens Park Rangers. Meanwhile, they were still under threat of expulsion from the league. Scenarios like these playing out often tell us as much about the lack of governance and structures at the football authorities as they do about the mismanagement at the clubs involved. Albert Scardino, Notts County's acting chairman, a former Bill Clinton 'adviser' and Pulitzer Prize winner, warned that the club could be forced into administration or even liquidation within two weeks following Nottingham City Council's refusal to guarantee a £1.7m bank loan. His tenure was on the basis of a hire purchase type arrangement from the ageing previous owner who had struggled to find a buyer. It was the type of brinkmanship you might expect to come from the West Wing, not seen in Robin Hood territory.

In order to overcome £5m of debt, the club had also approached Nottinghamshire County Council in the hope that they would guarantee a further £1.7m. They too refused to act as a loan guarantor. In an attempt to restructure its crippling short-term debts into a more manageable figure to be paid off over a number of years, the club had planned to mortgage their £8m Meadow Lane stadium.

Scardino pleaded, 'We own our stadium, but we can't pay our bills with the stadium, that is a liability to us. We need the value of it, a small part of the value, in cash, to pay the people who have done business with us in good faith.' He commented in what was a common theme at many clubs. We have assets but we have no cash. In many other cases, such as at York City, once the ground has been split from the club the struggle becomes even harder. The final saga at County meant that if the administrators were unable to take the club out of administration by 9 December, County would be withdrawn from the league. The clock was running down, and it did look that the end was finally in sight.

In 2001–02, Notts County were nailed on for another relegation but, with just 11 games remaining, something incredible began. When the gates were about to close, a consortium helped by the £250,000 that the supporters had raised emerged. The investor was local entrepreneur Haydn Green who stepped forward and added his shares to those of the supporters which gave the supporters a majority shareholding of over 60 per cent.

It made for a great story, the oldest club in the league being owned by the fans, but ownership proved a challenge for the supporters. The club was stable and debt free but there were always opportunists wanting to sell the conventional dream of taking the club to a higher plateau. Even the official club history indicates that much of this had been driven by the infighting and lack of creditability of the supporters' trust.

In the summer of 2009, Notts moved into a new and exciting era when it was revealed that an ambitious consortium wanted to gain control and invest significant – some might say ridiculous – sums of cash into the club. A media circus unravelled at Meadow Lane and the supporters' trust voted overwhelmingly to gift their shares to Munto Finance. Peter Trembling became executive chairman with immediate effect and, less than two weeks later, the arrival of former England and Mexico manager Sven-Goran Eriksson as Director of Football had Notts fans pinching themselves. More big names followed, with the addition of Kasper Schmeichel, son of Manchester United legend Peter, and former Arsenal and England international Sol Campbell – all eyes were on the Magpies. The bubble soon burst and, eventually, a consortium led by Ray Trew purchased the club for £1 and took on the overwhelming debts of the previous regime to ultimately save the world's oldest Football League club.

Rumours of administration circled but the decision was made to tackle the money owed head on and Notts County, after many years of uncertainty, had some stability. Another local entrepreneur who thought he could square the circle was Alan Hardy who owned design company Paragon Interiors Group. BBC Radio Nottingham reported the company lent money to buy and fund the club as part of Hardy's takeover deal in January 2017. On 4 May 2019, Notts County were relegated from the English Football League for the first time in their 157-year history following a 3–1 defeat away at Swindon Town. Administration followed but as we know, clubs don't die, so it was a relief that on 26 July 2019, the club was sold to Danish businessmen Alexander and Christoffer Reedtz. The next chapter in the history of this old lady is now waiting to be written and from the outside it does look a bit more promising!

### The Story of Bury FC: Twice shaken to the core

Known as 'The Shakers', the team play in Greater Manchester almost in the shadows of the two world giants of the game, United and City. Gigg Lane is one of the world's oldest football grounds and has been the club's home venue since 1885. It is said to be one of those grounds that real football fans fall in love with and a playing surface players fall in love with.

The club struggled in recent times and the late 1980s brought a 'wealthy fan investor' to the club in the shape of a former partner at the highly regarded City financial company Phillips & Drew called Hugh Eaves. Alas, things went spectacularly wrong when the Eaves gravy train hit the station buffers in 1999. Some serious financial irregularities emerged from his former employers, and he confessed to his partners that they had 'lost' large sums of money from the proceeds of the sale to UBS, which he was responsible for managing. He vanished without trace and was last heard of in the Far East. In echoes of the Nick Lesson story, the plot thickened when Bury were sued on behalf of Eaves' former partners who then sought to recover their money which included £750,000 that poor old Bury were being asked to find. Selling the club was not an easy option as they could approve any takeover deals – presumably to be first in line for the £750,000 that they didn't have and then were saddled with the famous old stadium at Gigg Lane having a substantial mortgage on it to Lloyds TSB. They were a bank who desperately wanted to get out of football so support in that direction was always going to be limited.

A song of the time had Bonnie Tyler 'holding out for a hero' and of course stepped forward another likely lad in the shape of a soon to be disgraced solicitor, Richard Prentis, who offered the club £1 million. The only wee problem was that his guaranteed annual return of 15 per cent on 'fully secured loans' scheme was soon to be exposed as a scam. In May 2000, Prentis advanced Bury a 12-month loan of £1m secured on Gigg Lane and a fortnight later his company was closed down and he was eventually struck off by the Law Society.

The High Court then judged that the recovery process should be done on behalf of the many people who gave Prentis the original loans. In court, documents were generated that instigated proceedings to repossess Gigg

Lane in May 2001.

Bury did manage to get a stay of execution by notifying the court to delay moving on the ground as Bury claimed Mansport Developments were negotiating to buy the club. In desperate times a lot of sharks seem to circle football clubs with the sniff of blood in the water. Mansport was only formed in January of that year and is registered at the Manchester office of David Jones, who has been Swinton's secretary since 1995. All the initial paperwork showed that the sole director was Paul Barrett. Step forward Jones, who offered to become Bury's company secretary, to facilitate the Mansport deal. Ashurst Morris Crisp, the company acting on behalf of the creditors, treated Mansport as preferred bidder and, when Robinson resigned from Bury at the end of January, he said it had a deal ready to sign. It really is great to have friends with influence. Of course, during all these backdoor manoeuvres the most important people at the club, the fans, never got told anything.

Eventually it came to pass that the *Manchester Evening News* revealed that Jones and Barrett had been convicted together in 1997 of obtaining services by deception and imprisoned for 18 months – reduced to 12 on appeal – and eight months respectively. Several of Barrett's companies have also been put into liquidation and are under investigation by the Department of Trade and Industry. It highlighted the weaknesses in the fit and proper test at the English Football League.

The successful 'Save our Shakers' campaign that was brilliantly orchestrated by the wonderfully named Neville Neville is now part of Shakers history and the hope was that it signalled a significant change in the fortunes of the football club. From the Seat Sale campaign through to bucket collections, made not only at Gigg Lane but at many league grounds around the country, Neville (father of Gary and Phil) tirelessly organised supporters' groups, gave media interviews, worked closely with the administrators and finally arranged a deal which would ultimately save the Shakers from extinction. The supporters captured it beautifully, 'We owe him a huge debt'. The efforts were rewarded with a seat on the board, and they found a benefactor who bought the stadium and gave it rent-free for two years. Everything in the garden looked rosy. An army of supporters was mobilised and funds were frantically raised in a desperate attempt to save their football club. The collecting buckets used now deserve as prominent a place in the Gigg Lane trophy cabinet as our two FA Cups.

The PFA lent £170,000, its largest sum, to meet wages, and the Save Our Shakers supporters' campaign raised £128,000. All is well that ends well. In this case sadly not.

# IN ENGLAND'S PLEASANT LAND – THE WHITE KNIGHTS COME CALLING

*Shaken again in 2019 and still not stirred in 2023*

Bury really had to do something significant to become a main feature story on the BBC main news bulletins. Having just been promoted to Division One it was a shock to the system but not a surprise when the news emerged that Bury were in trouble again. Even then in their hour of need, when coverage on the BBC can generate significant exposure for a cause and potentially tease out any potential saviours, Bury ran out of luck. The news that Bolton Wanderers had also crashed and burned meant that the coverage they might ordinarily get was immediately diluted and the chance to find another white knight lessened.

The BBC coverage, when it did come, allowed us all access to the funeral of this famous old club. 'It's like a death', says one distraught supporter outside the home ground, on the day that Bury FC was officially expelled from the EFL, August 2019.

Sadly, Bury was another club that ended up succumbing to the lure of wealth that could drive the club forward, after being saved by fans the first time around. It all happened so fast and in the full vision of the EFL. During August 2019, owner of Bury FC Steve Dale went back on his CVA agreement (Company Voluntary Arrangement) to settle £5m worth of Bury Football Club debts. This meant that the famous football club Bury FC, winner of two FA Cups in its 135-year history, had been expelled from the EFL.

Dale had bought the club for the grand price of £1 from previous owner Stewart Day during a December 2018 takeover bid. Dale had a track record of owning companies in financial difficulties and even before the takeover had happened the EFL raised its eyebrows about the authenticity of Dale's funds. Steve Dale promised to settle the club's £5m debts, however as the club went into liquidation, supervisor of the CVA case Steven Wiseglass found that Dale did not have enough funds to provide anywhere near enough money to save the club from going into administration. Wiseglass carried out the usual actions of a CVA supervisor, which first involves assessing the funds available to the club and if these are not available then the assets held by the club become liquidated.

Dale was questioned by a number of newspapers at the time after fans were absolutely distraught to find out that one of the oldest clubs in English football had been expelled due to financial mismanagement and greed. He stated that 'lies' were being told about the situation of the club. Gigg Lane, the home ground of Bury, had to be repossessed, however, the 'phoenix club', a group of Bury supporters, attempted to clump together to claim it back.

Being the owner of the club, Dale owed ex-players and staff £4m in transfers and wages, but missed the deadline to pay this after being granted a further six-month extension by the CVA authorities to provide the money. Previous owner Day had loaned the club £3.6m, but after the takeover from Dale, that money was owed to him rather than Day. Companies and sponsors which supported Bury went into administration which further plunged the club into financial disarray.

After manager Ryan Lowe had led the team to League One promotion in the 2018/19 season, signs were there that the football club was moving in the right direction. However, players had not been paid for a prolonged period of time and this meant that the wheels started to fall off. Dale had promised to pay off the debt after giving multiple interviews to reporters when the CVA case opened. This seemed to be false and after the CVA case was complete, the administration process went ahead and due to a lack of proper funding and direction, Bury FC were kicked out of the Football League. A new side emerged owned by the fans, Bury Association Football Club. It was established in December 2019 as a phoenix of Bury FC, which had recently been expelled from the EFL. Sadly there were two separate supporters' groups involved and they had different visions for getting football back in Bury. One group set up a phoenix side, the other group concentrated on getting the Gigg Lane ground back.

In October 2022 supporters were urged to vote in a poll regarding a potential amalgamation of the Bury Football Club Supporters' Society (BFCSS, who owned Gigg Lane and the 'Bury FC' trading name) and the Shakers Community Society (who owned Bury AFC). If the merger was agreed, a new society – The Football Supporters' Society of Bury – would be formed, based at Gigg Lane, while Bury AFC would change its playing name to Bury Football Club. However, the proposals failed to reach the required 66 per cent threshold from both societies; the Shakers Community Society voted 94 per cent in favour while the BFCSS vote in favour fell short, at 63 per cent. In late December it emerged that a second vote would be proposed that might finally bring the two sides together in 2024. In Chapter 7 we will look at the Bury attempts at community ownership.

## A Fans' Guide for the Reasons That Clubs Fail

1. NOT ENOUGH CASH, RESERVES SPENT – AN ESTIMATED 90 PER CENT OF INSOLVENCIES

The vast majority of cases below fall into this category where clubs have simply spent more than they can afford. In the example at Leeds United, having won the league title they anticipated winning the Champions League or at the very least qualifying for the following season. They built a team that cost a pretty penny but as a consequence of the on-field failings, quite quickly had to conduct a fire sale of assets. The downwards spiral came quickly both on and off the park and led to the inevitable conclusion of administration. Another Yorkshire club with a small fan base but huge costs was Bradford City who had a wage to turnover ratio that had them heading to the debt status of a third world nation. They plied their trade in the pre-TV bonanza age in the Premier League and made ends meet, but as soon as they were relegated, despite the cushion of parachute payments they were unable to survive.

2. INSUFFICIENT COLLECTIVE RESOURCES OR HAD NOT PLANNED ON RELEGATION

As we have explored in earlier chapters there comes a time when there is recognition that there are just not enough resources to take the club forward. There have been various instances where owners' business circumstances just changed, either their external business has suffered or in the case that we found when trying to buy Stirling Albion, the owner was 83 years old and had lost a few fellow directors who had passed away. He just ran out of steam, support and cash. Fortunately, administration was avoided. Morton on the other hand suffered two quick relegations and simply ran out of directors with cash. Community ownership is not always the answer and at clubs like Bury and York City it opened the doors to opportunists who did far worse than the fans would ever have done. Some like Brentford showed better judgement in selling to a fan who worked with the supporters and had the resources to build a sustainable, community-focused club.

3. OPPORTUNISTS IN CHARGE OF THE CLUB

This is probably the most interesting category in what could easily be a rogues gallery of football directors. Not all of the club directors end up in prison, but many do, as we saw at the first Bury administration event and at York City, Portsmouth and Chesterfield. There are many other supporters who would argue that crooks and con men have been in charge at their clubs, although jail sentencing is pretty rare and is usually about more than just the activities at the football club. There is always the risk that a snake oil salesman or opportunist can manage to get through the door and quickly get their feet under the table. At Rangers, Craig Whyte was followed by Charles Green, both attracted by the vast fan base and the opportunity to make a killing from the ruins of the famous old club. There are many who believe that David Murray was just as much to blame for his tax avoidance schemes and running up debts of £76 million during his tenure. There are many Rangers fans that still hanker for him being stripped of his knighthood.

In July 2025 Murray for the first time in a decade appeared in public to promote his autobiography. He continued to claim that he was duped by Whyte. The journalists who interviewed him just didn't buy it and did their job by forcing him to apologise to the Gers fans who deserved better.

## 4. DEATH OF AN OWNER

Whilst Gretna's collapse was not caused directly by Brooks Mileson's death, as it preceded it. It was the prospect of his death that was the problem, as the vast sums he lent to the club would have been subject to Inheritance Tax on his imminent death. The SPL moved heaven and earth to keep them going to the end of the season, including giving them all the money they would have received from central funds at the end of the season, plus the following season's parachute payment – despite the club not making into that season Sadly even with the financial support of the league to play its players, it saw out its fixtures before going into administration being unsustainable without such a kind benefactor. Of course, Gretna 2008 emerged from that disaster as a smaller, sustainable community-owned club that ensured that football lived on in the area. In December 2019 having completed his purchase of Partick Thistle, multi-millionaire lottery winner Colin Weir sadly passed away leaving the fans' group Thistle for Ever waiting in the wings for the settlement of all of his affairs before being given his shares. It was indeed fortunate that in these circumstances the club was debt free and well managed off the park, despite being in its worst on-field position for ten years. Although a further saga emerged, that we will feature elsewhere.

## 5. CATASTROPHIC EVENTS FROM OUTSIDE FOOTBALL

When the ITV Digital collapse happened in 2002 it took with it several clubs who had banked on the revenues that were going to be coming to their bottom line. Sadly, it overpaid for the broadcast rights and crashed, taking 1,500 jobs with it. At the time it was reported that up to 30 clubs were in danger of going out of business, though it was estimated in the end that probably no more than four or five clubs, such as Notts County, were tipped into administration.

In 2020, the global economic meltdown due to the pandemic caused by the COVID-19 virus had massive consequences for the game globally and led to significant turmoil.

Many clubs are unable to prevent the inevitable decline following overspends. There is the old adage that the easiest way for a millionaire to lose a fortune is to 'invest' in a football club. Only a tiny percentage of clubs are able to win something, with the win being almost immediately confined to the history books within days of the achievement. In England, the chance of getting to the Premiership in recent years has fuelled debt mountains almost the size of some small countries, all in the hope that they can increase their revenue by £150 million.

This debt mountain is not just in the Championship; Divisions One and Two have also seen the growth of debt on the premise that an upward trajectory will help recover any outstanding spend. They can of course but dream of that conclusion. Sadly, the list of club failures is the equivalent of a Scapa Flow of famous names of clubs who were too big or too successful to sink.

## England and Wales: Some Notable Administration Events

Bradford City 1983
Charlton Athletic 1984
Middlesbrough 1986
Tranmere Rovers 1987
Newport County 1989
Walsall 1990
Northampton 1992
Kettering Town 1992
Aldershot 1992
Maidstone Utd 1992
Hartlepool Utd 1994
Barnet 1994
Exeter City
Gillingham 1995
Doncaster Rovers 1997
Millwall 1997
Bournemouth 1997
Darlington 1998 – practically disappeared as a club
Crystal Palace 1998–2000
Chester City 1998–99

Barrow 1999
Portsmouth 1998–2008
Swindon 2000
Hull City 2001
QPR 2001–2002
Lincoln City 2002
Halifax Town 2002–2003
Bradford City 2002
Notts County 2002
Barnsley 2002
MK Dons 2003
Leicester City 2002–2003
Port Vale 2002–2003
York City 2002–2003
Derby County 2002–2003
Ipswich Town 2002
Wimbledon 2003–2004
Darlington (again) 2003–2004
Wrexham 2004–2006
Cambridge Utd 2005
Rotherham Utd 2006
Crawley Town 2006–2007
Boston Utd 2006–2007
Leeds Utd 2007
Luton Town 2007–2008
Bournemouth 2008
Stockport County 2009–2010
Chester City 2009–2010
Salisbury City 2009–2010
Weymouth 2009
Plymouth Argyle 2011
Rushden and Diamonds 2011 – disappeared
Port Vale 2012
Coventry City 2013
Aldershot Town 2013–2014
Bolton Wanderers 2019
Bury 2019
Derby County 2020
Torquay United 2024

CHAPTER SIX

# In Scotland – Armageddon and All That

*I was primarily duped, my advisers were duped, the bank was duped, the shareholders were duped. We've all been duped.*—David Murray on selling Rangers FC for £1 to Craig Whyte

## Changing Times Bring Different Issues to the Fore

A RECURRING THEME is that as fans we all know that football is a business like no other. Conventional businesses are all interested in growth and maximising the profits in the market they operate in. Football is different; it is not an ordinary business, and it operates in an unconventional industry. All the energy at a club is not designed to turn a profit but to turn a group of players into a winning team. Success in football is defined by winning on the park; off the park not being bankrupt is deemed sufficient. When success is achieved in any given season, for most clubs it is no more than a passing phase that will be marked in the annals of history. Celebrations that will be captured in a book, on a special limited-edition DVD or merit a montage of clips on YouTube surrounded by the music of the day. Few clubs have had the ability to capitalise on success to create a dynasty that can keep them at the top forever more. Even those successful dynasties know that success is transient and often there are many uncontrollable factors that can influence what happens next.

In ordinary businesses the shareholders would want to see a return or dividend for any financial investment that they make. Not so in football, where it is rare for football clubs to provide any annual financial reward to their shareholder. If we reflect on how many clubs have gone bust over the years, we can also see that there is a huge amount of money pumped into the football economy that is lost forever. Occasionally there is a legacy, a new grandstand or training complex left behind but more often than not it is frittered away on players' wages. Only occasionally is the original investment ever returned on the actual sale of the club. In recent times Steven Thompson at Dundee United escaped but with less than his family originally put in, whereas the wise old entrepreneur Sir Tom Farmer sold his beloved Hibs and made a profit along the way which is without doubt his advisor Rod Petrie's greatest (or only, some would argue) football achievement. The statistics show few investors are so fortunate no matter how successful they have been in previous businesses. Not that all clubs are successful of course, but the lure of achieving where others have failed keeps bringing investors to the fore.

The focus is less about the bottom line and more about where the team sits on a league table at 4.45pm on a Saturday. Every August sees the start of a race to the top, the bottom or the middle, where you have just a small chance of securing success through promotion or winning a championship. Success will have to be measured in other ways. With so many distractions and football pressures being brought to bear, things often start creaking at football clubs and that always has an impact on financial stability. There have been many close shaves along the way for Scottish clubs nearly going under that are never reported. There are many who have just missed an entry onto the *administration roll of honour* by the skin of their teeth. We will also never know about the various times that benefactors have had to open up their wallets to keep a club afloat or to keep things moving until the next SFA or SPFL cash distribution is scheduled. What we do know is that directors giving cash loans to clubs is a regular occurrence. What the Covid pandemic showed us was that many clubs are very heavily reliant on supporters to keep going in times of financial stress. Several million pounds were raised by fans in this time of financial distress, in addition to most fans writing off asking for refunds for the unexpired part of season tickets. As one award-winning journalist said to me during this period:

> There is an aspect to selling season tickets to supporters during the ensuing depression caused by the pandemic that has to be morally questioned – can you really take money off of people who are struggling for a product as yet to be defined?

It is a valid point but as we know, football supporters really are customers like no other. At the Scottish Football Supporters Association nobody has come to us to complain about being asked to buy a season ticket in these circumstances.

Bryan Jackson, the administrator, is often known to refer to football supporters as 'the bank of last request'. When any club is in distress there is often only one joker left to play and it is the supporters who you can rely upon, even if there is little obvious return for them. Fear kicks in and it feels that if they don't dig deep then things will go from bad to worse. Of course, as we saw in the death throes of the Romanov dynasty at Heart of Midlothian, a share issue in a time of crisis raised £1 million only for the club to crash a few months later, taking the fans' hard-earned cash with it. If any other business had done that, they would never have survived for treating fans so shamefully. In fact, just months after that event Gavin Masterton, then owner at Dunfermline Athletic, tried to do the same thing as he desperately tried to raise £500,000 to keep his sinking empire solvent. Thankfully it failed but not without causing me a lot of grief along the way.

As we know, the loyalty of football fans has boundaries that seem to push towards infinity and beyond and no matter how badly they are treated it rarely takes them from the club they love. They might go less or even not go at all but what they don't do is shop elsewhere; that is a line you simply can't cross. It is not just at the small clubs that this happens, in recent times we have seen things that we would not have expected to see in my lifetime – at Ibrox we had Rangers fans selling scarves to help stave off financial meltdown, having seen their once bullish owner depart with a solitary pound in his pocket. At Celtic we saw fans protesting to evict the families who had a connection with the club for over a century and led them to their greatest ever achievement in the heat of Lisbon. To me, growing up in the 1960s and 1970s, the very thought of our two biggest clubs being in turmoil like this would have been unthinkable.

Celtic had a fairly typical structure with two family dynasties holding the majority shares and passing the honour on from father to son. The Kelly and White dynasties had been in place for many decades and, by the time the third or fourth generations were coming to the end of their tenure, the family fortunes had eroded at a similar pace to the faith that the Celtic fans had in their ability to lead. The significance of the family involvement should not be underestimated. One of the original Celtic players from 1888 was a certain James Kelly. He joined the club from then undisputed World Champions, Renton FC, where he was their original club captain. Kelly was regarded as a tough tackling centre half who went onto become Celtic's first captain and eventually after his playing career ended became chairman of the club. He was the father of Sir Robert Kelly who replaced him on his death in 1931 and also became chairman in 1947, a position he held until 1971. To say the family connection was deep at Celtic is no understatement and in the cold light of day it is remarkable that the connection lasted for nearly 100 years. Not many people can face up to that type of history and win – but Fergus McCann played a belter.

Much dark humour abounded around Celtic FC's empty biscuit tin that was empty when Fergus McCann arrived. It was said that not even a rich tea biscuit was left for Fergus never mind a Tunnock's teacake. Backing McCann might have seemed like a risk at the time, but the real risk was in having a dilapidated, crumbling stadium, no cash and rivals who were about to leave you behind on and off the park. Fergus McCann was well worth a punt, and he proved to be a shrewd businessman as well as a real fan and a man of the people. He also knew that if he was to be successful, he had to connect to the people who provided the club with its heart and its financial muscle – the ordinary fan. This was not your typical foreign investor coming in to see what they could get out of the club; he knew and understood the club and knew that with the right investment there was huge potential. He restructured and took advantage of new share issues to start the process that has led to the club being the sound business that it is today. He also departed these shores far richer than he arrived, but few cared about that. Dave King (who managed to be deemed a fit and proper person despite his 41 South African tax and finance convictions) thought he might be able to replicate this feat at Rangers, but the reality was that the task he inherited was too large. Unlike Fergus who came back to Glasgow for the duration of the project, King could not give the project the time, energy or financial input that it needed, and he departed back to South Africa in early 2020. The main difference was the size of the debt and ongoing trading deficits, easily repayable in the case of Celtic, impossibly so with Rangers. The best he could claim was Rangers were in a better place than when he found them.

Near neighbours Partick Thistle only escaped the liquidators' noose with the help of a highly successful Save the Jags campaign that raised over £100,000 from fans' fundraising activity. The Maryhill Magyars had a lot of celebrity fan backers such as Robert Carlyle and Justin Currie from Del Amitri who supported the fans' efforts. We know how important this type of support is when campaigning to buy a club. Thistle also sold on tranches of unallocated shares £1,000 for 10,000, which the wealthier fans purchased to bring in fresh investment. This resulted in the fans owning around 15 per cent of the club and having what was claimed to be the first fan elected to the board of a football club in the UK. Sadly, by the time the third fan was elected a few years later, the mood of the Save the Jags campaign had been forgotten. Having become one of the first, if not the first, club in the UK to have an elected fan on the board, they then went over a decade without a fan on the board. There was a combination of reasons why this happened, a new chairman who doubted fans having a value in the boardroom, the 'wrong' type of fan being elected to the position and the structure of the fans' organisation that had ceased to have a functioning relationship with the club.

# IN SCOTLAND – ARMAGEDDON AND ALL THAT

Scotland, as we know, is a very different footballing country to England. The geography of the country and our population size has meant since the early days of the game there were always more opportunities for players south of the border. A bigger marketplace, larger cities, larger clubs meant there was a well-trodden path for players. The sale of these assets is very often the difference between financial success and failure. Despite these human footballing exports leaving our shores, our clubs prospered in the pre-television era with huge audiences and minimal outgoings on infrastructure.

When Harold Macmillan, British Prime Minister came out with his famous quote in 1957 it could easily have applied to the next decade or so of Scottish football. He said, 'You will see a state of prosperity such as we have never had in my lifetime – nor indeed in the history of this country. Indeed let us be frank about it – most of our people have never had it so good'.

Until the early 1970s Scottish football prospered on and off the park. The conveyor belt of football talent seeking an escape from the dark, heavy industries of coal, steel and shipbuilding to brighten up our Saturday afternoons was spectacular and seemingly endless. Our clubs took in the talent and could sell the odd player south of the border but could still mould talent into a format that would see the halcyon days of our teams in Europe. Aside from famous Celtic and Rangers European triumphs, we have Hibernian, Kilmarnock, St Johnstone, Dundee and Dunfermline Athletic performing beyond what their size and status should merit against some of the giants of the game. Only a fleeting success in the 1980s during the New Firm, where Aberdeen and Dundee United excelled, has brought any semblance of prestige since. Although, of course, Celtic and Rangers have both reached and been defeated in European finals since the start of the new century.

## Additional Factors Affecting the Slide to Administration in Scotland

A succession of seismic changes have affected the game in Scotland since those glory days that have led to some of our clubs' slide towards administration:

1. The formation of the Premier Division in 1975 – in one fell swoop, eight decent sized 'provincial' clubs were dropped from the earning potential of the top division with several having to adjust to part-time football. Aspiring to get back to that elite group of ten clubs (now 12) is expensive and relegation is always a very real threat when you do so.

Running a topflight with ten clubs in theory should have made the bigger clubs richer but in the fullness of time the staleness of the competition led to fewer fans turning up. One of the biggest frustrations for fans is that they consistently say they want bigger leagues and not to be playing the same teams four times a season. The most recent research by the Scottish Football Supporters Association published in May 2023 as part of the League Reconstruction debate saw 78 per cent of supporters reject the notion that clubs should play each other four times a season. We are constantly being told this cannot be done as Sky TV insist that there have to be four Old Firm games each season. Yet through the Armageddon season with Rangers out of the topflight, this was never discussed or never seemed to be an issue to the broadcasters.

2. The change in the redistribution of funds where gates were not shared meant that the support from the larger clubs to the smaller was decreased thus putting clubs under more financial pressure. This often meant that smaller provincial clubs were willing to sell young players sooner than they would have ordinarily liked and often for less cash.

3. The Taylor report following the Hillsborough disaster put a huge financial burden on clubs to modernise and upgrade stadia quickly. This came at a significant cost to many who borrowed to do so.

4. New owners with lofty ambitions 'investing' money arriving on the scene. Attracted by the idea of owning one of Scotland's highest-profile football clubs, on 23 November 1988 David Murray secured the purchase of Rangers from the club's then owner, the Nevada-based Lawrence Marlborough, for a sum of £6,000,000. Dundee had the Marr Brothers, Motherwell had holiday and airline entrepreneur John Boyle and of course, Dunfermline Athletic had the former Treasurer and Managing Director of the Bank of Scotland Gavin Masterton. These lofty entrepreneurs, all successful in their own areas of expertise, changed the dynamics at these clubs. There were indeed significant improvements on the park and high entertainment value along the way but as the time ran out on all these newly created empires all four clubs ended up in administration.

5. The Heysel disaster might have seemed remote from our shores, but it did have a significant effect in Scotland. It resulted in all English football clubs being banned from playing in Europe for five years. Fourteen Liverpool fans were found guilty of manslaughter and each

jailed for three years. As a result of this ban. It fuelled a race to the top, highlighted by the David Murray quote about Celtic that 'if they spend £5, we will spend £10'. Of course, it later transpired it was not his money that he was spending and, like many before him and many since, he was failing to run the club in a sustainable way. However, his spending spree bringing high quality international players that we attracted to Scotland to play in Europe started a race to financial meltdown. Rangers were not alone. Clubs, like Dundee and Motherwell, had wages to turnover ratios at 130 per cent, much of it spent on players' wages that the clubs could simply not afford. The 'safe' recommended level for wages to turnover is now regarded as being around 65 per cent.

6. A willing lender was on hand in the shape of the Bank of Scotland who had most of the Scottish football clubs in its portfolio. Football clubs don't fail, do they? With huge debt mountains that were secured against assets that had limited value, the debt was allowed to rise virtually unchecked, and it was not until the world banking crisis of 2008 that we saw the reformed bank become a minor part of the Lloyds Banking Group. Football was then deemed to be rather toxic and a determined effort to exit this sector was made by those in charge of a bank that was now only Scottish in name. Huge debts were eventually written off at Dundee, Dunfermline Athletic and significantly at Kilmarnock, where Michael Johnston bought the club with £10 million of debt for £1 and managed to exit with a handsome reward years later having had the debt written off. A conservative estimate of 'lost money' from write offs and football administrations has the Bank of Scotland loss at £70 to £90 million – but it might be more!

7. The emergence of the Premier League in England moved the value of the broadcaster deals into the stratosphere and by default moved the SPFL offering as a mere slot filler. Previous turmoil with ITV Digital in England and Wales and the Setanta collapse left Scotland to grab what little it could.

8. The change in the sponsorship market with the demise of big corporate brands with HQs in Scotland and the changing dynamic to global activity left the SPFL and SFA in an uncomfortable place. With little chance to increase revenue from this source, it meant the clubs

were spending more but had little chance of getting a significant uplift in this market. In 2019 there was a growth of 5 per cent according to a new report from marketing intelligence firm WARC who had estimated a 23 per cent growth in the previous five years. Prior to the arrival of the Bookmakers en masse in 2011, finding sponsorship was a struggle for Scottish football. In 2010/11 there was no Scottish Cup sponsor at all. In May 2022 a global sponsorship think tank was estimating the global sponsorship market shrinking by 39 per cent by 2024.

## Jackson: From Grim Reaper to Club Saviour

There is nobody in Scotland better placed to understand why clubs fail in Scotland than Bryan Jackson. When we launched the idea of fan ownership at Partick Thistle, I invited Bryan to share the platform with me to help with the task of explaining that fans owning clubs was nothing to be feared. Some Jags fans did wonder why I asked along an expert in football club administrations to sell the concept of community ownership, but it didn't take too long for them to be inspired. Bryan had been given the title of Scottish Football's Grim Reaper a few years before by one of our tabloid's headline writers. This was to reflect how many of our clubs he had been involved in after they had gone bust.

As his own profile increased, he said to me that it is difficult to just go to a game on a Saturday as a fan. If he is spotted in the stand at Somerset Park or at the Falkirk stadium, there is bound to be someone putting two and two together and coming up with five thinking an administration 'event' might be imminent. Blair Nimmo was another administrator I met a few years back who also felt awkward going to games for the same reasons but as a Falkirk season ticket holder, he got away with it. What the audience gathered that night in Maryhill was that over the years his many experiences of seeing clubs in distress had led Bryan to now believe in supporters owning football clubs. His opening line that night said it all. 'Fans owning clubs marks the future for football in Scotland.'

I first met Bryan when he was the administrator who had been called in to help Dundee with its second financial meltdown in eight years in season 2010/11. The first game he had in charge was against Stirling Albion at Forthbank. As the fans had just taken over the Binos to become the first senior fan-owned club in Scotland we felt it important that we donate to Stuart Murphy, Dundee FC Supporters' Society's representative on the Dens board, to help the Dark Blues' bid for survival. Bryan saw first-hand how important the football community was when it worked together. It started a long association with Bryan that saw us work together at Dunfermline Athletic and Heart of Midlothian when I was working for the Scottish Government. He continues to help us at the Scottish Football Supporters Association as a willing volunteer advising clubs and fans' groups.

In those days just a few years after the financial crash and the implosion of some of our biggest clubs with Rangers, Hearts and Dunfermline Athletic in tatters, Bryan completely understood one of the most important football dynamics. Football fans are very unique customers who have an almost religious belief in 'their' club. Rather than seek out the latest maverick owner with an ego the size of a planet, he saw that the type of platform we created at Stirling Albion was not just something that would work in smaller clubs but that it was completely scalable. I remember sitting at the café at Stirling Railway Station one morning a few nights after I had been on BBC *Newsnight* talking about how I thought Rangers could become fan-owned. Bryan and I talked for ages about it, and he had already started to look at how the larger clubs in Germany operated. Sadly, his first conversion to community ownership at Dundee did not last that long. In Chapter 7 I will explore in a bit more detail why community ownership at Dundee failed.

At Hearts it was very different scenario, with a very positive outcome. Jackson will tell you he was just doing his job as best he could, but he has pretty much got hero status for his efforts to get Hearts on the pathway to community ownership. As a business restructuring specialist with BDO, he was placed in charge when Hearts entered administration in 2013 and had the task at the same time of righting the collapsed Dunfermline Athletic ship after its owner Gavin Masterton let it sink. At Hearts there were sleepless nights and battles with problematic Lithuanian administrators who didn't really want to talk to him. It led to off the record chats with the then First Minister Alex Salmond, flights to Eastern Europe for meetings organised by Lord George Foulkes and the constant threat of liquidation during a year of relentless stress and tension.

Having introduced him to the Foundation of Hearts (FoH) fan group his belief quickly came about that, with the financial support of Ann Budge, the fans could eventually get the club out of administration. Working with a dedicated team around him, his belief was that the community ownership model was the best option for the Jambos. There is no doubt that it was his belief which made it all possible. It was a huge gamble given that there were several other potential bids on the table and one of the main roles of an administrator is to give any restricted business the best chance of survival after the initial crisis is over. It was no easy task working with the club's majority shareholding from bankrupt Lithuanian companies UBIG and Ūkio Bankas, who saw Hearts as a minor irritant given the bigger financial mess that Romanov left in his wake; not just in Lithuania but also in Russia where rumour has it, he is now in hiding after his financial meltdown.

Ann Budge's £2.5 million loan was crucial to underpinning the concept, as were donations from supporters which saw FoH become a major part of the landscape. However, there is a huge debt that Scottish football owes Jackson for his faith in taking the concept to the next level. If he had not seen the gem of an idea that we had at Stirling Albion (where key fans gave a £200,000 loan towards buying the club) turning Hearts into the UK's biggest fan-owned club might never have happened. It was his belief in fans that allowed Hearts and Dunfermline to move towards community ownership. One of his previous teams Motherwell soon followed on that pathway.

Bryan spoke at Firhill about how the Hearts process worked and how it led to the opening of the new stand funded by the fans, ironically at a game against Thistle in April 2017. It is fantastic for community ownership to have such an advocate who believes in the concept.

Bryan put it this way, 'You asked me why clubs crash? That is really probably the easiest question to answer as it is a scenario that I have seen repeated in football. In simple terms it is down to the lack of financial discipline over a period of time.'

## Scotland's Horror Stories

Bryan has written a fantastic play based on his own experiences called *The Pieman Cometh* that looks back on his experiences in football and is now in the process of following that success up with a second play following the fortunes of the appropriately named Alan Ledger. As we look at some of the biggest cases in financial mismanagement across the Scottish leagues Bryan was there as our guide.

### Third Lanark FC – The Death of a Legendary Club

The Third Lanark Athletic Football Club were one of our original clubs. Legend has it that they were established by several players who had attended the first Scotland v England game at Hamilton Crescent, home of the West of Scotland Cricket Club in Partick. The team, made up of Queen's Park players, included fellow Third Lanarkshire Rifle Volunteers members Billy

Dickson and Joseph Taylor. Inspired by what they saw, they convinced their reservist soldier colleagues to join as they founded in 1872 as an offshoot of the Third Lanarkshire Rifle Volunteers. They were founder members of the Scottish Football Association (SFA) in 1873 and the Scottish Football League (SFL) in 1890. The club was formed as 3rd Lanark Rifle Volunteers Athletic Club, despite the correct name of the irregular battalion being 3rd Lanarkshire Rifle Volunteers. It was incorporated in July 1903 as Third Lanark Athletic Club Ltd.

The club quickly ascended to success, winning two Scottish cups, four Glasgow cups and even a First Division title in 1904. They are nicknamed the Hi-Hi, due to the chant that the crowds would use to intimidate teams visiting their home ground Cathkin Park, the site of the second Hampden Park. Post World War 2, the club's supporters founded a supporters' association to raise funds to help run the club, a great example of how progressive this club was and how close it was to the community. This type of fundraising was very uncommon at the time.

By the beginning of the '50s, the club was consolidated as a yo-yo club between the First and Second Divisions. It was during this period that Bill Hiddleston, a local businessman, first became involved in the club as a director and also for a brief spell as manager (we have to assume there was an ego at play in that decision). However, following financial irregularities and the approval of an unsanctioned £500 transfer (which he was later made to pay), Hiddleston was booted from the board of directors and left the club.

In the 1960/61 season, things were looking up for the club after a third-place finish in the First Division saw them qualify for Europe for the first time in their history. Unfortunately for the Hi-His, it would all be downhill from this point forward. These were the halcyon days but sadly nobody knew it at the time. Dark clouds were gathering and in 1962, Hiddleston returned as a major shareholder and stood for election to the board. The manager at the time, the legendary ex-Rangers and Scotland Captain George Young, promised to resign if Hiddleston was voted in. Hiddleston won, becoming chairman and Young was true to his word. Director Robert Martin also quit on the spot saying: 'Good luck to the Thirds and God help them.' Profound and sadly accurate words.

It is rumoured that he wanted to sell the site of Cathkin Park for development, making a small fortune, while moving the club to the new booming commuter towns of East Kilbride or Cumbernauld. One way to force this through would be to run the club into the ground, leaving them no choice but to sell the land. The summer after Hiddleston's return saw 34 players released and the club was soon relegated in the 1964/65 season.

Players' wages were often unpaid or cut. When players were paid, it was generally in coins, obviously taken straight from the turnstiles which meant the taxman was being diddled as well. Players were forced to make their own way to away matches and the electricity at Cathkin Park was cut. Money raised by the supporters' association would simply disappear and prizes from the club's lottery were never given out. Much of this unscrupulous activity was unseen to the general public and to fans.

As the crisis started to emerge, supporters refused to give their money to Hiddleston and attendances dropped. Unlike now where 43 per cent of revenue in the Premiership is generated by fans paying at the gate, in the early 1960s this figure was around 90 per cent. If you lose the fans, you lose your revenue. During that third-place finish in the season of 1961, over 555,000 spectators came through the gates at Cathkin Park. In their final season in 1967, this was little over 55,000. If there was ever a poster boy for ruining a football club, then you could look no further than the occupant at Cathkin Park.

About a fortnight after the final match against Dumbarton at Boghead Park, it was announced that Glasgow Corporation (the forerunner to the Council) had received an offer from the Third Lanark board to sell them the land at Cathkin Park for housing. The board acknowledged that a lack of funds had made this move inevitable. However, not surprisingly it had not wanted to make an iconic club homeless, so Glasgow City Council blocked this by refusing to give planning permission. Around the same time, the Thirds board also announced they were negotiating with an estate company to build a new stadium at Bishopbriggs to the north of Glasgow. In the end, the stadium was never built. These were all the desperate manoeuvrings of the club chairman Bill Hiddleston as he tried to extract an economic value for himself.

In those days when wrongdoing was suspected in the collapse of companies there was an investigation through a Government body called a Board of Trade investigation which conducted an enquiry into Third Lanark's affairs – which was published in November 1968 – revealing that the blame for the demise of the club lay very firmly at the hands of the owner, Director Hiddleston. Corruption was rife, constantly robbing Peter to pay Paul, failing in the basic governance of the club that allowed him to pay, or often not pay, players in cash and use the club's lottery fund as his own personal bank.

All of these events finally took their toll; on 7 June 1967, Lord Fraser in the Court of Session in Edinburgh issued a winding-up order and appointed an official liquidator. The petition to wind up the club had been brought by a Glasgow building company which claimed that the club owed them more than £2,000 for work done on the new stand at Cathkin Park. The judge accepted figures submitted on behalf of the provisional liquidator which showed that the club's liabilities exceeded its liquid assets by £40,000 in preference to those presented by the club.

On 26 June 1967, it was announced that Third Lanark's membership of the Scottish Football League had ceased. All the players signed to the club at that time were put up for transfer with any proceeds going to the liquidator. The Board of Trade enquiry found four former directors of Third Lanark guilty of contravening the Companies Act 1948 by failing to keep proper books of account during the two years preceding the liquidation of Third Lanark and fined £100 each. The investigation by the Board of Trade accused Club Chairman Bill Hiddleston of blatant corruption and found that 'the circumstances (merited) police inquiry'. Hiddleston never saw the justice that the Hi-Hi fans felt that his actions merited as he died in November 1967. With his death, the chances of really finding out what his tenure was all about died with him. The irony that was not lost on the Thirds fans was that he died from a heart attack when many believed that this was impossible given that he had no heart.

The excellent BBC Alba TV programme explores the role of Chairman Hiddleston in the club's liquidation that was, and remains, the subject of debate among those close to Third Lanark. He may have wished to profit personally from the sale of Cathkin Park for property development. Cathkin Park was sold for housing during the 1967 close season, but Glasgow City Council refused planning permission. On the other hand, he built a new grandstand for the club in 1963, an unlikely thing to do if Hiddleston intended to put the club out of business. Another allegation was that Hiddleston wanted to force the club to move to either Cumbernauld or East Kilbride, the then booming 'new towns' in the Glasgow commuter belt, which at that time had no senior sides of their own. Four days after their last-ever match, played on 28 April 1967, the players reported to Cathkin Park to be told the floodlights, which were already being used sparingly, would never flicker again.

This was Scottish football's first major liquidation since the Second World War, making it a very unusual circumstance although similar administration events had occurred at St Bernards, Leith Athletic and for Raith Rovers entered voluntary liquidation in 1947. In addition, the success of clubs like Celtic, Dundee, Hibernian, Dunfermline Athletic, Rangers and Kilmarnock in Europe distracted from the plight of Third Lanark. This combined with a complete disinterest from the support after years of decline contributed to there being no formation of a phoenix club. However, there are plans for a new stadium at Cathkin Park and a new amateur team was founded in 1996. They stated an interest in joining the SFL in 2008 after the demise of Gretna, however never formally applied. How high the phoenix club will fly we will just need to wait and see. For a full and comprehensive understanding of what happened at Third Lanark I recommend that you read *Third Lanark: Life and Death of the Hi Hi* (2010).

## Dundee FC: Two Administrations for the Price of One

Dundee were one of the first of our bigger clubs to go into administration in 2003. They went into the history books by becoming one of the few who survived two administration events when they managed to repeat this feat again in 2011. Only Darlington FC have a better score with three administrations to their name. The first administration in 2003 saw Ernst and Young, who had previously completed turnarounds at Portsmouth and Gillingham, be called in. When the administrator referred to a critical situation, they pointed to the mountain of debt that stood at over £20 million and monthly overspends of £400,000. Once they started counting, they revised the amount owed to £23 million.

The start of the 21st century saw an influx of foreign players to the SPL, with clubs often paying large salaries to attract them. This practice was most prevalent at the big city clubs; however, the likes of Dundee and Motherwell were keen to do similar. A run through the team sheet shows where the cash was going at Dundee, with Fabrizio Ravanelli, Nacho Novo, Craig Burley alongside Carrazana, Sara and Caballero being joined by Scotland internationalists Gavin Rae and Lee Wilkie. Dundee's new foreign signings did see some footballing success, with a Scottish Cup Final, an appearance in Europe and two top six finishes in the years leading up to administration but how the Marr Brothers who owned the club expected to balance the books, nobody will ever know.

The club was massively over-spending. Crowds didn't increase as much as was hoped, and star players were sold on for less than expected. This caused the club to lose a lot of money and run up staggering debts. There was also mystery around the Italian businessman Giovanni De Stefano who was reputed to be bringing in multimillions of investments in the process. They were placed into administration in November 2003. Thankfully the club had supportive creditors. The club sold Dens Park, restructured completely and supporters' groups raised significant sums to help the cause. Despite relegation in 2005, the club was deemed to be debt-free by 2006. The second administration was not that far away and although it was less spectacular, it was equally as painful.

In September 2010 a second administration came calling when the club failed to find £365,000 that was needed to pay tax. It was a period when

HM Revenue and Customs started to lose its patience with football clubs and their special place in society. Dundee scrambled around and offered £100,000 immediately, but it was rejected by the tax man and the second administration event arrived like an unwelcome guest. In fairness, the debts of just £2 million were a mere drop in the ocean compared to the first implosion at the club in 2003. Much of this was accumulated by the age-old football strategy of 'investing in the playing side' to get to the Premier League where income would more than double. It is staggering to think that having succumbed to the charms and potential investments from De Stefano the first time around that the club would fall into the same trap again just a few years later when Aberdonian businessman Calum Melville invested with few strings attached and money was spent that he and the club simply did not have.

Thanks to investment from the Dark Blues Business Trust and the Dundee FC Supporters' Society, the club was able to pay off HMRC. The remaining debts were exclusively football debt, which gave them more flexibility in repaying. In 2011, the club came out of administration under majority ownership of the Dundee FC Supporters' Society, who ran the club alongside a director selected by the Dark Blues Business Trust. The club was now fully democratic, with any supporter society member over 15 possessing voting rights. The club's new CEO, Harry Mclean said: 'We can't simply copy what has gone on at other clubs but we need to write a new way of doing things with the help of the whole community.' Sadly he would never get a chance to do that, as a few months later he left the board alongside his fellow director and former club chairman Stuart Murphy.

The supporter-owned club had the benefit of an unexpected promotion to the Premier League when they replaced Rangers but when they slipped back down again, they failed to see progress and looked for inward investment. The club remained supporter-owned until a takeover from American investors in the 2013–14 season. Despite this, the supporters' society still owns a 20 per cent stake in the club and gives voting rights to members. We will further explore why supporter ownership failed to take hold at Dundee in Chapter 7.

## Dunfermline Athletic FC (DAFC): Administration in 2013 – What Happened, Governor?

The fall from grace at East End Park was almost as spectacular as what happened at Ibrox, given that the club was owned by the former Treasurer and Managing Director of the Bank of Scotland. In 1999 Dunfermline's owner Gavin Masterton appointed John Yorkston as the club's new chairman. With

Yorkston and Masterton at the helm, the club stepped up its spending as it sought to bring back the European glory days of the 1960s. A spell of success followed, with the club returning to the Premier League. They also competed in the 2006 League Cup Final, as well as the 2004 and 2007 Scottish Cup Finals, seeing them qualify, albeit briefly, for the UEFA Cup. The reality was that spending was increasing without any subsequent uplift in revenue being generated. The financial mismanagement ran deep and in 2012 Yorkston and Masterton saw the signs of an inevitable failure when it emerged that they had an outstanding tax bill of £134,000 owed to HMRC. It is rumoured that at this time, the club's total external debt was in the region of £8m. Masterton had a web of companies set up all feeding each other and tried to find a way out of his problems by having a share issue for fans.

The hope of a share issue bringing in £500k of new capital was scuppered as the supporters were getting little in return aside from a debt mountain, much of it owed to the bank and Masterton himself. The club was placed into administration in April 2013. The 2012–13 season saw the club forced to make the majority of their senior players, as well as some non-playing staff, redundant. This saw the SFL deduct 15 points from the Pars, leading to their eventual relegation to the third tier via the play offs. Fortunately, the majority of the club's debts were voluntarily waived by creditors in July 2013.

After a failed takeover attempt by the Pars Supporters Trust (PST), Pars United was formed to issue a second bid. Pars United, a Community Interest Company, was an umbrella organisation uniting the efforts of wealthy supporters, small supporters' groups and the PST.

PST successfully acquired 94 per cent of the club in October 2013. The administrator Bryan Jackson said: 'It was the devotion and loyalty of the fans, team, staff, management and of course, Pars United which helped get this over the line.' Two months later, on 13 December 2013, Dunfermline officially exited administration. The Pars United takeover left the PST as the club's largest shareholder with 28 per cent of the club. The rest of the club is owned by 200 individual shareholders, with no one owning more than 6.5 per cent. The fans will never know just how much work that finance expert Ross McArthur and his team put in to get the club back in order. It was a massive collective effort with thousands of man-hours on the task. I am proud to have helped them in the task and I have always had a very warm welcome back to East End Park any time I visit.

In July 2021 when the club welcomed DAFC Fussball GmbH's purchase of a 75.1 per cent holding in the East End Park club, Thomas Meggle, Damir Keretic, Nick Teller and Dr Albrecht Gundermann became the SPFL's newest owners. It was said at the time that the quartet would bring fresh capital, lofty aspirations and a fine pedigree in sport and business to Fife. From what we have seen so far, the jury is very much out on what exactly they have achieved and in September 2024 they put the club up for sale.

## Falkirk FC: Administration and Provisional Liquidation, 1996–98

For the most part, Falkirk fans look back on the '90s as one of the better times in the club's history with exciting youngsters coming through regularly and an entertaining brand of football on display. Despite playing the majority of the decade's seasons in the second tier, the club often caused upsets in numerous cup runs. However, off the pitch, the club was fairing far worse. The costs of an entertaining team were too large for the income of a club playing in the second tier, resulting in annual operating losses and growing debts. With a Premier League of just ten clubs, trying to become an elite club and staying in the top league was a huge problem for most provincial clubs.

By 1996, the club had amassed debts of around £2.7 million and was placed into the administration process which was handled by Donald McGruther, a lovely gentleman who tells the story with great eloquence. By March 1998 the struggling club was put into provisional liquidation as it was unable to agree deals to pay off its outstanding debts. In May 1998, a local consortium of Falkirk-supporting businessmen and women raised over £600,000 to purchase the club's shares and take control of the club. One consortium member of the Major Shareholder Group (MSG), Douglas Macintyre, said at the time that had the group not promised to pay off the club's debts, Falkirk would have ceased to exist. We of course know that the chances of a club like Falkirk disappearing were remote but in times of stress and impending failure many a Churchill-inspired speech has been heard on the doorsteps of our football clubs.

Through investment from the new MSG, prize money for a second-place finish in the second tier and revenue from cup runs in '97 and '98, the club was able to pay off the majority of their debts. The club went on to become debt-free a few years later after the sale of former ground Brockville Park in the centre of the town for redevelopment as a supermarket. The subsequent development of a successful community programme and the laying of an artificial surface all meant the club was heading for success off the park. On the park was a different story, with controversies surrounding the closure of the Academy and the failure of the MSG to sell their shareholding to the Falkirk fans' group 'Back the Bairns' who had pledges of over £850k secured and ready to action. More on that story in Chapter 13.

## Motherwell FC: The Long, Slow Administration, 2002–2004

Motherwell enjoyed a good spell throughout most of the 1990s which saw second and third-place finishes in the SPL. It was hard to see just what could go wrong. They were run by one of Scotland's leading entrepreneurs, John Boyle, who had sold his travel business and started Zoom Airlines. Backed by those lovers of Scottish football, the Bank of Scotland, Zoom fitted into the low-cost transatlantic market once occupied by its pioneer Sir Freddie Laker.

In August 1998, the club was bought by John Boyle, who became the new chairman. Just as he had a vision for transatlantic low-cost aviation, Boyle had a vision of a strong Motherwell that could compete with any of the big city clubs at the time. At a time when Scottish clubs were increasing expenditure to bring in foreign talents, Boyle's Motherwell would be no exception. The club paid large wages and transfer fees with little success in return. Unlike the travel business where customers would swap airlines or tour operators at the drop of a hat, Boyle completely misunderstood the dynamics of fan loyalty and the fact that no matter how hard he tried or how good the football on offer was, converting lapsed fans who have got out of the habit or finding new fans is impossible to do in the short term.

According to the CEO at the time, Pat Nevin, Boyle picked a playing budget that was guaranteed to create significant annual losses. He said:

> You have to go back to when John took over at the club and he asked me to help look after it for him. Firstly, I said 'Don't be stupid' then I did three different costings. I did the first that really wasn't going to cost us any money. It basically left them round about relegation or just above it but we'd build the youth development. The second was to spend X amount, be pretty safe in the league and build a plan around that. The third was the all-singing, all-dancing version, getting up towards £2m a year and combining that with building your academy. Much to my amazement, he went for the latter. I said, 'Are you off your head!?'

With massive annual losses and growing debts, April 2002 saw Boyle place the club into administration and put it up for sale. The club finished last during the 2002/3 SPL season but avoided relegation due to First Division champions Falkirk not meeting minimum stadia requirements. If Motherwell had gone down, it could have been a very different story. At the time, Boyle didn't accept that the club's precarious position was a result of massive over-spending and cited the collapse of a TV deal and the loss of long-term sponsor Motorolla.

After two years of administration, the club still had no buyer. However, in April of 2004, the club left administration. With no other buyer in sight, Bryan Jackson sold the club back to Boyle when he waived the club's debt to become his personal debts. The club was then debt-free thanks to this move and the sale of star players such as Stuart Pearson and James McFadyen.

The eventual successful move to community ownership is another story to be discussed elsewhere.

## Rangers FC: A Complex Story With Poor Governance Unwinds

There have been many books written about the rise and fall of Rangers that will be able to give fans more detail and analysis than I can offer here in this short summary. They were one of Scotland's biggest clubs with a knight of the realm driving them forward. When the then relatively unknown David Murray took over Rangers it was described as 'business as usual' as he bought out Lawrence Marlborough, the grandson of the famous Glasgow Builder John Lawrence, who had been at the helm in the late 1960s and 1970s and had an association with the club going back to the 1940s. Business as usual did not last very long as Rangers' availability had been brought to Murray's attention by his friend Graeme Souness, who at 35 was looking for a 'project' following his exit from a successful spell in Italy with Sampdoria. Souness took a seat on the board along with a 10 per cent shareholding – estimated to have cost him £500,000. He was occupying the most unique role in British football. No club had ever had a player, manager, director on its books and that little bit of trivia will go down in history as something that is unlikely to be repeated again.

The price which Murray paid to seize control was viewed as surprisingly low for one of the biggest clubs in Britain. Within a few months of Murray's arrival, Rangers had recruited their first high-profile Roman Catholic player. Mo Johnston joined in the summer of 1989 having reneged on a promise to re-join Celtic. The Ibrox club also embarked on a mission to win the European Cup. But the revolution had begun during Marlborough's tenure, who had tasked one of his house-building executives, David Holmes, with running the day-to-day affairs at the club. Holmes recruited Souness in an audacious move more than two years earlier with almost instant success.

Although Murray was already making waves as an industrialist, he was known, if at all, by football fans for a failed bid to buy Ayr United earlier that same year. That failure at Ayr did not impress the Rangers fans. 'Most fans will be disappointed, if he is not good enough for Ayr is he good enough for us?', said one Rangers supporter interviewed in a bar by STV on the day of his arrival. Murray promised investment 'at least as big as had gone before'. What had gone before was helping change British football's landscape. Investment triggered by Marlborough combined with a ban on English clubs competing in Europe following the Heysel Stadium disaster in 1985 meant Rangers were able to reverse the established practice of the best Scottish players heading to the English league. They attracted top English talent north. These signings included the iconic England skipper Terry Butcher, and many international stars would follow.

Liquidation, while it occurred on Whyte's watch, is largely viewed as the result of extravagance combined with a ruinous Employment Benefit Tax scheme pursued in the Murray years. Whyte, of course, did not have any resources but had a cunning plan to use future revenue generated from season ticket sales from the broking firm Ticketus to fund his purchase. On the departure of Murray, the previous owner Marlborough said in a newspaper interview,

> Anyone who owns a club comes in and says they never want to leave but once the novelty wears off, it becomes very hard work – a grind even. David did very well in the beginning but then after a period you could tell that it wasn't working. The magic wears off.

But his on-field legacy is 35 trophies – including the longed-for nine titles in a row between 1989 and 1997 which equalled Celtic's run. The debate about whether many of these honours are tainted due to the tax issue – players were paid through side contracts – will run into the next century, probably beyond, with fans of most clubs seeing it for what it was. Spending money you don't have to give your team a competitive advantage is unfair. The Rangers fans still feel the pain of the administration and the years of turmoil that followed with the Whyte, Green, Easdale and King eras failing to heal what was the biggest failing in Scottish football. On the steps of Hampden Park, the CEOs of the SPFL and the SFA warned us that Armageddon was approaching unless Rangers were brought back immediately to the Premier League. Fans disagreed, sporting integrity was upheld and Rangers fans started the process of redistributing funds throughout the lower leagues, giving a huge economic benefit to clubs the length and breadth of the country. Many felt it was karma for what had gone before.

One positive by-product of the Rangers crash was that for the first time, Scottish football fans used the financial power that they held to threaten their clubs with refusal to buy season tickets. Messrs Doncaster and Regan tried to push through a vote that would see a newly formed Rangers stay in the Premier League for commercial reasons. They had traction with clubs who are driven by self-preservation and maximising revenue. We were told that if it did not happen it would be Armageddon for Scottish football. Instead, the fans revolted and said that sporting integrity was far more important than giving Rangers preferential treatment. The economic benefit of Rangers in the lower leagues proved a huge boost to just about every club in Scotland as the Gers licked their wounds and climbed back to the top.

Holding football to account is no easy task but in this instance, the fans knew our game would survive and they stepped forward to ensure the cries of Armageddon be ignored and the sporting integrity of the game be its primary concern.

*A footnote in football history – some noticeable Scottish cases where clubs went under whilst members of the SFL – there have many others in the lower leagues too:*

Port Glasgow Athletic 1912
Abercorn 1920
Lochgelly United 1928
Clydebank 1931
Clackmannan FC 1931
Broxburn United 1932
Armadale 1935
Bathgate 1938
Galston FC 1940
St Bernards 1943
Bo'ness FC 1945
Kings Park FC 1945
Solway Star 1947
Leith Athletic 1955
Third Lanark FC 1967
Queens Park FC 2000
Greenock Morton FC 2000–2001
Airdrieonians FC 2002
Clydebank FC 2002
Motherwell FC 2002–2004
Dundee FC 2003–2004 and 2010–2011
Livingston FC 2004–2005 and 2009
Gretna FC 2008

Rangers 2012
Dunfermline Athletic FC 2013
Heart of Midlothian FC 2013–2014
Edinburgh City 2023
Dumbarton 2025
Inverness Caledonian Thistle 2025

CHAPTER 7

# Learning From Mistakes – Following Out of Love

*Success is no accident, it is hard work, perseverance, learning, studying, sacrifice and most of all; love of what you are doing or learning to do.*—Pelé

MY GRANDMOTHER ALWAYS used to extol the virtue that, 'God loves a trier'. I am not sure where she got those words of wisdom, but I don't think it was from the Bible. This gem was usually given to me as some of my football exploits were falling short of my own high expectations. I remember hearing it loud and clear at my early Scottish Schoolboy trials down at Largs that failed to get me signed up for a top side or get down to the final 24 players. In another football context, I remember my father's favourite player at Partick Thistle never being the star of the team. I found it quite peculiar and have never come across any other fan who thought like him.

When I was a wee lad idolising Alan Rough, Jimmy Bone or Alan Hansen he preferred some of the journeymen professionals at the club such as Tommy Rae and Bobby Law. When I questioned his football judgement it all came down to the fact that 'they were triers'. What I took from that was that he knew they were not great players but were real team men who were always seen to give their best. Consistently there for the team, but never the star performer. I guess it is not a bad attribute for a player to bring to any team.

There is no doubt that there is a lot of positivity for those who try to make things happen in all walks of life, none more so in football and in the area of fan ownership. We all know that there can be no success without failure and here we hope to highlight some of the issues as to why the clubs who have tried community ownership have *failed*. Building on this knowledge will allow us to help ensure the mistakes made by others can be used to develop better plans in the future. What these examples tend to illustrate is that it is not so much the failure of community ownership as a model but more the given circumstances that dictated moving back to the benefactor scheme.

Where there is planning and preparation, community ownership works well. Moving out of community ownership is not necessarily a failure of the model but tends to be driven by a lack of resources or having the opportunity of fresh inward investment. There are some who of course regret passing up the opportunity, such as we are seeing again at Chesterfield, who are now looking at taking the club back again. There are arguments too that, for example, at Dundee where ownership was traded for fresh inward investment from abroad, that the club has not performed any better than if it had remained community-owned. In that case, the promise of a new stadium, a better team and new training facilities remain undelivered.

## Bury FC

In 2000 Bury were in trouble – as we saw in Chapter 5 – when a succession of *white knights* came calling. The fans at Bury inherited several million pounds of debt due to previous owners' overspends. In May of that year, Prentis, the majority shareholder advanced Bury a 12-month loan of £1m secured on Gigg Lane and a fortnight later his company was closed down and he was eventually struck off by the Law Society. Bury FC reached an agreement that saw them move out of administration and transfer control of the club to the fans' trust group. It meant that the Shakers had to sign a four-year Creditors Voluntary Arrangement (CVA) which saw the cash-strapped club pay just 10p to the pound of their debts to unsecured creditors. The club were originally given just two weeks in which to find a buyer.

The agreement enabled the transfer of the club to the 'Save Our Shakers Trust', a fans' group originally set up to raise money to see Bury through to the end of the previous season. Bury FC came under supporter ownership in 2002 after the club entered administration, split between Save Our Shakers Trust (63.8 per cent) and the Bury FC Supporters' Society Ltd (Forever Bury) (11 per cent) At the time Matt Dunham, of the club's joint administrators RSM Robson Rhodes, said: 'This represents a potential way forward for clubs to deal with current cash flow crises, the failure of ITV Digital and the general financial uncertainty that many face'. He went on to say, in the words that many an administrator of football clubs might say, 'Without the hard work of the supporters and their fundraising efforts it is probable that the club would by now be closed'.

The administrator had really high hopes for not only Bury but for others that might follow in their footsteps. It was almost as if he was a forerunner to Bryan Jackson.

By selling the club to the supporters it enables it to become an integral part of the community and allows supporters to direct the future of the club. This solution could well provide the basis for other clubs to deal with the difficulties they are currently facing. It is a tremendous result.

The fans' group will now control all of the day-to-day running of Bury as they prepare for life in Division Three.

### Life for Bury as a Community-owned Club

Property entrepreneur Stewart Day bought the fans' stake in 2013 following financial difficulties for the club, which had necessitated taking out a PFA loan to pay players' wages and the club being placed under a transfer embargo. Initially, by all accounts Day did a good job for the club but after nearly five years the club was accumulating debt, and he was running out of money. Day put the club up for sale and struggled to find any interested party, until another likely lad in the shape of Steve Dale emerged on the scene. It later transpired that 43 of the 51 companies Dale had been associated with had been liquidated in the past but he had promised to work closely with the community to ensure the club became financially viable after years of cash problems. That seemed to be good enough for the EFL who admitted after the club went under that they did not put him through the usual process of due diligence when he took control because the club's future was under threat at the time. There are warning signs when anyone buys a football club for £1.

Sure enough, within days of getting the keys, Dale made it clear that he wanted to sell the club, and initially came up with an asking price of £2 million. There were reportedly four interested groups looking to buy Bury, but a deal could not be agreed with any of them at that asking price and Dale hung on to eventually go down with the ship. Sadly, Bury FC became the first club to drop out of the league since Maidstone. I do hope that given all the lessons that can be learned from how community ownership can work that Bury fans look to the likes of FC United and AFC Wimbledon and come back owned by the supporters.

### Reasons for failure

- Failure of the fit and proper test at the League and FA allowed someone with 43 previous business failures to be allowed into the club.
- An undeveloped concept, so there were few guidelines to follow or examples to learn from.
- Inherited the initial problem (a club in administration) without

much warning so there was little opportunity to plan, with the main focus being on the rattling of buckets to ensure immediate safety.
- Unable to develop a long-term strategic plan that would have held the club in the community for the longer term.
- Fear of the unknown led to the failure of a big vision. Instead, almost immediately there was the desire to revert to type – looking for investor/philanthropist/rich Bury-centric entrepreneur to take the lead.
- Divided fans' groups which, even in 2023, years after the crash, have struggled to work together for the greater good.
- No natural leader in the fans' ranks who had the confidence to develop the plan and lead from the front.
- No ongoing income generation as is seen in Germany with club memberships or at clubs like Hearts, Dunfermline Athletic or Motherwell.

## Brentford FC

Bees United (the Brentford FC Supporters Trust) used to own 60.3 per cent of the shares of Brentford FC and have the main representation on the board. Matthew Benham, a successful entrepreneur, himself a fan and a member of the Bee United Trust owned 30.7 per cent of the shares of Brentford FC, with other supporters owning 9 per cent. The supporters' trust did a deal at a time of crisis at the club with spiralling debts and a crumbling stadium and eventually sold their entire shareholding to Matthew Benham, who also acquired all other minority shareholding to own nearly 100 per cent of the shares.

The reasons for the sell-out are not that dissimilar to those at Portsmouth. The club had been relatively successful under community ownership, indeed described by Benham as being stable. However, with a decaying stadium, few inward investment opportunities and being in a highly competitive market, there seemed to be no real opportunity to move forward. They also had the added benefit of working with Matthew Benham and getting to know him. It was a comfort to know that as well as being super wealthy, he is a lifelong Brentford fan, who owns two betting and statistic companies, Smartodds and Matchbook. His initial involvement came in 2006, when the supporters' trust, Bees United, needed another £500k to complete their takeover.

Brentford FC owned the freehold of its stadium, Griffin Park, where it had played for over 100 years. However, Griffin Park lacked modern facilities for spectators and non-football revenue generation. The club found it virtually impossible to generate sufficient revenue to break even with a playing budget that enabled it to compete successfully at its current level in the Championship. Griffin Park was a stadium in a residential area, hemmed in by housing; it was not a suitable site for developing a modern stadium with sufficient capacity and associated commercial revenue generating facilities to enable the club to compete on the pitch and get to a point where it could break even.

You can start to see a theme emerging when fans take on football clubs. More often than not the *opportunity* to take over a club only emerges when the clubs are in distress, often at short notice or with little warning. Given that few clubs heading in that direction will be open or transparent makes planning and preparation that much harder. Even in cases where disaster is looming, such as we saw at Heart of Midlothian or Dunfermline Athletic, there was not a lot of lead time for fans to campaign effectively. Fortunately, at Hearts the team that created the Foundation of Hearts had looked at a plan to buy the club as a long-term solution and were well established and ready to act swiftly. If they hadn't been so organised the successful takeover might never have happened.

The warning signs are there if we hear that any club is for sale for £1; you know that there is a pretty obvious reason why. What it tends to tell us is that someone, who we can assume is or was a successful businessperson (the seller), has accumulated a significant debt and is not in the position to continue to support the club. There always tends to be someone else (the buyer) who has the ego to think that they can do something different and turn things around. As we saw at Bury with Steve Dale and Rangers with Craig Whyte, they come in with a plan that seldom works.

At Brentford it was different. Prior to the Bees United takeover in 2006 the club had run up a bank overdraft in the order of £5 million in the days when banks were allowing clubs to have security against the stadium freehold. In most cases, stadiums were overvalued as their use was restricted to sport, yet many were valued as if they were real estate that could attract a shopping centre or a significant housing development. I remember being in a meeting with Gavin Masterton as the Pars were staring at the abyss and he told me that East End Park was valued at *over* £22 million. Where that number came from is anybody's guess but was probably based on the belief that a new supermarket might want to buy the site. Even looking at the sale at Brockville and Love Street this did seem a tad overvalued.

At Brentford, Bees United twice refinanced the debt with the help of Matthew Benham and in 2010 concluded an agreement with that supporter to provide substantial equity funding for a five-year period, in order to stabilise the club until a new stadium could be developed. At that time, Brentford were in deep financial trouble. As former Chairman Greg Dyke said, 'It is fair to say that without Bees United there would probably not have been a club for Matthew to take over.' Benham is the man that has brought financial stability to Brentford where he injected £5 million of new capital between 2009 and 2012 when he took over Bees United's 96 per cent shareholding.

The Bees have huge challenges to face competing as a small club in a huge city, in a league structure that is highly competitive and populated by multi-millionaires. The days of spending money that they did not have and borrowing money that they could not repay are long gone for this club. Having Matthew Benham and his money has removed them from the hand-to-mouth existence that they endured for many a year. The additional benefits are that he is a real supporter and having worked with the fans during the initial purchase period, he understands the value of supporters and the community. He continues to have fans on the board of the club and a 'special golden share' that safeguards its long-term future.

Benham's financial commitment to Brentford was estimated to be up to £100 million. The long-term aim is clearly to create a sustainable club, but for the time being its ability to maintain a competitive presence in the Championship is almost entirely reliant on the owner's generosity.

The state-of-the-art new Brentford Community Stadium opened in season 2020/21 and the club reached the dream of being a successful Premier League side. As Benham said: 'Our new stadium is one of the most significant and exciting developments in the history of Brentford Football Club. The cornerstone of our long-term vision, it will help ensure a sustainable future for the Club'. It is hard to argue that community ownership actually failed at Brentford. In reality, there was never a level playing field for the fans to work with. They inherited £5 million of debt, got the club stable and entered a partnership with a multi-millionaire supporter of the club. At the Bees, they have an owner who is a genuine fan who has the best interests of the club at heart and works with the fans' group to build confidence and capacity. In many ways this is a far better position than fans at Portsmouth find themselves in, where they have sold to an overseas investor who is far more likely to want a return on his investment than Matthew Benham.

## *Reasons for a change from community ownership*

- Fans inherited a club in financial meltdown with £5 million of debt.
- Stadium was in a state of disrepair with no long-term plan to allow modernisation and with limited options to move given land values in London.
- Realisation that the financial task for a fans' group with a club of this size was challenging.
- The changing market dynamic where the push and pull from the riches of the Premier League meant that the knock-on effect in the lower league saw competitors attract significant foreign investors. As these clubs pushed towards the top of the Championship it added a huge pressure on the clubs with aspirations to try to compete against them.
- A genuine positive partnership emerged between benefactor and fans' group as they worked together to develop the club.

## Chesterfield FC

The late '90s were a successful time for the club after the 1994/95 season saw them promoted to the Second Division where they continued to punch above their weight. They would remain in this league until the inevitable relegation finally arrived in 2000.

Following relegation, the cry from the board was for new investment to be made. This would enable them to push back up the league from where they had come. In stepped local businessman-made-good Darren Brown who took the club over and appointed himself as chairman.

The recurring theme of individuals buying a football club, passing the football authorities' fit and proper person test and turning out to be anything but fit and proper, is one that we know only too well. In a scene reminiscent of *Groundhog Day*, it is something that just seems to keep happening. Maybe one day someone in authority who really cares for the game will devise a more robust approach before allowing any maverick to walk into our clubs without significant checks and balances being in place. You would have thought lessons might have been learned over the years but apparently not. Interestingly, the failure at Chesterfield was one of the reasons why the fit and proper test was established in football, sadly with many further failures since then it remains far from fit and proper itself.

In no time at all it would become apparent to all the Chesterfield fans that Brown was not fit to run a professional football club. Soon after his takeover, he attempted to avoid paying Chester City a transfer fee, resulting in the club being docked nine points for financial irregularities by the league. The following months would see the club rack up debts of over £1.6m under Brown's leadership. Brown was also subject to mounting accusations of fraud and he was forced to sell the club to Andy Cooke.

Eventually the club was bought by Chesterfield Football Supporters Society (CFSS) in 2001 from Darren Brown, who had run the club to the brink of insolvency (and was later jailed for crimes committed during his tenure at the club). The CFSS had held a meeting to discuss the perilous state of the club in March 2001, and a collection of funds yielded £6,000, which was used to buy the club several days later. A fan at the time suggested that this was £5,999 more than the club was actually worth given the state that Brown had left it in. Cooke immediately sold the club to the Chesterfield Football Supporters Society for just £6,240. The CFSS was founded just 16 days beforehand and already amassed 3,000 members contributing £300,000 collectively. Impressive for a club with average crowds of no more than 4,500. The club entered insolvency as a result of the Brown-era financial mismanagement.

The CFSS spent the next while raising funds and managed to agree deals to write off some of the club's debts, but the legacy of Brown's tenure was still haunting the club. Recognising that the club needed additional investment, the CFSS agreed to give control of the day-to-day running of the club to a group of wealthy supporters in return for investment. However, the CFSS would remain as the club's legal owners. This arrangement suffered difficulties initially, but the involved parties managed to make it work and the club was successfully turned around.

The CFSS remained owners until 2012 when Dave Allen took control of the club after four years of investing. In a scenario that mirrored what happened at Brentford, Chesterfield showed that community bids can be successful in saving crisis-hit football clubs and Brown's disastrous reign led to the FA introducing a fit and proper test for prospective club owners.

In June 2020 it emerged that the Chesterfield fans have decided to mount a bid to bring the club back into community ownership to ensure its long-term security. They stated that the club would more secure if it was in the hands of those who love it most – the fans. Shares were sold for £250. Alas the excitement was not to last and the majority shares were sold to brothers Phil and Ashley Kirk in March 2024 having invested a total of £3 million on the club.

Brothers Phil and Ashley Kirk were introduced to shareholders at the

Annual General Meeting as new investors who would put an initial £1m into the club in 2020 with a view to help the Spireites Trust keep its ownership of the club in a perfect community and business partnership to make the club more sustainable https://spireitestrust.org.uk/

Phil, who made his fortune in the oil industry, explained:

> We've agreed to put a million pounds into the club. Half the money is going to general and then half the money at the moment we're looking to help build the sports bar and get that off the ground.
>
> I'm so proud of the town, proud of Derbyshire and proud of the team and just to be able to put some money in and help is great. Our only wish is to do good for the town and the club.

It's a partnership that seems to have worked in once of the UK's oldest clubs that remains in fan ownership in 2025.

## Reasons for a change from community ownership

- Failure of the Fit and Proper Test to protect the club from a predator.
- The club inherited financial mismanagement and structural chaos.
- There was very little support or indeed understanding in these early days of community ownership.
- The fans' organisation was a fledgling organisation with little time to have in place the resources or structure in the initial phase.
- There was no ongoing fans' investment plan in place similar to the membership schemes in Germany or Spain or as we have seen at the Foundation of Hearts.
- The size and scale of the financial need called for additional resources.
- A positive relationship developed with the investor who was also a proven fan, and it was seen as an easier route to eventually cede control in return for additional investment. It would be hoped that the strength that endures with that partnership would ensure that the longer-term health of the club would always be community focused in the years ahead.

## Portsmouth FC

Portsmouth became the largest fan-owned football club in England, after the Pompey Supporters Trust (PST) successfully gained possession of Fratton Park in April 2013. However, in May 2017, the PST members voted in favour of selling its ownership to former Disney Chief Executive, Michael Eisner, his value estimated to be at €5.67 million. What happened at Portsmouth was described to me by Colin Farmery, the trust and then club Communications Manager who lived and breathed the whole experience. He gives a really good insight into the Pompey situation. He feels that it could be a bit unfair me putting Portsmouth into the failed community ownership chapter. He says:

> What the supporters did for several years was to ensure that the club ran effectively and efficiently and within its means. We went from a situation where we were near death's door to stability with improvements on and off the park and, most importantly financial sustainability. Things changed only in that to get to the next level we needed additional resources that a benefactor might bring.

Portsmouth, in a move similar to what happened at Brentford, found that benefactor in Michael Eisner who appreciated the fan ownership background and is very much working in partnership with the supporters. The main difference is Eisner is no local-boy-done-good and so far, we have not seen just how deep his pockets are or whether Fratton Park will have the major redevelopment that it so badly needs. Ten years on from him successfully buying the club back from the fans, they have stability but the much-anticipated drive towards the land of milk and honey of the Premier League has never materialised. On reaching the tenth anniversary, Eisner, who is now 80, suggested that it is a project that his sons might now take on.

### Reasons for a change from community ownership

- The pain of many years of financial meltdown had a significant impact on the ability of the fanbase to see a longer-term plan that was supporter dependent.
- Inward investment required for stadium redevelopment.
- Aspirations to be a Championship level club (at least) meant that there were not the funds available to facilitate this desire in what is a hugely competitive market.

- Supporters felt comfortable with the new owner having been courted by several others.
- The lure of getting back to the Premier League made the change more likely.

## Scarborough Town FC

This was a second supporter-owned 'phoenix' club formed after the liquidation of Scarborough, and essentially competed with the larger Scarborough Athletic FC for former Scarborough FC fans, though focused more upon a youth team rather than a senior one. It eventually folded. The club was run on a democratic basis by a management committee. Membership was open to everyone by payment of an annual fee. All adult members had an equal vote and were encouraged to use this vote at every AGM and EGM (Extraordinary General Meeting). It had two complete seasons, the first in the Wearside Football League, then being promoted to the Humber Premier League, Division One. The club were champions of both leagues and were very well attended. Despite this success, financial problems overcame the club during its final year, resulting in its records for that season being expunged.

*Reasons for a change from community ownership*

- Size of the task too large.
- Could not generate enough income.
- Did not own any assets.
- Divided fan base.

## Stockport County FC

The club was purchased in 2005 by the Stockport County Supporters Co-operative but was sold to an investment group in 2009 after near-bankruptcy. A long-term goal of the Supporters Co-operative is to buy the ground and buy back the club. Stockport County FC first joined the English Football League in 1900 and remained a member for almost all of their history from that point forward. In 2003, the club was bought over by wealthy businessman Brian Kennedy, a person whose name often appeared as an interested party during the period Rangers had collapsed. He was often referred to as someone who might be a white knight for them. Kennedy, who was also the owner of

Sale Sharks, combined both the rugby union club, football club and Edgeley Park under the one company. This was known as Cheshire Sports. However, the move proved a bad one for Kennedy financially. He was rumoured to have lost in the region of £4m as a result of the venture and in 2005 he put Stockport County up for sale. County supporters saw an opportunity to dictate the future of their club and formed the Stockport County Supporters Co-operative, which in July 2005 bought 98 per cent of the football club. Crucially, however, Kennedy kept ownership of the club's ground, Edgeley Park.

Stockport agreed a deal with Kennedy to remain at the ground, but this left the club with very little disposable income. With no real assets and the cost of renting their own stadium, the club was broken. In 2008, they had to take out a loan to cover the cost of desperately needed training ground renovations. This debt of around £300,000 as well as £250,000 owed to HMRC led to the club entering administration in April 2009. With the club up for sale, takeovers were attempted and failed, with the club remaining in administration for over a year. They finally exited in June 2010 when a consortium known as the 2015 group, formally took ownership of the club.

## Reasons for a change from community ownership

- No real preparation time to develop the strategy.
- Did not own the assets.
- Rent and rates too expensive to make it sustainable.
- Owner more focused on profit than the club.

## MyFootballClub.com

Being first to market is always really important in any business and football is no different. With the birth of the World Wide Web and of social media channels, an opportunity arose to do something different with football club ownership.

Into this space arrived MyFootballClub.com, which claimed to be the dawn of a new age of football fandom. The whole premise was based on the fact that football is a world sport and that most ordinary football fans had no real say in how the club that they followed week in week out was run. The concept was in essence the ultimate Fantasy Football that combined all the excitement and traction of football gaming with Electronic Arts FIFA and the Football Manager games through engaging with this global online community. It offered fans around the globe the chance to play the role of being part manager and chairman with all the responsibilities that it would bring. You could be involved in sanctioning transfers, selecting the match day squad at a real team, propelling a little-known club up the league pyramid. It was Fantasy Football for armchair experts, based on a loose notion of community ownership that eventually ran out of steam.

The visionary who dreamt big was a journalist and copywriter. Will Brooks, a Fulham fan and a huge Football Manager fan wondered if he could harness the power of the web to make a communal football club come alive. The concept started off in rather vague terms with MyFootballClub growing from a one-page website which offered contributors the opportunity to buy as yet unnamed clubs, to the eventual official takeover of a Conference side. Fuelled by a significant feature on the BBC, within three months 53,000 people had registered their interest in the scheme. When push came to shove there were 32,000 members signed up for what was to be a unique community ownership journey that offered them the chance to pick the team on a Saturday. Rumours of discussions with Leeds United and Nottingham Forest, both then in the Championship, helped fuel the excitement of the new global football community. The reality of the situation was that when a deal was eventually done, it was the purchase of non-league club Ebbsfleet United that will always be the first professional sports club owned and run by an online community.

MyFootballClub's interest in Ebbsfleet was officially announced in November 2007, and after three months of negotiations, a deal was completed in February 2008. Democracy is not a word usually associated with football clubs but, in this case, the global vote was pursued and it resulted in 95.89 per cent of members in favour of making their dream come true, as they and their fellow fans took a long journey into the unknown. It was not going to be a smooth ride.

With members from 120 countries all wanting a say and an existing fan base to satisfy, the fanciful notion of fans actually picking the team never came to pass, as the weekly vote on who should actually pick the team always sided with the manager, the seasoned professional Liam Daish. It seems that even the most sophisticated of keyboard warriors knew their limits. A positive start saw Ebbsfleet win the FA Trophy just months after the takeover, beating Torquay United 1–0 in front of a crowd of 40,186 at Wembley with many of the new global fans taking the opportunity to see the team in action for the first time.

Despite the gift of a positive start with a win at Wembley and a range of innovative marketing plans with player interviews, interactive content and live streaming of matches, the inevitable happened and the memberships started to fall dramatically. The concept was always about fun and novelty and once it translated into the reality of running a new professional football side that was not part of your loyal football DNA, many lost interest.

The dream began to die and as Will Brooks said in his interview in *The Blizzard* magazine:

> One of my biggest conclusions is that perhaps the idea was more exciting than the reality. I think people loved the idea of it, and the media loved the idea of it, but then when you announce that you've bought a Conference club and nobody's heard of the players, then people began to potentially switch off a bit. As soon as we were running out of money it became more difficult.

By the time the 2012–13 season was due to kick off, there were just 1,300 members left and the dream of attempting to transform football ownership was coming to a sad conclusion. In April 2013, MyFootballClub's members voted in favour of handing two-thirds of their shares to the Fleet Trust, and the other third to one of the club's major shareholders. KEH Sports Ltd, a group of Kuwaiti investors, arrived to take over within a month and remain in place to this day.

*Reasons for a change from community ownership*

- Poor integration of virtual fans and real fans.
- Ownership dream for members was for a far more prestigious club.
- No sustainable longer-term business plan.
- Novelty factor soon wore off.
- Club had no real history to work with.
- Timing not right.

## Dundee FC

'Dundee fans decide on their future showing that democracy in football can work' read the headline in *The Courier*. Meanwhile, that doyen of Tayside Broadcasting, Jim Spence, asked on BBC Scotland, 'Is this the end of fan ownership in Scottish football?' Jim of course was trying to highlight just some of the concerns that surrounded what was Dundee's short-lived foray into the previously unchartered waters of fans' ownership. He was hinting that if Dundee became lost to fans' ownership, that the game was a bogey for fans wanting to own their club. Jim liked to play the devil's advocate but he knew that the other four smaller senior community-owned clubs in Scotland were managing just fine at that time, being run effectively and most importantly, sustainably. He also knew that many other fans' groups at clubs such as Hearts, St Mirren and Motherwell still saw this as a real way forward and would not be put off if the Dundee fans decided to change ownership of their club.

It is not that the benefactor model has in recent times worked particularly well for the Dee, with a spectacular £23 million of debt in 2003 and the vanishing chequebook of Aberdonian Calum Melville causing their collapse in 2011. Coming into community ownership seemed like a sensible option given that the administrator Bryan Jackson had failed to find any interested parties willing to take a punt on the club. The fans were, of course, the bank of last resort and the club had to continue. By the time that the club had converted to community ownership, I had left Stirling Albion and was being funded by the Scottish Government through their investment in fans' affairs after the Rangers collapse. For a short period in time Dundee FC were actually the biggest fan-owned club in the UK.

It's just too easy to say fans can't run clubs but as our colleagues in Sweden and Germany know, that is just not the case where it is the norm. However, one of the major challenges for supporter-owned clubs is operating in an unsustainable environment that is the rest of the football landscape.

On reflection, I think it is fair to say that Dundee stumbled into community ownership rather than embracing it with gusto. Just as we had seen in other parts of the UK, if there is no forewarning of a crisis, it is really hard to prepare for it. Dundee were in the gutter, had no suitors given their track record and fan ownership offered a way forward. I attended several public meetings at Dens Park, and I was struck almost immediately with the lack of excitement about owning and running the club. Having had the excitement of taking Stirling Albion into community ownership, I was shocked at the lack of enthusiasm for the local people to own the club. Aside from the size of the club, there should have been no real difference. I recognised that with a larger support there would be more willing workers but what I could not see is that there were also many more people wanting a say and bringing previous history with them too. There were also many more potential leaders and many who carried grudges and feuds, some of them relating back to the first administration.

I do not know the inside story of the personalities or processes that fan ownership at the club took but having met many of the people involved at that time, it was clear that the support was far from unified. Not just on the terraces but also in the boardroom. So often it is the case that expectation continues to exceed the reality of what any given club can hope to achieve. In the changing landscape of our football economy, paying players what you can afford to pay based on your actual income is starting to rebalance the game. Having failed to do so for some considerable time, Dundee struggled to come to their new economic reality. They also had an older generation brought up in the halcyon days of Bob Shankly winning them titles with stars like Ure, Gilzean and Cooke, and reaching the European Cup semi-finals. There is no doubt that in the scramble to save the club from its second administration, there were many things done to get the deal across the line that in the cold light of day should have been done differently with a more considered governance structure.

My report from the time makes interesting reading:

> At the Dundee fans' meeting I attended on Saturday there was a real mix of emotions in the room. Disappointment at the way the club and the society had been run, concern about how the investment process had been played out in public and a very real anxiety that having twice been in administration, what the landscape might be if the new investors decide in a few years that it's not for them anymore. Due diligence will not be able to predict or help with this kind of decision. The most important thing is that there are safeguards put in place so that if the marriage does not work out, a suitable pre-nuptial agreement means that the Dundee fans, who will always be there supporting their team, have the opportunity to buy back the shares they are currently selling to the American investors.
>
> A Dundee fan at the same meeting asked why I was against the investment. I didn't get a chance to respond at the time as the mood in the room worked against me but, for the record, I am not against new investment in Dundee. What I wanted the fans to be aware of is just what they would be giving up (ownership and control) to get the investment. If the Dundee fans do decide they want new owners, then at least that is the decision they have made.
>
> Whatever decision is reached it proves the point that democracy in football can work. What it will not do is put off the many other fans who do want control of the club that they call their own.

The Dundee Football Club Supporters' Society have had three places on the board since they have had a majority shareholding in the club. The club on the park had the unexpected bonus of promotion to the SPL last season as a result of the Rangers liquidation. The club were ill prepared for this and as a consequence it was not surprising that the club were relegated from the SPL. The dramatic shortfall in income from £1.2 million down to approximately £65,000 this coming season in Division One is part of the reason why an SPL 2 breakaway was threatened and has now been overcome with the new league structure. However, such a massive drop in income is something that few 'normal' businesses could accommodate.

## *Reasons for a change from community ownership*

- History of two painful administration events had eroded a lot of trust.
- Failure of a natural leader to emerge able to unite factions.
- Poor governance of previous fans' groups.
- Too many personal battles.
- Too many folks unwilling to take advice.
- A very recent history of failure at the club.
- Various groups failed to merge to form a Foundation of Hearts-style new organisation leaving factions with agendas.
- No membership income stream developed.
- Failure to adapt to the new norm – the club does not have a given right to play in the topflight despite its history and size. Over the last 40 years it has been a Championship side for as long as it has been a Premiership side.
- A CEO who was working against the community ownership model – presumably as the inward investment would make his job easier/more exciting.

In April 2024 Dundee posted debts of £2.9m for the second season in a row under American ownership.

## Wrexham AFC

The Welsh club had been on a rollercoaster ride way before the Hollywood jet set of McElhenney and Reynolds made headlines when they completed their takeover of the club in 2021, with ambitions of taking the Welsh side to the Premier League. At the time of the takeover, Wrexham had been languishing outside the top four divisions of the English Football League for over a decade. It was, however, a decade of stability and sustainability after the horrors of various owners who used the club as a plaything. The fantastic article in *FourFourTwo* magazine (see References) goes into the whole sordid history in splendid detail and I highly recommend grabbing a coffee and sitting back and enjoying the read. It really does tell of a fantastic club, from its near-death experiences to the joys of the Superstar takeover.

I will never be able to do the story justice here but in summary: December 2004 saw the Welsh side make history by becoming the first to be docked ten points by the Football League. This was the result of the club having gone into administration with debts of more than £4 million. By the end of the season, they'd plunged into the fourth tier by a margin of eight points. This was the bottom of the barrel time for the club after a succession of dubious charlatan owners (many of whom ended up in the dock). With a club as low as that, the only investors available are the ones who love the club the most – the fans. Step forward Wrexham Supporters Trust (WST) who started the fundraising with a simple yet compelling proposition that had real health benefits too. They started a 'donate a beer' scheme where fans would hand over the weekly equivalent of a pint to raise money for the club. That group would later play a seismic role in the Red Dragons' future. It was a moment when fans and the wider community united and believed they could do it themselves. Many felt they couldn't do it any worse than what had gone before. They bought the club in 2011. The club thrived and despite no more than stability on the park, it was a huge success to be celebrated that ordinary fans had, in the space of three years, paid off all the debts and they had broken even. Nine years later a star-studded approach changed the club in the most unexpected way.

In November 2020, Canadian actor Ryan Reynolds and American actor Rob McElhenney, through the RR McReynolds Company LLC, bought the club. The deal received the backing of 98.6 per cent of the 2,000 members of the Wrexham Supporters Trust that voted. While many fans rejoiced, there were the 1.4 per cent who were concerned that they were part of a strange TV experiment. A football version of *The Truman Show*, perhaps. They wanted evidence of a plan beyond the new owners' goodwill community gestures and celebrity waves. There was concern that all the boring old stability of fans' ownership was being sacrificed to allow the super cool handsome dudes from Hollywood to make cash from the club.

Following the takeover, a docuseries called *Welcome to Wrexham* was announced to be in production for FX with Boardwalk Pictures. The series debuted on 24 August 2022 in the USA, followed by a release on Disney+ in the United Kingdom and Ireland. The documentary shows the stars not only enjoying themselves but engaging in a way that many club owners have failed to do. It is still very much early days but in the many interviews that they have done, they do seem to have completely bought into the exceptional community ethos that almost ten years of community ownership had brought. The performances on the park have also improved with the arrival of the stardust and an exceptional FA Cup run has worked wonders too.

Given where the club was before they came in, I would not be surprised if years from now the exit strategy might not see the club given back to the community that they bought it from. Now that really would be a great end to the documentary series. I have to admit that I do love the theatre of the Disney Plus series *Welcome to Wrexham* and of course the lead characters have made the community the focus of the story. If you have to come out of Community Ownership then finding Hollywood superstars to buy and three promotions can't be a bad thing.

## *Reasons for a change from community ownership*

- No obvious strategy to move beyond the comfort of the existing basic sustainability.
- A very recent history of failure at the club. In 2019–20, the club finished 19th on points per game after the season was ended early due to the COVID-19 pandemic, the lowest position in the club's 150-year history.
- Membership income stream not enough to take the club forward.
- The community ownership model was established in a crisis and served its purpose of ensuring stability but as the club had underperformed on the park in the 15 years since the purchase there was always going to be a risk to the survival of the model.
- Inward investment would make the job easier/more exciting moving up the leagues.
- Hollywood excitement made it a once in a lifetime opportunity.

## Community Ownership Does Not Work for All

It is easy for those who fear or oppose community ownership to point to the failings when clubs have become community-owned and have not stuck with the model. What is different here is there is little money, and the supporters have no option but to invest as the fans have become *the bank of last resort*. In many instances, the crisis at the club has been complex and camouflaged in a web that has been deliberately difficult to untangle. In many of these situations it can be hard for fans who take over to make a success of it as they probably were not battle ready for the challenge.

Often these club failures are shrouded in secrecy and if the supporters are not ready for them, they have less time to prepare. The administration process is designed to get the business turned around as quickly as possible and this also adds a huge time pressure to the process. An important point that one of my colleagues in England raised to me was that some of these administrations were handled by companies who had little experience of football clubs, which certainly did not help them. There are not that many in the profession with the very significant and unique experiences of Bryan Jackson or his long-time colleague Trevor Birch.

The specialist knowledge that comes from understanding the football business is invaluable.

In the situation described at Stirling Albion, we knew the club was for sale and had a successful Saving the Albion campaign team in place that raised £100,000 in just over a year. That built confidence in the seller and others who were not early adopters of the scheme that there just might be the capacity to do something with the fans. Likewise in Edinburgh, the fans at Hearts knew that they had to find a long-term solution to the Romanov problem of a disengaged foreign owner and a growing debt mountain. The FoH had almost two years of preparation for the task in hand. That was why several influential figures of an emerging Hearts supporters' group spent time coming to investigate and seek advice from myself at Stirling Albion after the club had become fan-owned. These fans listened, learned and took away confidence, along with all the documentation we gave them – they decided to form a group that would eventually become the Foundation of Hearts.

There is no doubt that the preparation and planning process gave them a huge advantage when it came to getting in a position to take the club forward. If they had not been in that position, there is no way that the administrator would have had faith in selling them the club. In many of the failures that we see listed here, fans don't have the luxury of the time afforded to the likes of Stirling Albion or Heart of Midlothian to prepare for the ensuing disaster ahead. In both of these cases, the campaign groups had attracted key personnel with legal, financial and marketing muscle and had a vision for what they wanted to achieve. In cases where the implosion was less obvious in coming, such as at Notts County, Bury, Dundee and Chester City where the fans had little time to prepare, despite raising significant funds community ownership failed to get established. If they had the German model in place that Hearts adopted with season ticket sales being supplemented by a monthly membership fee, then they might not have had to rely upon finding new benefactors to support them.

Having a lack of financial resources to meet the challenge is something that is a stumbling block not just for supporters but also for any perspective new owner. Timing is critical and with the Binos we had luck on our side. Having already managed to raise a lot of money for such a small club, we got the call to say that we had to find £300,000 in a matter of days. It set forward a bizarre chain of events, certainly in my household. Everyone knew that we had £100,000 in the bank and when Jim McGinn, the trust lawyer and old university football teammate of mine, asked where the other £200,000 was coming from, he nearly fell off his seat when I told him I would cover it. I had just sold my house and was waiting on planning permission for a new build and had the cash in the bank. I of course had chatted to Steven Leiper and Topher Nairn who were my closest confidants in the campaign and they quickly said they too would throw in significant sums in the order of £25,000 each as loans. The problem was they couldn't get the cash right away. That meant in the short term we needed £200,000 and to find £125,000 to pay me back. With a huge leap of faith, mostly from a very supportive wife, we got the deal across the line. With proof of funds in the bank, it allowed the deal to be concluded and, thankfully, after visiting several farms and houses around Stirling with our super salesman David McFarlane, we had pledges that would arrive over the next six months to reduce my liability. Although it was a mad few days, it allowed the concept of the fans and a benefactor working together to develop. This was successfully employed by Hearts (Ann Budge) and Motherwell (Les Hutchinson) in the years that followed.

Prior to the first Bury administration, they achieved promotion. Likewise, at the time of the Stirling Albion fans' buy-out, the club had just obtained promotion to the Championship but had racked up a debt of £300,000 to the bank, covered by a secured overdraft. They also owed £240,000 to their landlords Stirling Council for various disputed rent and rates payments. Even allowing for the increased revenues that would be generated by playing in the Championship, there would simply be no way of recovering the accumulated debt hanging over the club. Fortunately, the fans purchased the club for £300,000 and agreed to take over the outstanding disputed Council debt. That faith in doing things differently prevented any chance of an administration event happening at Forthbank. Many of the debts were accrued from having run a budget that was considerably larger than the other clubs in Division One that year.

The gamble paid off on this occasion as the revenue from the season with games against the likes of Partick Thistle, Dundee and Dunfermline Athletic allowed the fans to gamble that they could repay the £200,000 that they had from benefactors. The difference with community ownership is that the supporters knew all about what was happening at the club financially and were told before the season started what the budget would be. It was almost half what it had been the season they had won the Division One title because the dream changed from trying to stay in a league competing against full-time teams to paying back the fans who facilitated the purchase of the club. Transparency is the first rule of community ownership – being honest with the stakeholders.

I remember us breaking the news to over 200 fans crammed into the King Robert Hotel in Bannockburn. A season in the Championship would be very exciting for the fans BUT we were cutting the budget and were the only part-time team in the league, meaning that going down was almost certain. Relegation was almost an inevitable consequence but not really a worry to the fans who had seen the same thing happen in the previous seasons that the club had been promoted. The difference this time was that as owners they had the openness and transparency that meant that they knew what was happening and that the club would not be taking on any more debt in the process. At the end of the relegation season, we had paid back nearly £60,000 from the original £200,000 borrowed and were running sustainably.

## In Conclusion: What We Learned from the Model

- Supporter investment will always be capped based on the size of the support of the club.
- Timing is everything; if you are unprepared for a crisis and it emerges then we know that fans will always rally around but you need long-term commitment.
- Building capacity like in case of Stirling Albion with the Save the Albion campaign or with Hearts with the Foundation of Hearts, activity is the key to success. If the fans have a chance to campaign, they can build infrastructure and credibility with others.

Having many fans' groups is a problem that can be resolved with a new clean organisation, such as we saw with the Foundation of Hearts eventually getting the support of the G10 group of fan groups at the club. Existing organisations can continue to do what they do but having a leader can help overcome some of the problems of the past. We need to always be aware of the politics of any given supporter base and with independent input help them overcome them. If you all love the team, then you all have to work together to make it work.

The benefits of the new group:

- Not tied to baggage of any of the existing groups.
- Unifying force with defined ( new) leadership.
- New name and identity gives marketing opportunities.
- Creates a sense of excitement and often urgency.
- Makes it easier to attract media attention at an important time.

CHAPTER 8

# Fans – 'Who are you?'

*Football is the most important of the less important things in the world.—*
Carlo Ancelotti

WE KNOW THAT football fans' primary concern is about what happens on a Saturday afternoon. What is important is the almost religious ritual of watching as their heroes try to write another chapter of sporting history for the club. However, over the recent years, there has been a significant change to that dynamic as fans have had to understand just how a football club works as a business. When it comes to the inner workings of football clubs, their finances and the politics at your club and at the football authorities are now essential. One of the themes throughout this book is that the strength of a community can potentially offer a greater, longer sustainable future for a football club than individuals or small groups of businesspeople. At the very least, we hope that by the time you close the final page of this book, we have demonstrated that football supporters can be equally adept at running clubs as anyone else. What was unconventional, untried and radical is becoming something that is now an important part of the new football economy. As knowledge and understanding grow so too does the confidence.

## Fans: The Changing Audience

If we look at the wider football landscape over the past 30 years, there are plenty of examples of clubs going out of business. As a result of the turmoil that ensues from such calamitous events, the ordinary football fan has had to learn about how clubs work or, in these cases, what has caused them to spectacularly fail. Fans of course need to know what has gone wrong and how it can be avoided in the future. Having to step forward in these circumstances is not often the best preparation for future success and the few times that community ownership has failed was in situations where the fans' groups were just not prepared or organised in such a way that they were capable of running a football club. If we wound the clock back 30 years ago, it would be highly unlikely that you would find any knowledge or indeed interest in the details of how football clubs were managed. Only in times of crisis would there have been any insight from behind the curtain that guarded the daily friend of football operations – otherwise the clubs just ran like normal.

Many clubs moved away from being driven by smaller local family businesses that were often connected with the club through generations to larger business operators. With that changing dynamic, we saw a move from concern about the community that their businesses had served for generations to the more corporate world where a profit motive or ego would often drive the strategy. In these cases it put a distance between the ordinary fan and the knowledge about how their football club was being run.

In Scotland over the past few years, we have seen high-profile business failures at Rangers, Heart of Midlothian, Dundee, Motherwell, Livingston and Dunfermline Athletic, to mention just a few. In England in the last few years, Bolton Wanderers and Bury have joined Derby County as the off-field disasters have become national news. Supporters now have a real understanding of just what happens behind the scenes in football. As we live in an era of instant communications, it means that information is quickly gathered and opinions are freely shared in the supporter community. Fans have had to learn about the fit and proper test, CVAs, administration, liquidation and the governing bodies' relationship with all of the above. Even those who claim only to be interested in what happens on the park can't exclude the information flow that now comes minute by minute.

The once held notion that the ordinary fan knew nothing about what went on behind closed doors in football clubs has gone forever. Over the years it has been a frustration to me when I come across 'football people' who are dismissive of ordinary football fans. It is almost as if they have a mental image of a packed Hampden Park, full of cloth-capped heavy industry workers of the 1940s or 1950s, educated only in the way of the shipyards or coal mines. They were the uneducated and the unwashed or 'pond life' as one club chairman suggested to me when describing his own supporters. Maybe those sepia-tinged images and the more recent recollections of the 1980s hooligan culture have been so deeply ingrained in their minds that fans will never be truly accepted. Society has changed beyond all recognition in the last five years and so have football fans who have moved with the times. In 1950, just 17,500 students were awarded university degrees across the United Kingdom. In 2018–19, there were 2.38 million students studying at UK higher education institutions according to the statistics given by the official educational body Universities UK. In 2019, the statistics tell us that 42 per cent of the UK population have completed higher education. That is a lot of very clever and experienced people out there and guess what – many of they are ordinary football fans.

One of the most dramatic changes over the past 30 years has seen the growth of women attending football matches. This important part of the audience has largely been ignored and has had little recognition by the football authorities or indeed by many clubs. Smaller clubs often have an excuse in that they don't have the resources but at the League and FA level it really has not had the attention it deserves. My own anecdote around this came when the SFSA were conducting research into the Women in Football. When asked about how many women supporters there were in the Scottish game, neither the SFA nor the SPFL were able to give the BBC any indication of the size of the audience. Fortunately, with nearly 30,000 individual members we knew that 8 per cent of them were female fans. We had also conducted a major benchmarking exercise in 2017 with nearly 17,000 respondents and 8 per cent of those who completed the survey were women. That stat has been used numerous times since then and is now seen as gospel.

When BBC Radio Scotland asked me about my own personal experiences of the female audience, I recalled a tumbleweed moment that was followed by laughter behind the goals at Firhill. In the mid-1960s I was a wee lad sitting on the concrete crush barrier with my dad and his mates from his shipyard days. When there was a break in play and an unusual moment of hush surrounded our group, I managed to create a level of laughter that I have failed to achieve in many years of trying since. All because this wee six-year-old boy pointed out to all there gathered, 'Look Dad there is a woman down there!' It was the St Andrews Ambulance first aider and so rare was it to see a lady at a game that my observation brought a lot of laughter.

Since those days, the growth of the female following can be seen to have risen substantially and will continue to do so in the years ahead. This growth has undoubtedly been the result of some key factors.

The overall growth of the game and the glamour of its top stars have had an influence on making the game more accessible. It is a sport that is exciting, with international box office appeal. Football now offers a feast of international soap opera proportions available to watch in the comfort of your own home.

From the arrival in the 1960s of the fifth Beatle George Best to the dramas of Cristiano Ronaldo, as a sport football has sex, money, fashion and celebrity appeal far beyond other ordinary sports.

Since the demise of the hooligan culture of the 1980s, football has become more accessible to everyone but in particular families and women. Aside from certain circumstances, there is a lot less fear about going to watch football.

The growth of girls playing football, where it continues to be the fastest growing sport in Europe. If you get that love of the game through playing it, you are far more likely to watch it too.

The growth of TV coverage means it is an easier way of getting into football without having to endure what many see as almost a rite of passage – the 'Tuesday night cup tie in January away at Forfar Athletic'.

Post the Ibrox, Hillsborough and Bradford City disasters, the Taylor report saw a huge improvement of the facilities at football grounds across the UK. We know from our SFSA Research that there is still huge disparity around the grounds but the overall standards of accommodation at clubs have improved considerably.

Society has changed. When I was a kid in the 1960s, football was pretty much exclusively for dads and boys but nowadays, with a change to the sexual stereotypes, this has been confined to the history books alongside the macaroon bars and spearmint chewing gum being peddled around the open terraces.

With a change in social structures and blended families becoming more of the norm, there have been changes that have led to more influences. Our research also heard from many women who, because of being a single parent, had ventured into taking kids to football, entering an arena that might previously have been the domain of a father figure.

The rise of social media has also had a key role to play in understanding the changing football landscape and empowering fans to campaign successfully. I don't believe for a minute that the iconic Glasgow club Third Lanark would ever have gone out of business if the disaster that emerged were to happen today. Of course, although clubs rarely die, the challenge is to get them off the life support machine as soon as possible and preserve what they have or risk a long winding road to take you back to where you started. We have seen this drama unfold recently in England where Bolton Wanderers got a last-minute reprieve following collapse, took a points deduction and preserved their league status. Sadly, at Gigg Lane, poor Bury had no such reprieve and were bumped out of the league structure completely. The only way back for them is to re-emerge as a phoenix club and work their way through the league pyramid structure. Often in these circumstances, it is about timing or just how attractive a club is to save. So, Bolton Wanderers with its pedigree and scale was a far more attractive proposition for new investors than poor wee Bury. So, the landscape in football has changed and supporters now recognise that as well as being 'a club' the team is also a business that has to be run in an efficient manner, just like any other limited company. What supporters don't want to see is the corporate world that identifies them as just customers. They are far more important than that, being the heart and soul of the operation. Of course, if you are running a business, even one as unique as a football club, you do have to know and understand your audience.

## Understanding the Fans – Someone Has To!

I think I know a wee bit about fans and what makes them tick, given that one way or another I have been involved in marketing to them for over 25 years. However, in all that time, including ten successful years helping Nationwide with its sponsorship of the England team, no one I ever met really understood the real dynamic of fans' unique characteristics. There have been several academic papers on the subject, but I never felt they really captured the essence of the football supporters that I knew and understood. I was privileged to walk the corridors of power at the FA and then for a wee while to help Gordon Smith secure some significant commercial deals when he was at the SFA, yet when talking to brands or commercial partners it seemed to me that fans were all classified as one big group.

More often than not, clubs I have spoken to only had basic categories such as season ticket holder, former season ticket holder, international fan etc. Over the past 15 years, the CRM (Customer Relationship Marketing) developments at clubs have seen a new level of database management come into play. Generally speaking, the larger the club the more that they have invested in database management and the segmentation of football supporters. However, most of this work is conducted in generic terms, aligning data management from the wider marketing world and adapting it into season ticket holder databases. There is a lot of information around the age, the postcode and the socio-economic grouping that fans belong to. This is supplemented by additional information, usually gathered via surveys and other research and added to provide fan profiling which helps clubs understand the customer and how much economic value they can bring to the club. Do the fans buy hospitality and if so, how often and at what category, do they have family members, how many years have they been season ticket holders? There are usually a multitude of other similar customer questions that the best resourced clubs have to be able to answer. What it does not do is dig deeper into fan culture. I am not an academic nor am I a market researcher, but I have been fascinated by how the unique loyalty of fans works, why they follow a certain club and how and when the relationship with the club might change in the fullness of time.

A few years back I wrote a less than memorable wee charity book called *Saving Scottish Football*. The one thing that grabs people's attention from it was the chapter in which I attempted to segment the fan base. Since then I have done a few guest lectures at several universities for Sports Management Undergraduates and Masters students where I have explored the different fan types.

From the discussions I had with many fans, I decided to try and develop a range of classifications of supporter types. So that by the time we launched the Scottish Football Supporters Association in April 2015, it allowed us to get any individual who joined the SFSA to self-select the type of fan they saw themselves as. The fan types of classifications are not perfect but what it does do is allow us to build a picture of the overall landscape and start to develop a real understanding of Scottish football fans. I do hope in the coming years that we can build on this and really help football to understand its audience better. One of the first exercises in 2023 was looking at the lifetime value of a fan and seeing just how important that is to the game. We know that in Scotland 43 per cent of revenue in the SPFL is generated through the turnstiles and that number increases to over 50 per cent in the divisions below, so understanding those exceptionally loyal customers is essential if you want to grow the business. My argument is: how can you grow your audience if we don't properly know who they are and how they consume their football? If you want to understand the importance of this, then look no further than the football academic Rogan Taylor who talks extensively about the unique love that fans have for their team. His quote to describe that unique loyalty says it all, 'You don't get customers at Tesco wanting to have their ashes scattered in the car park'.

## Fan Segmentation Factors

Various methods can be applied to segment fans into different categories and, in many cases, this has been the domain of academics who often don't know or understand fan culture as well as fans themselves. Our friends at FanQ in Germany looked at these factors which provide a sensible starting point for further exploration.

- Behavioural
- Demographic
- Geographic
- Psychographic (the qualitative methodology of studying consumers

based on psychological characteristics and traits such as values, desires, goals, interests, and lifestyle choices)
- Behavioural factors
- Product or service usage (live or TV)

Every fan who walks out of their door to attend a match seeks to extract something from that unique experience. Because of the connections and the collective emotions that are shared at games, it can never be categorised as just entertainment. Given that each fixture is different and that many groups of fans might choose to only attend certain types of fixtures, the dynamic can change with every game that is played over different seasons too.

Understanding fans as we (SFSA) do, we know that the vast majority of football fans just want to see the team winning, get the emotional buzz that is unique in football when visiting the home ground and, of course, hope to get some entertainment along the way. Football is unique, with few activities or events that can compare to it. It could be argued that some of the North American staple sports, like ice hockey, grid iron, basketball and baseball might run close but given the way that franchises are sold across the States, there is little to hold this argument together. Soccer, as they call it, has a deep loyalty that no other sport comes close to.

Most recently, Pep Guardiola when talking about the threat of playing behind closed doors (during the pandemic), compared football to the theatre. He is of course partially correct; it is just that every game is different, and it follows no script. Part of the appeal is that you might see the game of the season or the best goal ever, you just never know what the football gods might have lined up for you. That fact helps compensate for the many freezing cold winter nights that you have had to endure watching a turgid 0–0 draw. There are elements that money just simply can't buy. Of course, in this market there is always next week or if things are not too good then next season.

Some fans will be happy even after watching a match of dreadful quality, as long as their team win. Others will do the opposite and enjoy a good quality match even if their club lost. For most fans, however, it is a combination of the two aspects with the weight each has depending on the individual fan's preferences. Win seekers may totally alter their buying behaviour depending on the club's success on the pitch, while entertainment seekers may do the same depending on the players' flair or the level of excitement that has been generated.

Apart from their ticket, several fans like to purchase other products and services prior, during and after the game. From shirts and caps to beers and match programmes, a fan can spend money in various ways during their visit to the stadium. Of course, football products and services are also available outside the match day context too, with subscriptions to club radio and TV stations now commonplace in a way that stretches the whole experience beyond match day.

## Demographic Factors

A simple categorisation typically used by clubs would be a demographic segmentation which consists of dividing the fans into groups based on variables such as age, gender, income, family lifecycle and geography.

One of the problems that football in Scotland faces is the lack of data around all these factors. We also know that most of these variables are not static. So habits might change with age or through changes in your family lifestyle, just as your income and geography might change. All these factors thrown together make for a constantly moving and changing customer base that is very difficult to really get to know. That fact alone makes this process difficult for clubs to manage their customers. At Manchester City, with global aspirations they had a digital and marketing team of over 30; at Albion Rovers, who share the same objectives of bringing in more fans and getting those who come along to spend more, might be lucky to have someone in the boardroom who knows something about marketing.

Given the unique profile of a football customer, you can't quickly campaign to change clubs' customers. Every day should be a recruiting day for the club. If you think Sainsbury's is too expensive you can try Tesco, but changing a football fan from one team to another is virtually impossible. Even the greatest season ever on the park will only bring a small uplift in supporters and most of these will be from the existing wider fan base who might go more regularly or increase the number of away games they go to. There is no doubt on-field success will make it easier to recruit but the truth is that the making of a fan is more about a quasi-religious conversion than finding a *new customer*. Just as most religions thrive from indoctrination from family members so too does this make the best recruitment tool. Having the drive and determination to build a marketing plan around that is no easy task for our clubs.

Football fans are predominately male – the SFSA membership data shows that 92 per cent are in membership – but in recent years the number of female spectators has been increasing as we have seen above. If a club receives an extremely small percentage of its visits from women, it needs to look into the reason for that and try to find ways to penetrate the untapped female market. Sometimes the factors behind women not attending are overlooked by clubs. One of the most common reasons often quoted but rarely acted upon is the poor quality and cleanliness of WCs for women in the stadiums and the misogynous behaviour of fellow fans.

Income is also an important factor in how we determine fan types. The level of disposable income available to spend on football as a lifestyle/hobby will very often dictate just how much money and time can be invested in it. Supporters might like the idea of watching the team home and away but might not be able to afford it. A fan's family lifecycle is also of utmost importance. As do buyers in any conventional market, the majority of football fans vastly change their buying behaviour during their lifespan. We have explained this in further detail when looking at the individual fan types.

## Geographic Factors

This categorisation divides fans according to their geographical positioning. Distance may not necessarily affect a fan's preference on which team to support but it definitely has an enormous effect on his/her attendance level. The closer a fan lives to the club's stadium the more likely it is that they will attend matches and thus the more valuable he or she is to the club. It has been argued that the realistic catchment area of a football club includes the fans that live within a 60-minute distance from the stadium. This will of course vary from club to club and there will be many exceptions to it.

Another geographic aspect is the tendency of fans to support teams which are based in their hometown even though they primarily support another 'bigger' club. These 'second tier' fans are not as important as normal fans as they tend to spend the bulk of their football budget on their primary club and just leftovers for their hometown club. In many cases, local clubs find themselves unable to attract fans due to that factor. There is a belief, albeit anecdotal, that this used to be far more common in the 1960s and 1970s when transport to away games was not as easy and there was not the wall-to-wall coverage of football on TV that we now have. If you were, say, a Rangers season ticket holder living in Falkirk, if Rangers were away at Aberdeen, you might watch Falkirk at home just to see a game of football.

## Psychographic Factors

Loyalty is the main factor here. Unlike conventional markers, the football industry can boast it has one of the most (if not *the most*) loyal customer bases. It has an almost religious zeal that drives an audience to behave like no other customer group. Even when the supporter drops down the loyalty ladder due to age or a change in circumstances, they never desert the brand/club completely. There will remain the opportunity to still sell them something. It might not be a season ticket, but it could be a TV highlights package, a club shirt or a special occasion hospitality package. The nearest equivalent we can find for this dynamic is in religion where the 'Once a Catholic always a Catholic' adage applies to football fans – no matter what team they support – they can never truly escape from their origins.

The loyalty of football fans works in two distinct but very important ways.

### Club Loyalty

At the core of being a club supporter, this devotion prevents the fans from switching to other competitors in the same market (another club). However, this dynamic is not fixed; as the market has changed there are many fans who support other clubs in different countries. This might have been stimulated by a visit to a club on holiday or just through watching on TV. I have an annual trip down to Newcastle United once a season with a friend Andy Scott and his son Callum and my son Gregor just to get a bit of Premiership excitement. It always amazes me the number of Scots who now go down to watch United on a regular basis. Having a chat with many over the years I have met guys who are Hearts, Hibs, Dundee fans etc who have converted to watching the Magpies with only the occasional trip to see their English club. We have also seen a huge uplift in the number of fans from the UK going to watch a more traditional fan experience in Germany with cheap flights, cheap admission costs and the convenience of Airbnb. It could not have been predicted that we would have a St Pauli FC fans' club in Glasgow, but we do.

### Football Loyalty

FIFA are the custodians of the game globally and they tell us that the game attracts 7.2 billion people watching football during the World Cup. It has more participants than any other sport across a range of football participation categories. There is no doubt that this popularity cements its place as the most dominant world sport. Having a loyalty to it is a certain deterrent to the fans from switching to other services in the broader entertainment market (cinema, theatre etc). They of course don't consume football exclusively and will play and spend money on other sports and entertainments but love of the game tends to ensure that loyalty is virtually impossible to break. Even at the top of the game with the financial scandals and decisions to host tournaments in Russia and Qatar, FIFA rode the storm out as the love of the game far outweighed any of the negative self-inflicted PR disasters that they had created.

The game itself is always the most important thing.

## The Return on Investment is Far from Obvious

A wee while back I wrote a piece for the excellent *Nutmeg* magazine which I have based the rest of this chapter on. I have updated it and modified it to reflect the change in circumstances and the new data that I now have from ever-growing SFSA membership. Football is not a product, it is a lifestyle choice. Without significant structural change to the way clubs view fans, no matter what schemes you offer you will simply not be able to get enough new fans through the gates to justify the investment in these areas. So, what we have is what businesses call 'customer churn' where you are losing more fans than you are managing to bring in. Given how long it takes to build a loyal fan then you can see that the picture looks gloomy. When the SPFL have isolated the Premiership figures from the last few years it does look very rosy. However, over the past five seasons the picture is skewed with the return of Hearts, Rangers, Dundee United and Hibs to the topflight in recent seasons, and these figures mask the truth.

For the so-called provincial clubs, there is a dilemma in that there are football fans within their area that are only attracted to the two big successful clubs: Celtic and Rangers. I am sure that it would not take a major research paper into the psychology of the behaviour of sports fans to get to the bottom of why people want (and need) to follow successful clubs. In Scotland, we also have the history of the sectarian and religious issues that have blighted our game but have acted as a recruitment tool for others. It is important as a matter of research to understand how we become fans and how over the past 20 or 30 years this has changed.

Indeed, it is a journey that is now very much under the spotlight once again as football wrestles with the growth of the *Ultra* culture that has taken a grip on these shores, having grown across Europe. It brings with it a whole new raft of challenges regarding what is acceptable behaviour at football matches.

Every business worth its salt needs to understand their market and I am sorry to say that this is something that has been completely lacking in Scottish football given the lack of resources and importance this has been given. We are further hampered that as a business our football operates as a members' club that competes on the park, but those members are rarely brought together to work for the collective good of the game. Being so divided is a huge weakness for anyone that has a desire to improve the game. It really is cases of self-interest always trumping the common good.

Everything we are told about fans is based on a little knowledge, anecdotal evidence, some previous history and, of course, the age-old navel gazing and its sister, the gut feeling. No business in the world would go into such a dramatic period of change as when the leagues merged a few years back without the detailed knowledge of its customers.

There is no evidence to suggest that even if these basic foundations were in place those who control our game would take any notice of what the customers want or in this case need to stay engaged. But that, as they say, is another story. On this journey, we will start by looking at who the customers are and look to see what opportunities might exist to talk to them. This is important to fans as we want our clubs to be successful and vibrant with a good atmosphere, important to the clubs as it brings in more revenue and important to the league who want to make the proposition as attractive to the sponsors and TV companies too.

## The Route to Becoming a Football Fan

### The Family

The most common route to becoming a fan is to follow in your grandfather/father/uncle's footsteps and start your journey as part of your family birthright. Of course, when you break the link through the aforementioned churn you have far more difficulty in capturing the next generation of fans. Strangely enough, many football families have fallen away after mixed marriages where there is a fight to see which family club the offspring will support. Is it Hearts or is it Hibs? Worse still, marrying into a rugby or golf family could easily deprive your club of a future fan. Finding a fellow Dons fan to marry in Aberdeen might well be achievable but finding a fellow Rovers fan in Coatbridge might be more of a challenge.

However, even with a satisfactorily happy family connection, we can see that over the past 30 years in my family, there is a dilution in the loyalty which is a huge change from the previous generation. So many factors come to play, from the change in the community as a whole, to the diminishing importance of football as a part of the fabric of our society, to the many other alternative opportunities that exist to use the leisure time that once was the sole claim of the football industry. In this scenario, we can see where Scottish football has lost its way and for once it is not the fault of the game. What the game can be blamed for is not acting fast enough to address the consumer behaviour changes that have emerged and adapting to provide help to create a new audience.

### Location

There is no doubt that Scotland has some geographical and population disadvantages, and we are not just talking about the legendary wind in Arbroath that has scared the living daylights out of many a player or spectator. It is so much easier in larger countries like Spain, France, Germany or Italy, and to an extent England, where there are larger population centres to support their league structures. With large cities there is plenty of space for good-sized clubs to prosper. England has big one-city clubs like Newcastle United, Sunderland, Leeds United even down to the smaller cities like Norwich City or Leicester City. In Scotland, we just don't have the luxury of a large population and what we do have is skewed to a couple of large clubs who dominate our landscape. What would be ideal is for fans that live in say Falkirk to follow one of the local teams. Of course many do but, as we know, to the detriment of the game, far too many leave their hometowns to follow our two big clubs. It is a drain on local football that it seems we are unable to address. As they say – success breeds success. This is great for Celtic and Rangers, but undoubtedly bad for the economics of our game. Of course, if you are born in Hamilton, there is a good chance that you might end up being an Accies fan, which is a good starting point for each provincial club but as we know it is no guarantee.

### The Friendly Introduction

Quite often a friend will introduce somebody to the game or a club and that introduction will stick, whether it is as a second team or indeed as the primary team of choice of the individual. This season my son's pals have been to a few Partick Thistle games with me (kids go free) and some Stirling Albion games (our local club), and I would think if we continued to do so, these will become their teams of the future. Another interesting aspect is that of all my son's friends, very few have fathers who take sons along to games the way it happened in my generation. The worry is that there are so few parents now taking kids along to games that once this cycle is broken it will be lost. Habit is such an important part of keeping loyal fans.

### School and Workplace

Having pals at school who follow a team can open the door to football for fans who maybe have no previous family history of supporting a team.

There have been some great examples at Dumbarton and at Stenhousemuir of boys aged 14–16 who used to congregate at the local McDonalds on a Saturday taking the opportunity to sample the delights at their local club. It was a slow build-up to getting to understand a bit more about lower league football and indeed to be accepted by the original support. This was a bit of a challenge for these original supporters when the young team were developing their own Tifosi Ultra environment – well, bringing a big drum and singing a lot is a good starting point!

The workplace can also bring an entry point for some fans who have maybe not had any direct club influences. This is less prevalent now than in the days of heavy industry where the bonding and social interaction was very different to what we see now. Many a shipyard used to virtually have their own supporters club and in my early days of watching football, there was a whole section of ex-Barclay Curle shipyard workers who all gathered in the same part of the terracing as my dad. I have also seen the workplace introduction to football happen when staff have relocated and needed to find a local team to watch – going with someone in the office who follows a team is a great way of getting under the skin of a team rather than just flying solo.

## The Random Reason – Lady Luck Has a Say

### Away from Home

It might be a work placement or moving away from home to university or college that ignites a spark. One of our SFSA ambassadors runs a marketing agency in New York. He was brought up a Manchester City fan and studied at Glasgow University. Andy and several of his colleagues decided that watching Partick Thistle helped him feel part of the city and its unique football culture. Despite only contributing financially for a few years, he still feels emotionally tied to the club and his short-term adopted home.

*Other Particular Reasons*

Many will have heard that Stenhousemuir have a fantastic fan base in Norway. The Norwegian Warriors Supporters Club was set up almost 20 years ago and has in excess of 400 members. It is one of the largest foreign supporters clubs outside of the English Premiership and they have gone on to become shareholders at the club. The Norwegian Supporters Club has sponsored the football club in many ways since their inception and currently sponsors the main stand, now called the Norway Stand. They have also, among other things, sponsored the Youth Programme and organised a pre-season tour to Norway for the first team in recent years. It started in a similar way, with Norwegian workers being based in Larbert and falling in love with this cracking little community club and the fact they were known as The Warriors. From a marketing perspective, there is little that can be done to find support like this. They just need to find you.

## Scottish Fans Tell Us What Type of Fan (Customer) They Are

As we have been exploring, it is really important to build a strong, vibrant fan base across our game. So, before we can even think about trying to get more fans into our grounds it is essential that we try to understand our fans and how they fit into each club. There is no definitive version of this fan profiling and for Football Insights research purposes we believe that this is as complete a picture as possible to create. When anyone joins the SFSA they are asked to self-select what type of fan they are. This insight has given us a significant understanding of not just who our members are but more importantly just how valuable they are to the football economy. With over 30,000 individual fans segmented into these categories, we really have a much better understanding of how many fans fit into these different categories. These figures quoted below are accurate up to and including December 2023.

If you can imagine a loyalty ladder, then the higher up the ladder you go the more important the fan is to the club economically. The stronger the loyalty the more fervent their support and of course how much more valuable they are as an income stream, how much they can generate as income for the club. It should be noted that these categories and the percentages are of Scottish football fans. There is no doubt there will be similarities in other countries and other leagues but there would be significant differences depending on the factors discussed before such as the geography of the country and the wealth and of course the very history of fans within each domain.

## Football Diehards are 17 per cent of the Scottish Football Audience

This fan never misses a game home or away if they can help it. Without doubt, these are the most loyal of all fans. They would not miss a game except in extreme circumstances (serious family illness or bereavement, etc) or indeed if cost prohibits it. This is sometimes seen with Old Firm fans who can no longer afford the foreign trips that were once the norm. These diehards will always ensure that key decisions such as weddings or holidays are taken outwith the football season. This is a sector that is diminishing and, in our research, we have found fewer of these fans than we might have historically expected. There is no doubt that part of that is due to the wall-to-wall coverage of away games on TV.

In the national context, we find a subset of this group with Tartan Army devotees who never miss a game home or away but many of them have dropped down the loyalty ladder at club level to finance the important foreign excursions.

## Committed Regulars are 26 per cent of the Scottish Football Audience

Fans in this category are season ticket holders who, unlike the Diehards, do not need to see every game in the flesh. They take in the odd 'local' away match. For example, if you were a Partick Thistle fan you might go to see them away at Hamilton Accies or Kilmarnock but a trip to Dundee might be deemed too far. We found that with fans who supported a team who did not qualify for Europe every season, these fans would be a bit more selective and would try to add an away to Europe to their repertoire wherever possible. The key for all clubs with this group is to ensure that they don't drop down to become a Committed Occasional as this will take the revenue away from being guaranteed to become nothing more than just possible or probable income. In this category, we have fans who hate the idea of not having a season ticket.

## Committed Occasionals are 24 per cent of the Scottish Football Audience

Goes to around half the home games, or maybe less, but not enough to merit buying a season ticket at the club he or she loves. Would like to go to more games but other commitments such as family or work or finance means that this is not possible. These are the fans that football clubs should try to convert to buy a season ticket as they are the most likely to become a Committed Regular if their financial or family circumstances change positively. More often than not these fans will once have been a Committed Regular, who have fallen down the loyalty ladder.

*Historical Occasionals are 8 per cent of the Scottish Football Audience*

Always been a fan but only manages to go to a few games a season. They have dropped down the loyalty ladder and the income they subsequently give to the club has diminished. A very dangerous category to have fans in as they can quite easily fall down completely and become Lapsed Lovers. Most fickle of fans who find it easy to do other things on a Saturday and football is now just part of a repertoire of things they do rather than being the core of their weekend activity.

*Walk-ins or Visitors are 5 per cent of the Scottish Football Audience*

Loves football, just looking for a game in the area or a place they are visiting. 'So I am in Dumfries, and I wonder if the Queens are playing at home today, yip great I'll go along and see them.' These fans were much more prevalent in the halcyon days of the 1950s through to the early 1980s. Now, however, it is a rare sight and many of the futile marketing campaigns seen across the county are aimed at this market segment when they should be looking at others further up the loyalty ladder. There is scope within this category to look at options to attract tourists. Scotland has a year-round tourism industry and there are very real opportunities for all clubs to build on their unique story and attract more visitors who might not just come to the match but will buy the t-shirt too.

*Distant Lovers are 8 per cent of the Scottish Football Audience*

Fans in exile that don't get to matches as much as they would like. The danger with this category is that through time the passion wanes and this sector becomes the hardest to keep on side. Distance tends to erode the connectivity and it becomes harder to engage with them on a day-to-day basis. With this category, they may come a few times a season for big matches, but you are limited to what value you can extract from them. The internet has helped, as has social media, but it is hard to do much in this sector to maximise revenues for the clubs.

These two categories below have been the hardest to define and in the years ahead we hope to further define them with more research. There is a degree of crossover that needs further exploration, ie 'I am a lapsed fan, but I still try to watch my team on TV' etc.

### Lapsed Lovers are 3 per cent of the Scottish Football Audience

They used to watch the team and can be encouraged out for big occasions – such as cup finals, play offs or unique events (testimonials or celebratory events relating to past glories) –but apart from that you will never see them. When they die off, the family connections are often lost and history is broken and can't be reclaimed. If had a pound for every person who I met who told me their grandfather used to be a Thistle fan, I would be able to make a sizeable contribution to the club's playing budget. This is no urban myth, for if you look at the record attendance of 49,838 in the 1920s, then there were a lot of grandfathers and great-grandfathers to lose.

### Armchair Fans are 9 per cent of the Scottish Football Audience

They only watch games on TV. They are most likely to have previously found a place higher up the loyalty ladder, but dropped right off the spectrum probably from getting out of the habit of going to matches. Other circumstances such as taking up other sports, having a family, changes at the club, or indeed a general dissatisfaction with the game they used to love, takes them to the TV screens. From the League's perspective, the simple message is that you can't have it both ways and if fans drop off the loyalty ladder you just need to be thankful that they still buy a Sky Sports subscription. Of course, there is a danger that their loyalty to Scottish football will decline as they expand their horizons through watching the more glamorous Spanish and English leagues. If they have a few TV packages, they can be contributing a sizeable amount of money to the game, far more than some of the other categories above.

### Changing Times, Changing Habits

For work and entertainment, there are many who will attend football matches regularly, either for corporate reasons or because they work for the club or other football body. Some but not all will fit into one of the above categories and others will sadly not be converted to become fans no matter how many games they see.

We all know that people are living longer and in better health for a longer period of time. Most people in my generation born in the early 1960s will be able to recall grandparents being tired and really old by the time they retired at 65 – if indeed they were lucky enough to make it that long. Lifetimes in the shipyards, iron foundries, coal mines or other heavy industries, where health and safety hardly existed, made for a short and often painful retirement.

The over 50s currently account for 80 per cent of the wealth of the UK – some £300 billion – and spending by households including someone over the age of 65 is £109 billion. These figures will only get bigger as the shift towards an ageing population gathers pace, with the over 65s now nearly 19 per cent of the population. Today, there are over 11 million people in the UK aged over 65 and on current projections that will have increased to 16m by 2030.

Within that group, older segments are the fastest growing and by 2050 it is estimated that there will be more than a quarter of a million centenarians in the UK. Some of the facts that the charity Age UK highlight are worth noting. What the custodians of our game need to reflect on is how this changing demographic will have an impact on who is watching live football and how they cater for their needs. It really is worth reflecting on these numbers.

By 2030 it is anticipated there will be over 21,000 centenarians (ONS, 2018).

In 50 years there are projected to be an additional 8.6 million people aged 65 years and over – a population roughly equivalent to the size of London (ONS, 2018k).

By 2030, one in five people in the UK (21.8 per cent) will be aged 65 or over, 6.8 per cent will be aged 75+ and 3.2 per cent will be aged 85+ (ONS, 2017b).

The 85+ age group is the fastest growing and is set to double to 3.2 million by mid-2041 and treble by 2066 (5.1 million; 7 per cent of the UK population) (ONS, 2018k).

Since the start of the 19th century, the UK has seen mortality rates decline and life expectancy increase (ONS, 2018b).

Babies born in 2018 are (at birth) projected to have a period life expectancy of 79.9 years old (males) and 83.4 years old (females) (ONS, 2018k). Although a slowdown has been evident internationally, life expectancy in the UK is lower than many other comparable countries (ONS, 2018h).

Between 2011 and 2016 the UK's average annual life expectancy improvement was lower than the EU average, for both men and women (PHE, 2018a).

The causes of this slowdown are likely to be complex and are not yet clear; theories include austerity, health and care system integration challenges, and increased prevalence of conditions such as cardiovascular disease, obesity and dementia (The Kings Fund, 2018a).

Nothing stands still in life or in football and if we want to care and nurture our game for future generations, we should be working hard to develop our relationship with its supporters. Over the past few years I have shared this information with both the SPFL and the SFA. I do think with some further investment it could really help them market Scottish football to the next generation. This is exactly the type of initiative that the never-published Deloittes report was interested in. The door of the SFSA remains open if anyone wants to develop this work with us further.

Knowledge after all is power. Sadly, as many clubs have little specialist marketing resources and little budget then it is not something they have shown any more than a passing interest in. When talking to one club chairman about his club's marketing efforts as they struggled to get out of the Championship, he said, 'There is of course the old adage that you can't flog a dead horse and that is what it feels like here'.

CHAPTER 9

# A Wake-up Call at Westminster and Holyrood – the Long and Winding Road

*Maybe now is the time to put the supporters first?* —
Alison Johnstone, former Scottish Green MSP,
now Presiding Officer of the Scottish Parliament

OVER THE PAST 30 years there has been a recognition that football governance is well below the standards that would be deemed acceptable or indeed normal in other industries. Every now and then in the occasional electoral cycle noise is made about the plight of football supporters and the way that the game is managed. These football fans are all also voters.

Sport in Scotland is, of course, devolved to Holyrood and, in the rest of the UK, it is a matter reserved to Westminster. Neither Government likes to see the national game in crisis or to see famous institutions like Rangers, Hearts, Portsmouth or Leeds United crashing, but the initial efforts to engage in a process that might change the dynamic has been slow and problematic. Could community ownership play a role?

## In England and Wales

In the most recent of times, there has been a belief that the globalisation of football and iconic clubs changing hands into foreign ownership might not be a good thing for the game. It is a subject that is deeply divisive and is certainly not as black and white as it might initially appear. A good example might be Manchester City; a huge club that not that long ago was playing in front of just 15,000 fans in the third tier of English football, in a stadium (Maine Road) that was in desperate need of modernisation or demolition. City were always seen as the local Manchester side, unlike United who have attracted fans not just from within the British Isles but globally. United were the forerunner to Barcelona's successful drive to be a football tourist phenomenon.

Manchester United have fans from across the UK and many fans from abroad travelling on a regular basis to Old Trafford to watch the team. This love of United from afar came from the very real sympathies that the wider world had for the club following the 1958 Munich Air disaster. It was enhanced by the charm and charisma of the late great gentleman of the game, Sir Matt Busby and, of course, the coming of colour TV, winning regularly and having the first worldwide football sex symbol in George Best – a mantle that Ronaldo took on. These were just some of the contributing factors that made United different and helped maintain the City position of being everything their glamorous neighbours were not.

The biggest complaint or grudge that Manchester City fans held against their neighbour's fans was that 'You're not from Manchester'. This was the USP of the club; if you want all the showbiz stuff, it is available at United, if you want real football for the people of Manchester then you have to follow City. There were no protests, just some tears for past memories when their beloved Maine Road was bulldozed or when new billionaire owners moved City to a new stadium and developed on the park to become one of the best club sides in the world. What did that tell us about City fans? Were they just fickle fans or pragmatists who just want to win? The reality is that like fans of most clubs, they had virtually no say in what others were doing with their club.

The new owners of City knew the changes they were bringing were radical. They developed their Citizens' programme, starting in Manchester and now with a worldwide reach, aiming at giving something unique back to the supporters. It has been an award-winning success in fan and community engagement. Some might argue that having that level of financial resources behind them, this level of financial investment in the community would be expected. What it did do was make a connection and engaged with fans who went on a very successful journey with the club, whether they were season ticket holders from Moss Side or casual fans in Sydney.

Suffice it to say that there are not many Manchester City fans who would want to go back to the years before the multimillion Arab investment with poor facilities and a poor team. Has some of the soul of the club been lost, maybe, but not to the extent that the fans don't feel it is the same club. Now they are making history in a different way and thanks to the way the club has been run it is still very much part of the community. The only thing that has gone are the quips about United's international fans now that the Etihad stadium is also a similar tourist destination. Such has the change been that we still await the outcome of the charges brought against them by the Premier League for breaking over 100 financial rules between 2009 and 2018. This is now a very different club, with very different aspirations.

We can start to see that in England in particular, the football ownership dynamic has been changing and this multinational ownership alongside the plethora of administrations ensured that the Government would have more than a passing interest in football. As a former colleague of mine who worked at the FA for several years once said to me, 'For politicians football is an easy ball to kick.' Football is the national game and has a deep connection to the national psyche. It has always meant that the Government has to understand what is happening in the industry and how it might influence the voting public. Likewise, astute political policy makers know that football is our national game and if there is any angle that they can utilise then it can be worth pursuing, against an industry that is basically a complex anarchic members' organisation. In recent times, football has done itself no favours: local corruption, financial mismanagement, racism, match fixing, poor responses to drug testing, love affairs with gambling and alcohol sponsors and a blatant disregard for the supporter (customer). If you factor in the shocking vote rigging, financial irregularities and corruption at both UEFA and FIFA and their discredited leadership, then we can understand why challenging football is an open goal for our politicians.

## Westminster Begins to Wake Up

From 2010 to 2014 at Westminster, there were many politicians dabbling in football affairs, primarily concerned with the administration events that had seen their local clubs have ownership or indeed administration issues. The main problem area that was identified was the 'disconnect' between clubs and their local stakeholders, which often led to a lack of accountability and transparency and caused damage to the social value of clubs in their communities. This is not good news for politicians and they started to see corporate, group and individual ownership at clubs generally serve the interests of owners and shareholders, over the interests of supporters and local communities. There were calls for action to be taken. It was, of course, easy to see that there was a lack of democratic involvement and representation of supporters throughout the game, so something had to be done.

The answer finally came with the Coalition Government (remember them?) who felt that the time might be right to kick the doors of the FA who they felt were badly in need of reform. The second target was the Premier League (awash with cash and corporate greed). The idea was to set up an Expert Working Group to look at how this might evolve. The good news was that supporter ownership was getting on the agenda. The bad news was that it probably came 20 years too late to make any difference in England. The now-defunct Supporters Direct (SD) that led the charge had limited resources, was funded by the football authorities and was spending most of its time looking inwards rather than at the vastly changing landscape that had long passed the tipping point for large-scale community ownership.

Trying to get political buy-ins by the time that it was virtually impossible to compete against wealthy individuals – many being overseas investors – meant that community ownership would be left in the wake as the Westminster Government focused its efforts on the reform of the FA. In July 2011, the Culture, Media and Sport Committee published a report on Football Governance. The report focused on the game in England. It acknowledged the success of the Premier League and the Football League but also pointed out that this success had been accompanied by 'financial instability and increasing levels of debt, which remains a serious problem throughout the football pyramid'. The report recommended, among other things, reform of the Football Association. The Committee said that almost all of its recommendations for reforming football governance could be achieved through agreement between the football authorities. However, it also said that the Government should consider introducing legislation if substantive progress wasn't made. The Committee published a follow-up report (HC 509 2012–13) in January 2013. This said that the football authorities had not done enough on governance reforms and that the Government 'should introduce legislation as soon as practically possible'.

### *Proposed Expert Group Terms of Reference*

The idea was that supporters' groups such as SD and the Football Supporters' Federation Association (who in 2019 would merge with SD to become the Football Supporters' Association) would propose how the Expert Group should proceed. Helen Grant MP, the Minister for Sport, Tourism and Equalities was the recipient of this information as her Coalition Government's Programme for Government made a specific promise to '…encourage the reform of football governance rules to support the co-operative ownership of football clubs by supporters'. By the time that this work commenced, more pressing issues had hit the Coalition Governments and the revolving door that seemed to be installed in this office meant the long grass awaited any outcome.

Despite that, there had to be seen to be some action. As the Department for Culture, Media and Sport Select Committee Football Governance Inquiry (2011) and subsequent reports had recommended, there was a need to set up an Expert Working Group to explore the barriers to increased supporter share ownership and provide solutions. By 2013 the working group was still not set up and fans were starting to get agitated and demanded that it be set up before the start of the next season. The reality was that there was no significant push for community ownership from supporters as the money started to roll in in England and Wales. Things of course were very different in Scotland which had none of the TV and foreign investment and had the bitter recent memories of Rangers, Hearts, Dundee and Dunfermline Athletic to spur us into action.

The main focus for the working group was that they should look at developing practical approaches to the difficulties faced by supporter ownership schemes, including problems raising money, obtaining shares and defending against compulsory purchase orders. The aim of the Expert Group was, in simple terms, to identify solutions to legal and financial barriers of greater collective supporter share ownership of football clubs and potentially other sports. Supporters Direct, in an effort to broaden its reach and to secure more funds, moved from its original football heartland to other sports, where there were fewer financial barriers to having community ownership. Suddenly, Rugby League, Speedway and Ice Hockey were of interest as there were fewer barriers and potential revenue sources. It was a strategy I disagreed with as I believed that it was important for fans to be properly represented by a considered and professional organisation. Brian Burgess, the chairman at the time, disagreed with me and I recall him saying to me, 'We are first and foremost a business that is involved in football and now other sports'.

The reality was that this was the last real stab at pushing the community ownership model south of the border via the patronage or political manoeuvrings at Westminster. The window of opportunity was closing fast as the market had changed beyond all recognition. Supporters Direct was created with the direct intervention of former Labour Party Sports Minister Andy Burnham to help facilitate the opportunity in the wake of so many administrations and liquidations. With a funding model that relied on handouts from the Premier League and the FA and a shrinking opportunity, it was no surprise that with a remit of governance and community ownership, they eventually merged into the more robust structure of the Football Supporters' Association.

Far more pressing matters, such as the reform of the Football Association and the ongoing battle against racism and, to a lesser extent, homophobia, took political precedence for subsequent governments. We know that supporter ownership in England and Wales is alive and thrives in the lower leagues where there are less financial or practical barriers, and it has beacons in the likes of the superb Exeter City and AFC Wimbledon, but it seems unlikely that demands for community ownership legislation will ever get traction again at Westminster. However, this fans' foray into the world of politics did lead to far more significant implications following the arrival of the European Super League.

As the original Westminster saga was evolving at Holyrood, different circumstances led to a whole range of unique actions that I was to eventually play a role in.

## The Rangers Crisis and Political Involvement

When Rangers crashed there were few people who predicted that it might happen – surely, they were too big to fail? These were extraordinary times which resulted in extraordinary solutions. Nor were there many people at that time who would have predicted that it would lead to the Government investing in fans' affairs, but they did. I was employed to help get fans a voice after the Government and MSPs were bombarded by faxes, letters, emails and telephone calls imploring that fans have a say. The remit was challenging and difficult and was heavily political but having the resources allowed the fan ownership model to have a champion who had been over the course, thanks to my successful campaign at Stirling Albion.

The other significant factor that changed the football landscape was the period of Armageddon which the football authorities tried to sell as an economic argument for keeping Rangers in the topflight via the infamous five-way agreement. Of course, in economic terms, it made perfect sense to those suits charged with running the game; but from a sporting integrity point of view, fans of clubs in Scotland were not having it. With the game in Scotland being so heavily dependent on income through the turnstiles, it was a risk that Messrs Doncaster and Regan were prepared to take to get the clubs to vote it through. The only fans that they wanted to consider were the board members of their clubs that needed income from being in the topflight. With no national fans' organisation and nobody to speak up for fans, it was a low-risk strategy given the clubs *always* vote with their own self-interest and would not want to lose Rangers' income. The one dynamic that was not considered was that club chairmen up and down the country had to sell season tickets to supporters. The scale of financial misconduct that Rangers had engineered over a prolonged period was colossal and in simple terms, the message from the fans was that it was cheating and should be punished. What is often ignored is that many of the Rangers fans recognised this and as one described it, were 'reluctantly comfortable' in accepting their fate. Fans' disquiet started to emerge in Aberdeen and went down to Dundee and then through the Central Belt as fans galvanised and took the messages to club chairmen – if you back the Armageddon plan to keep Rangers in the league then we will NOT be buying season tickets.

Fans for once had a voice and I wanted to use it by creating a national fans' body that would properly represent them in the future. As I found out, if at first you don't succeed then try again.

## Putting the Fans in Control: The Fans First Campaign

Here in Scotland, things were very different from the attempts to get community ownership on the political agenda down south. Some of our biggest clubs had gone to the wall and the market had changed dramatically from what was happening in England and Wales. There were no Roman Abramovich's arriving at Glasgow or Edinburgh Airport wanting to invest in Scottish football and the television executives saw little glamour in a top league for the likes of Hamilton Accies v Dundee, in a stadium that might only be at 20 per cent capacity. In Scotland, the mantra for community ownership grew organically, out of the necessity of replacing either the family dynasties at clubs or the local butcher, baker and candlestick makers who couldn't support the original 'investment' that they had made in the club. The demands for supporter ownership of Scottish clubs came from satisfying a need rather than making demands of the politicians to help make it happen. Scotland was, in that regard, very much a different country with a very different pathway than our friends across the border. It was significant that before I was given the challenge, Supporters Direct had closed its doors in Scotland having failed to get any traction. In fact, their profile was so low that in a year of running the highly visible Saving the Albion campaign they had never contacted me.

Little did I know when we started the Saving the Albion campaign what might follow in our wake. It had started from humble beginnings by trying to prevent Stirling Albion from collapsing as the 83-year-old owner Peter McKenzie could no longer support it. As we got towards the finishing line, we were competing against a group of Edinburgh businessmen. The deal we were competing against was being organised by Rod Petrie, most recently the President of the SFA. Way before the talk of colt teams ever emerged, he was trying to buy Stirling Albion for Hibernian to use as a feeder club. Fortunately for our campaign team, the McKenzie family decided to take a risk with the fans to keep it in the community rather than take the easy cash from Edinburgh. That success was replicated elsewhere with Stenhousemuir, Clyde and East Stirlingshire soon following the likes of our phoenix sides Clydebank and Gretna 2008 in moving in this direction. Dundee tried and bailed out quite quickly but clubs like Dunfermline Athletic and Heart of Midlothian started to share a community vision for football in the hands of supporters. It was the type of momentum that a political party that was interested in making some positive news might wrestle with. Often known as being progressive and dynamic and looking for radical solutions, the Scottish Green Party soon had its shadow spokesperson for sport, Alison Johnstone MSP (now the Presiding Officer of the Scottish Parliament), look at the opportunity.

I worked with Alison and her team over the months to look and see if there was any potential opportunity to allow provision under the Land Reform and Community Empowerment Bill to allow football clubs to be bought by supporters. The theory was very simple: if the residents on the Isle of Eigg in the Hebrides could get preferential bidder status and buy their island, could provision be made to allow ordinary fans to buy their football club? It sounded far-fetched but looking back there is no doubt that this initiative started the ball rolling and is now a huge part of the community ownership story in Scotland. It showed that without any prompting by supporters that fans owning clubs was being discussed in the corridors of power at Holyrood. Of course, the SFA and SPFL hated it and it started making me an enemy, being the messenger for the concept.

For over 18 months, the Scottish Green Party had been championing the concept that community ownership of football clubs could become an accepted right for all football fans in Scotland. This has been driven through amendments to the Community Empowerment and Renewal Bill. They would extend the scope of the bill beyond land and physical assets to include clubs' membership shares. As important as stadiums are, it is these shares which give clubs the right to play in the various leagues.

Beyond that, the party proposed a number of additional measures to empower fans' official trusts or supporters' groups, including the right of first refusal when clubs come up for sale, the right to buy a proportion of the shares where they cannot afford the club's full value and eligibility for Scottish Government funding support.

## Proposals from Alison Johnstone MSP

I have detailed these below as they provide a real insight into the dynamics that have led to the changes outlined in Chapter 10 as this initial work had a significant role in helping supporters on the community ownership journey.

### THE START OF THE JOURNEY

Scottish Ministers are currently consulting on the Community Empowerment and Renewal Bill (CER), which will extend the community right-to-buy beyond the scope set out in the Land Reform (Scotland) Act 2003. However, the Scottish Greens, through working with the Communities Minister, has recently made significant progress and the bill is now progressing through the committee's stage with cross-party support. However, it seems unlikely that it will succeed in its current form. This paper has been produced to allow any interested party to have a wider understanding of this very specific area of football and the challenges and opportunities that it might offer for progressive policymaking.

The Scottish Greens believe football clubs are prone to suffering from many of the same problems tenants have historically had with absentee landlords, and that football clubs are frequently at the core of communities across Scotland. We believe that a right for fans to buy their clubs, either at any point or when their clubs get into financial difficulties, would be desirable in policy terms and also that the CER bill represents the ideal vehicle for such legislative changes.

This paper will therefore set out some options for amendments to the current bill, some or all of which may appear as part of a formal submission by the Green MSPs to the ongoing consultation process.

They identified that there were two major problems affecting the take-up of fan ownership:

- At present, owners are under no obligation to even deal with their supporters, let alone involve them in ownership and governance. As a result, fan ownership overwhelmingly comes about against a backdrop of corporate failure, where the lack of willingness of club owners to engage with supporters is followed by the openness of an insolvency practitioner to deal with anyone proposing a realistic rescue plan. However, as a result, most fan ownership arrives against a legacy of failure, debt and limited capital.

- Relatedly, a common model is for private owners/supporters to commit the club to spending money it cannot afford and to supplement revenue with their own resources. That means that without a wealthy benefactor, Scottish clubs are regularly faced with a dilemma in which sporting goals cannot be achieved through 'normal' trading, ie trading where expenditure is based on earned income.

As a result, financial success and sporting success are, for the vast majority of clubs, mutually exclusive. Under this model, clubs continue to be solvent only as long as their benefactors have the means to support them, but when such means are exhausted, the club quickly moves from apparently rude health to severe insolvency. It is this which lies at the root of the deep structural instability of the game, which has seen the majority of professional clubs in the UK go into formal insolvency over the past 20 years, most spectacularly at Rangers – 154 administrations in the UK since 2000.

While there are mechanisms which seek to address this in terms of controlling club expenditure, these efforts have had limited effects at best. The evidence is that expanded fan ownership is the only current option to go beyond those mechanisms in the interests of the sport at both a club and national level. Where the fans are in charge, unsustainable options are simply taken off the table; if the club has no wealthy benefactor, there is simply no way for it to be run other than as a 'normal' enterprise in which income and expenditure are linked in a sustainable manner.

A critical mass of fan-owned clubs would be the most effective way to achieve sustainable Scottish professional football, and sustainable football is also a necessary condition for successful and sustainable fan ownership.

A decisive break is required with the failed models of ownership. While the Scottish football authorities can address over-spending in a slow and incremental way, the governing bodies are creatures of their members and, as a result, regardless of the ways in which fan ownership helps deliver their stated goals of a more sustainable sport, the authorities inevitably cannot endorse it as an ownership model. They will remain structurally unable to drive greater fan ownership until such a time as a majority of clubs are fan-owned in order, ie when this objective is already largely achieved.

That leaves the Scottish Parliament as the only body with the means and ability to effect change.

In short, supporting fan ownership of football is an ideal opportunity to enhance the social, economic and environmental benefits clubs bring to their communities, and to boost local decision making and control.

The goal therefore is to enhance in legislation the definition of eligible assets or property to encompass the limited companies which own league membership shares in Scottish football governing bodies. This, ultimately, is what defines a Scottish football club, and is not dependent on whether a club's ultimate corporate parent has a registered office in Cumbernauld or the Cayman Islands.

## DETAILED OPTIONS

Beyond that, several other options should be considered, in part to reflect the diversity of Scottish clubs, in terms of scale, value, indebtedness and wealth of the community they are based in.

### *Right to buy when clubs are being sold.*
This would require a time limit to assemble funds – provisionally six months – and would probably also require a cooling-off period after any unsuccessful bids, perhaps two years, to reduce uncertainty for clubs. There could be an exception to the two-year restriction where the assessed price falls sufficiently far enough to allow the sum raised during the six-month period to be viable (eg if land is sold off or if a club is relegated).

### *Right to a say when clubs are sold.*
Where fans simply can't afford to buy a club, and where more than one bid meets that assessed price, the fans get to be involved in the decision. This would ensure bidders take account of fans' views and might include incentives to offer fans' trusts free shares, seats on the board, or other increased involvement.

### *Right to buy when clubs go into administration.*
We do not believe that changes to insolvency and company law would be required: those areas are reserved, but the relevant parts of this proposal would merely use insolvency as a trigger.

### *Right to buy a proportion of the shares at any point where a right to buy overall exists.*

A WAKE-UP CALL AT WESTMINSTER AND HOLYROOD

## The Fallout from the Scottish Green Party Proposals

Even the most devoted of advocates for community ownership of our football clubs, or the most dedicated of followers of the Scottish Green Party, were not expecting an easy journey for the proposals. I did my bit by lobbying Shona Robison, the then Sports Minister, Ruth Davidson, Willie Rennie and several influential Labour MSPs. The newly formed Scottish Football Supporters Association (SFSA) did a presentation for parliamentarians at both Westminster and Holyrood and pressed the case vigorously. The Scottish National Party in Government did have an alliance with the Scottish Green Party and were not going to be dismissive in public. However, having had their fingers badly burned with the Offensive Behaviour at Football and Threatening Communications Act legislation that made quite a number of football fans unlikely criminals, they didn't want to meddle further in fans' affairs. They also had a very cosy relationship with the football authorities who were against community ownership in any form as it broke from tradition. It also seems that they thought that it could lead to some sort of fan rebellion. The rationale being that if you had fans running teams the blazers in the boardrooms across the country would be changed to denim.

The Scottish Greens used their 'Fans First' campaign to try to get traction. They started to make some noise about the opportunities under the Land Reform Act but when the proposal came to Parliament the then Sports Minister Jamie Hepburn MSP agreed that a consultation with all the stakeholders in the game would be set up to discuss the issue further. Well-known football finance expert Professor Stephen Morrow was drafted in from the University of Stirling to head it up. Apart from the fact that the Scottish Government had no great desire to take it forward, they knew that this sideways step was enough to show the Scottish Green Party that it was being taken seriously. In reality, when I turned up to the first meeting, I should have brought my lawnmower so clear was the long grass that we were heading to. Just by looking at the invited guests list, I knew there was no chance that community ownership was being taken seriously. The SFA had Andrew McKinlay their COO, Darryl Broadfoot the Head of Communications and the SPFL had its CEO Neil Doncaster *in situ*. We were joined by Mel Young and Michael Kavanagh from Sports Scotland and the Scottish Government had Civil Servants Derek Grieve and David Hamilton in the room.

By the second meeting, it was clear in what direction the consultation was heading. The SFA had made it clear that they were not opposed to any club being community-owned, but they would not help them get there. Neil Doncaster of the SPFL summed up the wide gulf between where the

Greens wanted to go and where football stood. When I argued across the table that community ownership could be an important part of the football economic mix, Neil disagreed, 'I don't believe in community ownership, I don't think it will work. What we need is 42 Roy MacGregor's (Ross County owner/investor) that will support our clubs'. Against that backdrop, the three meetings did not really move in a direction that came even close to the spirit of what the Scottish Greens tried to propose. Prof Morrow did complete a report but by that time its terms of reference had been diluted to reflect on fans' affairs rather than anything meaningful, aside from the fact that the SFA agreed to implement having Supporter Liaison Officers at clubs to act as a link between clubs and the fans. It was hardly a victory as this had become a UEFA requirement, who had actually funded a programme to be put in place several years before. At the time of the Morrow Report, Scotland alongside a few smaller nations such as Albania, Kazakhstan etc, was one of the few countries who had not implemented it.

I attended two of the consultative meetings but by that time my tenure as Head of Supporters Direct Scotland was about to come to a spectacular end and I thought that my involvement in fans' affairs in Scotland would be over. Six months later, I returned with the launch of the Scottish Football Supporters Association ready to support community ownership properly. As part of the consultation process, the Scottish Government offered fans of all clubs the opportunity to contribute to the debate. As a fledgling organisation, we pushed the message out as far as we could and put in our own responses which added to the debate. We had 1,800 fans respond which was a great indication of just how the understanding and knowledge about community ownership was gathering traction.

## Options for Legislation from the Scottish Government

*1. What are your views on making a law to give supporters the right to influence their club?*

SFSA supports the right of football fans to influence their clubs, recognising the involvement of supporters as bringing huge benefits to clubs (and to the game as a whole) through their experience, passion, commitment and various levels and types of expertise. We believe that influence needs to be extended to direct stake holding and community ownership, as part of a 'mixed economy' to sustain the game into the future.

Participation in the form of influence should be an adjunct to, and not a substitute for, additional rights to governance, bidding and ownership.

We believe in the principle of partnership to enable the game to develop and improve. In some cases, this will involve a change of outlook and culture among those who currently own and run clubs, as well as the football authorities – towards seeing supporter influence, stake holding and ownership as beneficial for everyone involved in the game.

It is vital that clubs are open and transparent in all their operations, and that the ultimate beneficiaries of any ownership vehicles associated with a club should be public knowledge. We would like to see this achieved through agreement but, if necessary, with statutory backing. We concur that participation in the professional structures of football in Scotland should be conditional upon agreed standards of transparency and financial accountability.

The Scottish Football Supporters Association is already initiating Fans Awards and would provide the ideal vehicle for rewarding good practice in this and other areas across the game.

SFSA would welcome the extension and development of the Supporter Liaison Officer (SLO) system across the game, on the understanding that this is to supplement rather than replace other forms of participation in governance, influence and ownership. In terms of UEFA Supporter Liaison, it should be noted that SFSA offers, for the first time, recognised representation for Scottish fans within the European supporter structures.

*2. What are your views on making a law to give supporters the right to govern their club?*

We support the right of fans to participate in the governance of their clubs and would like to see a minimum 25 per cent supporter membership of boards, as well as a clear goal towards improved inclusion of women, disabled people and minority groups.

We would not support a two-tier directorship model that reduces supporter directors to a lower status or restricts voting rights.

We would welcome additional structures of representation and consultation throughout the game, but not as an alternative to directorships, stake holding and ownership – as appropriate in different circumstances – for fans.

We back the training, support and equipping of supporter directors as part of the professional development expected and required of all directors. SFSA provides an ideal vehicle for the establishment of a national fans' parliament.

*3. What are your views on making a law to give supporters the right to bid for their club?*

We support a formalised right to bid for supporters in the case of a club coming up for sale, to be extended to recognise supporter bodies, including trusts, CICs and community consortia. There should not be a restriction to trusts alone.

We welcome the idea that at the point of a sale, the supporters' body should be given the option to buy at least up to 25 per cent of the club. Owners and directors should be required to consult with supporters' bodies in the event of a club sale being proposed and to offer a priority bidding period before public notice.

More detailed consultation on mechanisms and safeguards will be required. We recognise the need to preserve the financial and trading stability of a club in the midst of bidding and acquisition processes.

We believe that transparency on registered assets is important, to support football stadia and facilities being recognised as assets of community value, and welcome the idea of the extension or adaptation of appropriate provisions of the 2011 Localism Act to Scotland, in accordance with parliamentary and democratic procedures.

*4. What are your views on making a law to give supporters the right to buy their club?*

In recognising the benefits of a 'mixed economy' of stake holding in the game overall, SFSA supports the extension and development of community ownership throughout Scottish football, noting the positive and successful example of the 51 per cent rule in Germany.

Starting from where we are, a more diverse ownership base can only be of benefit to the game in our view, with appropriate support, guidance and development.

We therefore support the principle of a statutorily backed right-to-buy for supporters in the instance of clubs coming up for sale, with appropriate safeguarding built into the process for the preservation of the financial and general stability of the club concerned. We note the partnership and transition potential of a recent example such as Heart of Midlothian.

The establishment of external support agencies needs to be done in such a way as to ensure that such agencies support the rights being established as well as ensuring the highest professional and financial practice.

*5. What are your views on raising the necessary funds, including the amount of time allowed for supporters to do so, to give supporters a right to buy their football club?*

The practical issue of timing needs to be considered in relation to the wide range of factors affecting the sale of a club. We recognise that there are important technical and commercial considerations involved in this, and would welcome involvement in further detailed and targeted consultation on this question.

SFSA is already involved in the establishment of a Fans Bank and other commercially-tuned vehicles for bringing resources into the Scottish game, and ensuring backing and a variety of loans are available for properly constituted supporter groups wishing to take full or part ownership of football clubs.

We believe that Government investment in community-based ownership, as part of a process of establishing clubs as hubs of community empowerment and well-being (as set out in our manifesto, 'Transforming Scottish Football') would be positive and beneficial.

It will also, of course, be necessary to secure further private investment and sponsorship on the basis of a renewed profile for the game and a dramatically improved use of its assets and resources for wider benefit.

An arms-length advisory and commercial commissioning body could be useful in this regard, established in an appropriately accountable way.

We would welcome consideration of tax breaks or incentives for majority community-owned clubs and supporter-owned consortia, without preference to one particular model.

Again the 'mixed economy' approach commends itself in considering these matters.

*6. What are your views on defining assets, in the context of making a law to give supporters rights in the decision making or ownership of their football club?*

Assets for a football club include the stadium, additional training facilities, invested materials from the company or companies involved in ownership, the identity and branding of the club and miscellaneous resources.

We would support the establishment of an Expert Working Group on this issue, to provide a broad definition, guidelines and transparency requirements (including consultation with supporters in agreeing an assets sheet). Also safeguarding of propriety for investors, as appropriate.

As noted earlier, SFSA supports either the extension of the Community

Empowerment Bill and/or incorporation and adaptation of elements of the 2011 Localism Bill to establish procedures for recognising the assets of football clubs, particularly stadia, as assets of community value.

*7. What are your views on how to define what is a football supporter and defining supporter groups, in the context of making a law to give supporters rights in the decision making or ownership of their football club?*

A workable definition could include a formally constituted group of season ticket holders, and more usually a supporters' trust, CIC, community consortium or other recognised fans' body (including umbrella organisations) constituted formally, legally and for public benefit. There will be a need for further specific consultation on this point.

*8. What are your views on rights of appeal, in the context of making a law to give supporters rights in the decision making or ownership of their football club?*

Any appeals process should be independent, transparent and with a clearly stated procedure, purpose and timetable. It should be constituted in a democratic way. It should be related to issues of misconduct, liability and breach of professional terms, and should not be constituted or made operative in such a way as to filibuster, block or obscure legal rights applying to supporters in relation to the issues set out in this consultation.

*9. Do you wish to make any other comments about supporter involvement in football?*

The Scottish Football Supporters Association welcomes this Scottish Government consultation on supporter involvement and, in particular, the serious consideration being given to statutory underpinning of rights to participate in the governance of the game, to bid and to buy.

As well as publishing and launching *Transforming Scottish Football: The Fans' Manifesto*, based on survey responses from 10,000 fans, SFSA is also in the process of establishing a democratic structure which will enable it to be a partner for the Scottish Government and the football authorities in determining the future of the game and enabling the formal representation and participation of fans at every level of the game in Scotland.

In addition, in the spirit of partnership needed for the development of the game we love, SFSA is reiterating its invitation to Supporters Direct

The origins of the SFSA – when football in Scotland found it too difficult to send a team to the Homeless World Cup, with the help of Scotland's HWC team and Hearts legend John Robertson, I managed the Scotland team in the tournament, only to fall in the final 3–2 to France.

Former Scotland Captain Gary McAllister helps us launch the SFSA on 9 April 2015 at the West of Scotland Cricket club where the first-ever international football match was played.

This year, we will create a new Community Sport Bond worth up to £5 million. We know that, for supporter and community groups, not having access to capital funds has been the main barrier to them being able to take ownership stakes in their local clubs when the opportunity has arisen. The Bond will empower communities and groups and strengthen local decision-making by giving groups the chance to acquire a share or control of their local sports club. To be eligible to apply for the Bond, groups must show clear community focus and support and, in particular, demonstrate how involvement in the running of their club would be used to support women and girls' participation in sports.

Co-founders of the SFSA Paul Goodwin and Simon Barrow, having just given a presentation about fan ownership to Dumbarton fans.

Scottish Government initial launch of what was to become the Fan Bank.

I first developed the concept of a fan bank in 2014 based on my experiences at Stirling Albion, Heart of Midlothian and Dunfermline Athletic, where fans had the opportunity to buy a club but not the funds. The Fan Bank allows them to borrow from the Scottish Government to activate share purchases for the community. The first scheme was launched by Humza Yousaf and myself when a deal was done that enabled the Falkirk Supporters Society to buy a tranche of shares to make them the biggest shareholders in the club.

Ian Murray, who we brought in to steady the ship and get the various Hearts groups to rally around The Foundation of Hearts. (Photo courtesy of Ian Murray)

Getting all the various groups together to follow one cause can be time consuming and challenging. At Hearts we succeeded but only with some huge support from David Southern the club CEO, then aided by Lawrence Broadie, who helped me by chairing some of the early meetings. The real key was bringing in Ian Murray MP to galvanise the support.

Creating a new fans' group is very often the best way to proceed as there are fewer baggage issues from previous campaigns. I always like getting the campaign in as part of the organisation name so you know what they want to do. Sadly the Hibernian one didn't last very long before it was closed down.

Author with Craig Hughes of the Well Society. Craig was a key appointment in growing the initial membership from 1,000 to 4,000.

Launching the campaign — for the Save the Albion campaign Bannockburn where Robert the Bruce saved Scotland from the auld enemy was a perfect location for the press call and a photo shoot. The BBC, Sky Sports News and STV sent teams to cover the event and we even featured on follow-up stories on ABC and NBC TV in the USA.

We generated a huge amount of interest in the Saving the Albion campaign with support from some unlikely quarters such as Andy Murray and Cristiano Ronaldo, not just getting the club into community ownership but then driving it as a community asset. With funds always at a premium we even wrote a book about our success — which sold out!

PR goes a long way — here we have Gregor Goodwin employed by his father to get the Buy Stirling Albion message out there.

Making the campaign work – you need a strong team around you. It is far easier now than it was for Stirling Albion, where pretty much everything we did was breaking new ground.

Success allows you time for a smile.

The power of football celebrity is a huge asset for your campaign. For the Thistle For Ever campaign we got Partick Thistle legend Jimmy Bone to help get the message out to the supporters.

Following on from Saturday's protests in the John Lambie Stand, various members of the support have decided to stage another protest against the handling of fan ownership on Saturday 26th of November. The intention of this is to empty the John Lambie Stand. Those protesting will not be entering the stadium.

We will be meeting at the canal bridge behind the John Lambie stand at 2:35pm before making our way down to Firhill Road opposite the Main Stand/Aitken Suite at approximately 2:40pm where we will gather displaying banners until kick off time. We will then make our way to the canal, where we will again be displaying banners and backing the team.

We welcome all Jags fans to join us in this protest. We ask any fans who wish to show solidarity with this protest but who still wish to attend the game to buy a ticket for the Jackie Husband Stand.

When a campaign hits a blockage it is often when fans start protesting that they get results. There was no movement at Thistle towards fan ownership until the fans started making some real noise. It worked at Dunfermline too but fizzled out at Kilmarnock and Hibs.

Gathering support – author with Maryhill MSP Bob Doris and the then Maryhill MP Patrick Grady.

The author presents the Dundee Chairman Stuart Murphy with a cheque from Stirling Albion fans who reached out to Dundee fans when they played in the first match after the Dee went into liquidation.

Getting a launch theme is important and I was very fortunate that both my brothers-in-law were fans of Community Owned Clubs. Gordon McAllister, St Mirren and Pat McCaughey, Motherwell, were on hand to help me launch the campaign to make Partick Thistle Community Owned. It also helped us convey the family aspect that fans owning clubs embodies.

Scotland, currently part of an organisation largely run from England, to join with us and our larger, wider membership in order to solidify the role of a fully autonomous, representative supporters' organisation across Scotland.

We see the extension of accountable ownership and transparent governance as crucial to the renewal, reform and regeneration of Scottish football. The issues raised in this consultation are therefore a crucial part of what we have called 'reclaiming the game' for supporters, communities and all who are willing to invest time, resources and labour into helping the game to flourish and grow on a financially sustainable, commercially innovative, participatory and democratic basis.

We therefore view the issues raised in this consultation as part of the need for a wider programme required for the regeneration of the game in Scotland, which in itself should be regarded as a national and community asset. The nine points set out in our crowdsourced manifesto provide a framework for the kind of national conversation/summit required to carry these renovations forward. They are:

## *Renew the Game*

- Bring back the fans through competitive pricing and family facilities at every club.
- Make football in Scotland media-friendly and innovative at every level.
- Re-market the Scottish game, pressing for financial fair shares and transparency.

## *Reform the Game*

- Rebuild the game with larger divisions, more variety and improved competition.
- Equip every club to be a 'community hub' for well-being and entertainment.
- Re-invest in youth through fresh plans for training and education.

## *Reclaim the Game*

- A 'diversity drive': 25 per cent fan representation on all governing bodies in five years, 50 per cent women, a permanent place for the national fans' body.
- Regular, independent auditing and review of the performance of governing bodies and clubs.

- Extend community and collaborative ownership, create a fans' right to bid or buy when clubs are for sale, create a fans bank.
- Lastly, we would point out that reform of the governance structures of Scottish football, and the full inclusion of supporters in the way they are established and run, is a vital corollary to the extension of influence, stake holding and ownership for supporters at club level.

## Outcome

These proposals were initially rejected, and the Scottish Government commissioned Stirling University's Professor Stephen Morrow to look at the wider issue of fan involvement. The Morrow Report specifically avoided looking at the pressing issue of community ownership of football clubs. Instead, it diverted its attention to the many areas previously looked at in the McLeish Report regarding the lack of fan engagement from both the league and the governing body. The exercise did no more than tick the box for the football authorities with no actionable outcomes deriving from them. Apart from the movement on the SLO programme, nothing tangible came from the report and fans and the community ownership concept was put back in its box.

CHAPTER 10

# The Governance Conundrum and the European Super League

*Football isn't just another business. It can't be treated like any other business. Football clubs are constituent parts of our communities. There is such a thing as society and the national game is a vital part of what makes it up.*—Gary Neville

### Sport and Politics Don't Mix, Do They?

ALTHOUGH THIS BOOK is primarily about community ownership in football, there is no escaping that fact that the new way of owning clubs has raised eyebrows with leagues and the football associations. As we know, the football industry has operated in a certain way for generations and it is rather resistant to change of any form. Yet, despite the 150-plus administrations (and counting) and the complete failure of football itself being able to address this one issue, as well as many others, we as fans are meant to just relax and let them get on with it. Easy, unless it is your team being torn apart by someone that they have approved as a fit and proper person. With so many of these interactions now very much in the public domain and supporters going to their MPs for help, it was only a matter of time before governments started to look under the bonnet of football. What they found was an unregulated industry that was unable to effectively control its component parts due to the inbuilt restrictions around club voting that ensured the ongoing need for self-interest prevailed.

Despite having the origins of the sport embedded into the community landscape, the football authorities in recent times have had to turn their attention to the relatively new concept of community ownership. In England, with some notable clubs participating, it suddenly was on the agenda as a different way of owning and running a football club. Talking to former directors of both Exeter City and Portsmouth, their view was that the FA and the Football League just saw them as an unconventional and somewhat loud (well, we are fans) but minor irritant. An FA insider of ten years standing told me that at the time of the initial Andy Burnham intervention in 2002, there was a concern that the new way of doing things could be problematic and was something to be wary of. The other side of that coin is that when clubs like Portsmouth FC are crumbling with reported debts of £117m like in 2010, then the threat from a new wave of community owners able to take on such vast challenges was unlikely.

Without the opportunity to press the reset button and put in a new structure, which is what happened with the new Bundesliga in 1962, the football authorities in England were relaxed in the knowledge that there were no major compulsory revisions that would effect change. Given that most of the clubs at the top of the game were stock market listed and the others were private limited companies, there was little fear of any further Government interference. The size and value of the market itself took the political parties' eyes away from the subject matter of community ownership and regulation around ownership in England.

The story in Scotland was completely different where both the SFA and the SPFL (actually some of the club owners) felt threatened by the emergence of community ownership and acted to try and suppress the concept and its champions. But more on that later.

*An election, a campaign group and a super league turbo charges action as football governance is put in the spotlight.*

The 2019 United Kingdom general election was held on Thursday 12 December 2019. It resulted in the Conservative Party receiving a landslide majority of 80 seats. The Conservatives made a net gain of 48 seats and won 43.6 per cent of the popular vote – the highest percentage for any party since 1979. The new Government was elected with a levelling up agenda that was key to winning the hearts and minds of the northern Red Wall seats. These were predominantly seats held in the traditional industrial heartlands of Northern England where the levelling up (redistribution of wealth from rich to poor areas) message was a dominant call during the election campaigns.

On securing the victory, the Conservative Government wanted to build on the pledges it had made, and football offered a relatively easy target to hit. There was a significant manifesto pledge designed to appeal to the football fan voters, where the long-desired call for a fundamental Review of Football would be delivered. Then Sports and Culture Minister Oliver Dowden MP picked up the baton that the dynamic football fan Tracey Crouch MP had started when she had held the post. His entry into the fray came on the back of the development of a significant campaign group, Our Beautiful Game, that included two former Ministers with responsibility for sport, Andy Burnham and Helen Grant, alongside the former Governor of the Bank of England, Sir Mervyn King, David Bernstein former chairman of the FA and former Manchester United and England star and football pundit Gary Neville.

Launched in October 2020 with a significant manifesto, the main call was for a fan-led review of the game in England. They were a diverse group of people who shared both a deep passion for English football and an equally profound concern about the current state of its management. One of the key aspects was the dominance of the Premier League which had been allowed to grow unchecked, meaning that there was no clear framework for the relationship between the Premier League and the rest of the game. The FA, who had overall responsibility, had its influence and moral authority as the *greatest league in the world* become the plaything of Arab states and billionaires.

There is no doubt that the COVID-19 pandemic rocked football to its core throughout the UK and the issues that had been bubbling under over the past ten years were now coming to a head. The Government had provided support directly to the National League in England as had the Scottish Government at Holyrood. It should, of course, never be forgotten that fans of clubs throughout the length and breadth of the UK did so too by significant fundraising as well as writing off money owed to them for season tickets, advertising, sponsorships and hospitality.

The Our Beautiful Game campaign group brought the overall arguments back to ask the fans what they felt about the game. When asked if fundamental reform of the game was needed 76 per cent of respondents said yes, 14 per cent were unsure and 10 per cent of respondents were comfortable with the status quo. When asked if the current English football model was sustainable, 78 per cent felt it was not, 13 per cent were unsure and only 9 per cent felt that the current situation was sustainable. These statistics are consistent with the findings that we have seen in surveys in Scotland too.

This heavyweight campaign group had spent a lot of time looking at the changing dynamic of the game and had the credibility of having significant input from the vast array of talented individuals that were available to consult with them. I would recommend that you read the manifesto in full as it is an excellent document – you can find a link in the References section at the back of this book.

What the group did was use their prestige and reputations to highlight the growing flaws in the English game where the FA was overlooked by the Premier League that had become all powerful. There were very real and growing fears that if it remained unchecked, the billionaires who owned the top clubs would continue to be self-centred and not properly support the football pyramid or indeed the grassroots that is at the heart and soul of the game. What they quickly established is the undeniable fact that as things stood there was no proper balance in the game.

The interesting aspect of this campaign was that it quickly established what the key issues were and made recommendations that would allow the UK Government to pick up the baton and deliver on it. The two aspects that were highlighted as key were:

- The first arises from the financial muscle of the EPL whose income is 12 times larger than that of the FA. With no direct mandates for the greater interest of the game, the flow of funds from the EPL to the pyramid and below needed addressed. It was also noted that it needed to be complemented by an effective and independent body to oversee the financial regulation of the game.
- The FA lacks credibility and has proved to be largely ineffective as a governing body. It has not modernised and is not sufficiently independent. It has been resistant to serious change.

It was obvious that those who had written this report had seen the problems of the preceding decade manifest themselves and wanted, and indeed demanded, action to resolve the underlying issues. They knew and understood the Westminster timeline that we have seen above and that the problems that had been discussed since 2010 just continued to remain unaddressed. The fundamental problem that we have seen throughout this book is that an industry that is left to self-regulate is pretty much incapable of deep and meaningful reforms. In this instance, the self-interest of the billionaire owners in the topflight of the English game were incapable of developing reforms that almost certainly would not directly benefit them as owners or as a club.

There was no second guessing what was required as the Our Beautiful Game team laid out its key findings.

The conclusion is crystal clear. Football has shown itself incapable of self-reform. The core issues are:

- Financial disparity and unsustainability;
- A power structure that is fundamentally out of balance;
- A range of consequential matters including, the embarrassing shortage of BAME coaches and managers at the top level, a general lack of diversity and the exploitation of clubs and fans.

If these are to be resolved, external involvement is required in the form of an independent regulator or commissioner supported by statutory powers. It also needs to be complemented by an effective and independent body to oversee the financial regulation of the game. Page 17 of the report (see References) gives the detailed recommendations and is worth reading.

What this campaign achieved was getting cross party support for change and of course galvanising the Conservative Party to act upon the manifesto pledges that it had already committed to. What the Our Beautiful Game team did not know was that a spectacular own goal was just about to be scored that would make their job so much easier.

## The Super League Provides the Spark

There had long been talk about some sort of breakaway league emerging and many of the top European clubs had been pushing UEFA to give them more power, more money and more control over European competitions. UEFA had over the years ceded a little bit but behind closed doors the billionaires in the English Premier League wanted more for themselves and decided to take matters into their own hands. When push came to shove they felt they had the winning cards and moved to officially create their own European Super League. They were so out of step with what real football fans wanted, even at their own clubs. It makes you wonder if they actually had done any internal research or maybe they believed their own publicity so much that they just assumed the fans would love it. Bigger is not always better. Wrong, wrong, wrong and for the only time in history did we see a continent united across borders and club rivalries send a message loud and clear. This was not needed or wanted.

Just a reminder in their own words what the super-rich were offering to European football.

> The Super League is a new European competition between 20 top clubs comprised of 15 founders and five annual qualifiers. There will be two groups of ten clubs each, playing home and away fixtures within the Group each year. By bringing together the best clubs and best players in the world, the Super League will deliver excitement and drama never before seen in football.

[This in itself is quite a claim].
Many claimed it was a power grab, intended to guarantee the clubs'

status and revenue, which some of them weren't currently earning from their performances on the pitch. The response forced Manchester United, Liverpool, Manchester City, Chelsea, Tottenham Hotspur, Arsenal, AC Milan, Inter Milan and Atletico Madrid to pull out, but Real Madrid, Barcelona and Juventus have remained active members and even in early 2023 they still saw hope for the doomed project. Real Madrid President Perez says fans are drifting away from football which is a ludicrous statement to be making from what we know about the game. Maybe he means that the TV money afforded to the top teams has hit a plateau and he needs to keep growing his revenues to stay on top both at home and in Europe.

Even in January 2024 the remaining clubs in the group were still hopeful and gave us a reminder in their own words what the super-rich were offering to European football. A22 Sports Management, the organisation now representing the three remaining clubs, believes a relaunch for the 2024–25 season is a 'reasonable' expectation. The thinking is clear from the video statements posted on their own website which is well worth watching. The key points they make are well worth reviewing as they give great insight into the mindset at these super-rich and empowered clubs.

'European club football is facing existential problems,' Reichart said in a video posted on A22's website. He continued:

> European football is losing its undisputed leadership position in global sports. It's not living up to its potential by not offering the best matches week after week.
> The current financial model in football is broken and unsustainable. Financial controls are inadequate and insufficiently enforced leading to competitive imbalances and financial stress.
> Clubs should be sovereign and master of their own destiny since they bear all risks and all investments. Today they are not allowed to freely organise themselves at European level, while almost every domestic league is run independently by clubs, governance of European competition resides only with UEFA… why?

What is incredible about this statement is that it is written in a way that ignores all the fall out of April 2021. Did it really happen? Never in the history of football has there been an outcry towards anything in football like the response to the new Super League concept. The protests began at the English clubs where fans immediately called out their clubs and started to protest at games. They were joined by all lovers of the game from former players, club icons, managers, coaches and, of course, the politicians who could see what was happening.

The Super League was a virtual closed shop where the clubs owned and operated by billionaires and global equity developed a plan that would make them stronger and richer and would exclude rather than include the wider football audience. Right across Europe the voice was united in a unique condemnation of the Super League. Yet in January 2023 the rump of these clubs were still pushing for their idea of a reform for the elite. What is even more ridiculous is that the scandals around the demise of Juventus are just casually ignored as if it is immaterial.

## The Westminster Timeline for Football Reform

As we have established football is like no other sport in the world. It truly is a global phenomenon that has allowed it special privileges in societies across the globe. We all know and recognise the power for good that it can bring from the grassroots to the pinnacle of the World Cup finals. Throughout the world, the unique place our teams and clubs hold near our hearts has built a passion that fuels the most positive and compelling human loyalty. Yet, for all the good that emanates from these daily interactions and commitments to our game, there is a darkness that power, money and ego can often bring.

Purists of our game would like to argue that there is no place for politics in the game that we love. This is an argument that emanates from a different era when the diet of news that the population had to consume came sanitised and channelled through just a very few limited sources. There was no local radio, no internet, no Google to hold and store each and every argument and counter-argument and, of course, no social media either.

The call to keep politics out of sport is a bit like the dummy tit argument. Up to the 1970s, nobody thought any different than to stick a dummy tit, or soother if you are American, in a baby's mouth when it cried. By the late 1970s, those academics in the know were expressing concern that all you were doing was blocking out an important communication tool for the toddler – even if it was making a parent's life a bit more bearable.

The arguments about keeping politics out of sport emerged in the same era when sport was deliberately used as a route for protest against the horrors of apartheid in particular. Governments have not been too shy at enforcing boycotts of major sporting events and the whole modern aspect of sports washing is now known and established as recent World Cups in Russia and Qatar have so easily demonstrated.

But look around and you will see sport using its reach on issues such as equal pay, fight against homophobia, racism and a whole range of societal issues. Let's not forget that taking the knee emanated from the actions of players in the National Football League (NFL) protesting against police brutality. The protests began in the NFL after San Francisco 49ers quarterback Colin Kaepernick sat and later knelt during the anthem before his team's pre-season games of 2016. On the global stage the dummy has been thrown out the pram and sport and politics are now intertwined, even if sometimes they are uncomfortable bedfellows; they will always be linked whether we like it or not.

At a local level, the politics around our clubs has always been there, but in the pre-digital era rarely did it see the light of day. As I have argued elsewhere, if Third Lanark were in the Scottish Premiership now it is highly unlikely that the man who took them under would have been able to get away with it so easily. And I am sure that a campaign to buy the club for the community would have quickly emerged too. Now there is no hiding place and the boardroom secrecy that was *in situ* across the land has been relegated to years gone by.

Of course, the need to find a route to accountability, openness and transparency in our game still exists and that more than anything is why reform is needed. The structure of the game is from a different era and despite the pleas of fans and politicians to embrace reform, it is incapable of doing so.

On the national level, governments have not been quick to interfere in the inner workings of football, although in more recent times they have dabbled around the edges. The current mayor of Manchester was recently in action to support Oldham Athletic which, along with another of his local clubs, Bury, had gone to the wall. Burnham had seen the dangers of football way back in 2002 where, as the then Sports Minister, he sought to help deliver community ownership through the creation of supporters' trust co-operatives that were funded by the Labour Government. It was felt at that time that a ground-up approach and giving the game real community support would help drive change from the bottom up. Sadly, that rather optimistic throw of the dice did little to effect change. What it did lead to was getting the football industry to pay for the national fans' organisations with the FA and EPL nudged to recognise the value of football supporters.

However, with an unregulated football industry that was in desperate need of modernisation, the patience of the Westminster politicians (of all parties) ran out. From 2010 there started a momentum that many believe will result in legislation finally having a White Paper in 2023 and moved to legislation in 2024. It has not been an easy journey and one that is not going to end anytime soon.

JULY 2011 The House of Commons' Culture Media and Sport Select Committee (CMS) recommended substantial reform to the governance and regulation of football and suggested that the Government introduce legislation to push through such reforms.

OCTOBER 2011 The Government declined to introduce legislation but asked the football authorities to work towards reform.

EARLY 2013 The House of Commons' CMS Select Committee published a follow-up report on Football Governance. They concluded that the limited reforms implemented had not gone far enough and the Government should therefore issue an ultimatum to the football authorities confirming that legislation would be introduced if adequate reforms were not implemented within 12 months.

LATE 2013 The Sports Minister of the time Sir Hugh Robertson restated that the Government had no plans to introduce legislation, but said he now expected reform from the football authorities themselves in the coming months.

JULY 2016 The then Sports Minister Tracey Crouch said the FA might lose its funding if it did not press ahead with governance reforms.

February 2017 MPs passed a (largely symbolic) House of Commons motion of no confidence in the FA's governance.

2019 The House of Commons' Digital, Culture, Media and Sport Select Committee published a further report into the administration of football following the expulsion of Bury FC from the EFL. The main recommendations were: the requirement of an Independent Licensing Regime and Reforms to the Fit and Proper test.

DECEMBER 2019 The Conservative Party Manifesto at the General Election committed the Party to establishing 'a fan-led review of football governance'.

JULY 2020 The House of Commons' Digital, Culture, Media and Sport Select Committee published a report into the 'Impact of COVID-19 on DCMS sectors', which included substantial reference to football governance and regulation. The Report determined that the current football business model is not sustainable and that the COVID-19 crisis had illustrated the financial issues within football, specifically in the leagues below the Premier League.

AUG 2020 The Football Supporters' Association launched their 'Sustain the Game!' campaign to protect the existence of clubs throughout football. The campaign called for: independent regulation of football clubs, greater transparency on club ownership, fairer and smarter distribution of football's riches and more of a voice for supporters.

APRIL 2021 European Super League is launched. Some of the top club sides in Europe decide to launch an audacious bid to outflank UEFA and their own leagues by creating what would be known as the European Super League.

Oliver Dowden, the Secretary of State for Digital, Culture, Media and Sport, has said the Government 'will do whatever it takes to stop plan' of the European Super League amid threats to withhold work permits and remove policing from grounds. The Cabinet Minister announced that there will be a 'fan-led review' into football in the UK, that will examine every element of the sport, 'root and branch'.

APRIL 2021 The Fan-Led Review of the Game in England is launched. The terms of reference for the review were issued on 22 April 2021. These charged the review with the aim to 'explore ways of improving the governance, ownership and financial sustainability of clubs in English football, building on the strengths of the football pyramid.' It came on the back of three different crises that eventually shaped the review.

JULY 2024 The Labour Government have committed to take forward the Independent Regulator Leglislation.

## Clubs in Crisis

The first was the collapse of Bury FC, a club founded in 1885, which ceased to exist in 2018–19 with a devastating impact on the local economy and leaving behind a devastated fan base.

The next crisis was COVID-19. For the first time since the Second World

War, club football was brought to a complete halt, threatening the continued existence of many professional football clubs. However, the pandemic and its effects laid bare the fragile nature of the finances of many clubs, as well as the structural challenges of the existing domestic football authorities.

The final crisis was the attempt to set up a European Super League (ESL) in April 2021. This new competition would have involved six English clubs as founding members, protected from relegation. It was a threat to the entire English football pyramid and led to an unprecedented outpouring of protests from fans, commentators, clubs and Government.

## The Fan-Led Review of the Game Findings

There is no doubt that the biggest and potentially most interesting recommendation coming from the findings is the call for an independent regulator to oversee the whole game. As a cultural industry that is wedded to the social fabric of the communities that it represents, there has been a massive disconnect with the audiences. Partially due to the inability of the football authorities to adapt and to regulate efficiently and partly due to the influx of TV wealth and the billionaire owners, many of whom come from areas where regulation and governance are maybe less exacting. Football has had a dismal track record of self-regulation and reform. It has also seen the wealth of clubs become the dominant factor in the game in England and what power the FA had as a regulator has been diminished due to the power shift towards the rich clubs.

Rules around owners' responsibilities and financial commitments would be beefed up under the report's recommendations, coming into line with practices more commonly applied to banks or media companies. The transfer levy, meanwhile, could see a tax of as much as 10 per cent put on Premier League deals, with the money redistributed. The review calculated that in the past five years a 10 per cent levy would have raised about £160m a year.

Other proposals include:

- A golden share, held by supporters, that could veto certain key changes in a football club – from changing the name to selling the ground.
- Shadow boards made up of fans who must be consulted by clubs on key decisions.
- Limits on the amount of money owners can put into a club, to prevent unsustainable practices and stop the distortion of competition, set according to the size of a club's existing finances.

- A reappraisal of parachute payments to be determined between the Premier League and Football League – and, if there is no solution, by the regulator.
- Compulsory relegation and promotion clauses in players' contracts.
- Compulsory equality, diversity and inclusion plans for every club, building on the success of the Football Association's leadership diversity code and the Premier League EDI standard.
- A review into the future of the women's game.
- Trials to allow the consumption of alcohol while watching a match.
- In 2026 the Football Regulator will be live and will have three key tasks.
- Club financial soundness – to protect and promote financial sustainability of regulated clubs, ensuring that clubs take sensible financial decisions and consider the long-term when taking risks.
- Systemic financial resilience – to protect and promote the financial resilience of English football as a whole, ensuring that systemic risks and structural issues like the distribution of revenue through the pyramid are managed appropriately.
- Heritage – to safeguard the traditional features of English football that matter most to the fans and local communities of clubs.

## In Scotland We Watch, Wait and Then Act

The long list of Westminster interactions that have taken place since 2010 are more than interesting to football fans and indeed some of the more astute politicians in Scotland. As we have discussed elsewhere, Sport in Scotland is devolved to the Scottish Parliament.

The pressure that has been cranking up over the years in England has of course produced some small but significant results. The SLO programme roll out, the fans' organisations having access to FA committees and of course the establishment of fans' funds that funded the Football Supporters' Federation, now the Football Supporters' Association. The SFSA, the national fans' organisation, has only been alive since 2015. Prior to that, the previous organisation that I ran, Supporters Direct Scotland, was stymied by the joint efforts of the SFA and SPFL who wanted to control the fans' narrative in Scotland. Sadly, few of the early successes in England have ever translated into positive actions in Scotland where the football authorities' interaction was once described by a leading fans' representative who knocked on the door at Hampden for many years as *'master and serf'*.

There always had been a painful disregard of the views of organised fans' groups. I know this only too well through my own interactions with the SFA and the SPFL. Although England is a different marketplace, what it has had is fully funded fans' organisations that have been able to lobby effectively. Here in Scotland, the history of the Scottish Football Supporters Association has been far more problematic. We are invited into Hampden Park occasionally but, in truth, the football authorities would like us to be a critical friend but without the critical part of the relationship ever being engaged. With organisations that are funded and run by volunteers, it has allowed the football authorities virtually a free pass, but more on that particular conundrum later.

There have been more than a few times that the football authorities have been called to Holyrood to defend themselves and not looked too clever. They have given evidence at committees on various topics including the football sex shame scandals, the inability to have a proper PVG (Protecting Vulnerable Groups) system in place, the ongoing blight of sectarianism on our game and the problem identified by The Children's Commissioner with kids 'slave' contracts. The usual cry of foul from Hampden Park when they have ever been close to being held to account, has been that governments can't interfere in football as it goes against the statutes that they adhere to that allow their ongoing membership of UEFA and FIFA. That argument was of course never really an argument at all and what limited credibility it was deemed to hold was well and truly blown out the water with the scandals that rocked the top of football at FIFA and to a lesser extent UEFA. One of the most intriguing examples of this remains the ongoing dispute around children's contracts that clubs have been using for years that are out of step with the United Nations.

PE1319 was lodged in March 2010 (during Session 3 of the Scottish Parliament) by Scott Robertson and Willie Smith on behalf of Realgrassroots. The petition called on the Scottish Parliament to urge the Scottish Government to investigate six areas in relation to youth football in Scotland:

- The legal status and appropriateness of professional Scottish Football Association (SFA) clubs entering into contracts with children under 16 years.
- Audit process and accountability of all public funds distributed by the SFA to its member clubs.
- Social, educational and psychological effects and legality of SFA member clubs prohibiting such children from participating in extracurricular activity.

- Appropriateness of 'compensation' payments between SFA member clubs for the transfer of young players under the age of 16 years.
- To increase the educational target from two hours curricular physical activity to four hours per week.
- Develop a long-term plan to provide quality artificial surface for training and playing football at all ages across all regions.

The petition has been under consideration by the Public Petitions Committee since 2010, with the issues raised being pursued by the Session 5 Committee and its predecessors in Sessions 3 and 4. The duration of consideration reflects the seriousness with which the issues raised have been addressed, the complex nature of some of these issues and the question of how these issues could or should be resolved. It has taken 12 years to get this process to a Final Report stage and the matter is still not resolved as we write this. The overall view from those on the Committee is that SFA and SPFL's 'time is up'. At the start of 2024 this issue still remains unresolved.

One of the main reasons for the lack of political will to seek reforms in the football industry has been the dominant position of the Scottish National Party at Holyrood and its previous failed venture into the world of football. This was the much maligned and divisive act known by football fans as *The Act*. This was The Offensive Behaviour at Football and Threatening Communications (Scotland) Act 2012 was an Act of the Scottish Parliament which created new criminal offences concerning sectarian behaviour at football games. It arose from a particularly difficult Old Firm encounter that started with touchline angst between the managers and leading to what many believed was a knee jerk reaction from the then First Minister Alex Salmond. For six years it put a barrier up between football fans and the Scottish Government and that allowed the football authorities to get a free pass on its poor governance.

Labour MSP James Kelly introduced the Offensive Behaviour at Football and Threatening Communications (Repeal) (Scotland) Bill on 21 June 2017. Kelly had described the 2012 legislation as having 'completely failed to tackle sectarianism' and as 'illiberal' which 'unfairly targets football fans', and was 'condemned by legal experts, human rights organisations and equality groups'. Professor Sir Tom Devine previously spoke of the Football Act as 'the most illiberal and counterproductive act passed by our young Parliament to date' and a 'stain on the reputation of the Scottish legal system for fair dealing'. Much was made of it when a Sheriff described the law as 'mince'. The Act was repealed on 20 April 2018 and the Government and the Scottish

National Party (SNP) have only ever tip-toed around the football industry since that poorly devised and failed intervention.

## Scotland is Different to England, but...

We have alluded to the history of the game in earlier chapters, and we all know that our game of football is inextricably linked to the game in England and always has been. Nothing gets the Scottish football historians backs up more than when England head to the Euro Championships or World Cups and are begged by the media to *bring football home*. Look out for a reaction from Scotland where documents and anecdotes abound about us being the football pioneers that took the game to the expectant world that contradict that England is the home of football.

What we do know is that since those early days of the knickerbocker-clad early adopters, both our nations have walked a similar path. Although our football industries are very different in size and scale, they are linked in so many ways to this common football bond. Both have a governance structure that is far from open, transparent or in any way accountable to the wider football community. As fans, we all believe it is our game but the reality is that we have no say in how it is run.

However, one of the main differences in the political landscape is that despite the various negative interactions between the football authorities and the Scottish Government there has been very limited parliamentary scrutiny over the lifetime of the parliament. Could it be that football governance in Scotland is so superior to what we have seen in England? Or could it be that the various Scottish Governments that have sat at Holyrood since 1999 have just had too many other priorities to deal with? Or that without a strong independent national fans' organisation to campaign, many of the major issues that football in Scotland has faced just fell through the cracks?

There is no doubt that Scottish football has successfully escaped the type of scrutiny that has emerged in England. As soon as there has been any push back there is the well-rehearsed line that governments are not allowed to interfere as UEFA/FIFA don't like it. No matter how strongly they play this card, it now holds little traction given the ongoing sagas that both these organisations have endured in the past decade.

## An Independent Review and the Wagons Circle

The Scottish Football Supporters Association was established in April 2015 and had grown to have over 40,000 members by 2017. Its members had major concerns about the governance of the game in Scotland which led to the organisation commissioning two highly respected German academics, Dr Prof Axel Faix and Dr Jochen Lammert, who had produced a significant body of football research to look at governance of the game in Scotland.

This resulted in nearly 17,000 respondents giving an almighty thumbs down to what they were seeing at the top of the game in Scotland. A summary of the results are shown in the press release below. Rather than accept the results, the football authorities circled the wagons and had no further dialogue with Scotland's national fans' association for over a year. A further reaction was to fund Supporters Direct Scotland who proudly claim to be, 'the official fans' organisation recognised by the SFA and the SPFL.' Our view at the SFSA is that we will always be independent, represent fans as best we can and fight for accountability, transparency and good governance. Not that we have ever been offered money from the football authorities but, if we had, it would be refused until they accept that they must take the views of their paying customers seriously.

**FIRST INDEPENDENT RESEARCH ON HOW SCOTTISH FOOTBALL IS RUN SHOWS BIG GULF BETWEEN FANS AND GOVERNING BODIES**

The results highlight a growing disconnect between supporters and the game's national and international governing bodies; improving relationships with individual clubs; and the stark reality that many fans could end up leaving the game for good unless change comes.

The research shows that all stakeholders want Scottish parliamentarians to pressure the Scottish governing bodies to improve, and that a majority rate the SPFL and the SFA lower than UEFA and FIFA in terms of their openness, honesty and trustworthiness.

The survey, which saw nearly 17,000 people participate during September, was carried out by the SFSA in partnership with Professor Dr Axel Faix and Dr Joachim Lammert, two respected German sports academics from the University of Applied Science and Arts in Dortmund and the University of Leipzig. Both have significant experience in carrying out similar evaluations in Germany and on a European level.

Key findings from the survey include:

**Stakeholders are very dissatisfied with the leadership of both the SFA and SPFL across a range of activities.**

73 per cent believe their own club is committed to the good of football;
65 per cent believe their own clubs are open and honest;
93 per cent believe that Scottish football should be overseen by an independent watchdog;
95 per cent of fans believe it is essential to have an independent national fans' body;
90 per cent feel that the Scottish Government should put pressure on football authorities to improve;
60.5 per cent said that they could lose interest in football in the future;
32.5 per cent attend fewer than ten games a season;
24.5 per cent said they never attend away games;
60.7 per cent said they attend between just one and ten away games a season;
92.5 per cent say football is important to them;
13.5 per cent don't think football is more important than their other leisure activities;
93.8 per cent want more supporter influence in the SPFL;
94.1 per cent want more supporter influence in the SFA.

There is little difference between the key stakeholders' opinions (players, managers, coaches, club officials, referees and supporters) throughout the research.

Unsurprisingly, there is also a growing concern about the performance of the national game, and what that reflects about the health of Scottish football as a whole.

Henry McLeish, a board member of the SFSA, commented:

This challenging independent research into how Scottish football governance is seen has uncovered some very concerning issues, but also provides a real opportunity for change. Robust research can form a platform for positive action for the future. The results of this survey are a healthy wake-up call for Scotland's game.

He continued:

The fact that over 60 per cent of fans say that they could end up leaving the game in the future rings a major alarm bell, as does the knowledge that almost a quarter say they never attend away games. Trust in the game's governing structures is worryingly low, so much so that a significant number now believe that the Scottish Government should be stepping in to help address the problem.

On a positive note, individual clubs seem to be making progress towards improving relationships with fans through greater engagement and transparency. The difference in the view fans have of their clubs compared to attitudes towards the governing bodies is noticeable.

What we appear to have is a big disconnect between the football authorities at Hampden Park and those who are essential to the flourishing of the game at a hands-on level, supporters certainly, but also players, coaches, managers and volunteers. Many key stakeholders have no real input into how their game is run at present. Greater involvement of those who love, resource and pay for the game is crucial in helping to turn it around.

Simon Barrow, chair of the SFSA, said:

This is the first fully independent, professional research into perceptions of how the Scottish game is run in 144 years. It highlights many areas of concern, but equally indicates that the time is ripe for change and supporter engagement. Rather than ignoring the worrying gulf between fans and governing bodies, we see this as an opportunity for them to build bridges with us.

Whether it's commercial aspects of the game, the performance of our national sides or overall governance and transparency, this is a challenge and chance to listen more carefully to what fans, who remain the game's vital customers, have to say and to offer. Played the right way, it could be football's democratic moment.

The intention of the SFSA is to run out this benchmarking exercise on a regular basis, so that a culture of engagement and continuous improvement can be developed.

Simon Barrow explained:

We would like to do that through helping to build new partnerships, to bridge the gap between grassroots and governance. What we are looking for is a 'big conversation' on the future of Scottish football, its ability to contribute to community well-being and its role as a key cultural industry for Scotland.

We are kick-starting this process through some practical work in three areas: governance, promoting the game, and performance. This will draw on creative minds and well-known figures across Scottish football. We will be inviting the governing authorities to engage positively with fans through our networks, and to consider reform in the way the game is run, promoted and developed.

After further digestion of the results of the new survey, the SFSA proceeded with short-life working parties comprised of former players, managers, coaches, referees and supporters, focused on alterative plans for some of the big issues the game is struggling with.

## October 2021: The Football Alliance is Launched in Scotland

Under the chairmanship of former First Minister Henry McLeish the SFSA established the Scottish Football Alliance which would talk to any stakeholder in the game who was interested in the growth of Scottish football. Its remit is to produce a paper looking at the necessary reviews that would allow Scottish football to learn and adapt from the proposal in England and offer suitable solutions for reform of the game.

As part of the task in hand, the Scottish Football Alliance reached out to football supporters to ask them what they wanted from the SFA/SPFL. Over 2,000 responses were gathered.

*Feelings for the football authorities*
Anger
Poor leadership
Distrust
Self-interest and conflict of interest
Not accountable
Disregard for supporters
Self-serving/contempt
Lack of empathy for the customer
Secrecy
No vision

*What do you want from the football authorities?*
Consultative/customer focused
Inclusive
Open/transparent
Accountable
Independent
Working for common good
Strategic
Innovative
Democratic
Commercially astute

*What do fans want to see? (based on six years of research data)*
Fan representation at highest level
Larger leagues
More competition in the top league
Stop playing same teams four times a season
Summer football
Alcohol allowed at games
An independent board to stop self-interest
End of excessive CEO salaries
A coherent SFA talent strategy for national teams
Better sponsors – over reliance on betting & alcohol
Influence in TV scheduling

The Scottish Football Alliance has also worked closely with colleagues at the Football Supporters Association and right across the political spectrum, recommendations were published in 2023 and these were debated at Holyrood on 31 January 2024. It was a significant day where the Scottish Parliament discussed independent regulation for the first time.

MSPs backed calls for real accountability and transparency and the Minister offered a Roundtable discussion to follow up this debate. This offer by Scottish Government opens the door to real reform as it acknowledged the importance of its central recommendation – the need for independent scrutiny and appropriate regulation of the finance, governance and conduct of the football authorities in Scotland.

I would encourage you to follow this closely as it will be a key discussion in Scottish Football in the years ahead.

The debate at Holyrood led to the Sports Minister Maree Todd MSP agreeing to a Roundtable discussion to take the debate further. The meeting was scheduled for 8 May and was to have a huge influence on where the future Governance of our game will go. Will the calls for openness, transparency and accountability with fans having a say in how the game is run be considered or will the closed members' organisation that has failed its members and the customers be allowed to continue as an inward-looking trade body. Sadly, an unexpected General Election put paid to the meeting which was rescheduled for 7 August and hopefully you will have been able to follow some successful developments around this.

It is certainly being watched by the Scottish Football Association. In late March 2024, they advised the SFSA (who let us remember are Scotland's National Fans' Association with over 82,000 members) that due to its stance on wanting an Independent Regulator in our game, they had advised all their departments not to deal with us! It was surprising that they actually put this in writing but it came at a time when we were supporting local referee associations with recruitment and were helping fundraise several of the disability teams. It also meant that we were denied access to the Scotland team and the National Fan Awards that we present annually were not able to be given out.

It really is a shocking way to treat supporters and if the politicians don't see that bullying tactic as an example of shambolic governance that needs reform, then we really are living in some sort of football twilight zone.

The revised General Election having been won by Labour saw them push forward in the King's Speech with Legislation of the Football Governance Bill thus heaping a huge amount of pressure on the Scottish Government to follow suit. Of course, Hampden Park will argue that Scotland is different from England and we have no problems here! As fans, I think we do know differently.

*The Scottish Football Supporters Association (SFSA) has welcomed the 'strong and determined' calls for accountability and transparency in the way Scottish football is run, as expressed by MSPs across all parties in a landmark parliamentary debate yesterday (31 January).*

Note:
The Round Table that was set up by Maree Todd MSP, the Sports Minister, in response to the Parliamentary debate has now met three times in 2024/5 and has not yet even debated the merits or otherwise of an Independent Regulator. It would appear that the only way that anything might happen in Scotland is if the SFSA apply pressure to all the political parties before the 2026 Holyrood election.

CHAPTER 11

# Community Ownership as a Viable Option

*Something happens when you feel ownership. You no longer act like a spectator or consumer, because you're an owner. Faith is at its best when it's that way too. It's best lived when it's owned.* —Bob Goff

WHAT HAS BEEN exciting for me to watch over the years is seeing the potential for community ownership becoming established and how these developments are changing the football landscape forever. It is what I fought so hard for against a system that did not want to adapt or change.

### A New Beginning for That Loving Football Relationship

Across the UK, football history has introduced us to a host of less than honourable villains who have used our clubs as playthings. What we know is that it is always the fans who are left to pick up the broken pieces from the many indiscretions that have occurred over the years. Now we don't need to have a major crisis for the model to be properly considered. Tailor-made solutions for each club means that we have started to see a return to the clubs being owned by communities rather than corporations or wealthy benefactors – who can have a very different level of benevolence based on their own objectives.

In simple terms, *love* is the only reason why clubs don't just survive but actually thrive. Just ask the fans of Gretna (2008) and Clydebank FC who still watch their club week in week out, no matter what level they are playing at. Both were Premiership sides in their day but now play at a far lower level to the same adoring fans. A noticeable consequence and significant fact is that in recent administrations the fans are now regarded as a real viable option to get the club back on an even keel, rather than administrators taking the risk on 'another' benefactor. Of course, part of that is a consequence of there being very few entrepreneurs who now think they can make money from football.

If they can't do that then you would expect that their objectives are vanity driven, unless you do have a genuine philanthropic desire to support the local Rovers or Athletic. That does not happen very often but, as we saw with the fantastic gesture to Partick Thistle by Colin Weir or when James Anderson the Edinburgh businessman offered assistance to football during the pandemic, it can happen. Both of these magnanimous gestures were made for the love of the game and not the slightest hint of any personal interest being involved.

The interesting dynamic that does seem to be emerging in Scotland is that without a significant number of buyers available, many clubs are rightly looking at what direction they might be going in. It was very interesting that just before James Anderson emerged to help our game, former international star Steve Archibald, who was involved in a takeover at Airdrie in 2000, emerged to tell the BBC that due to the pandemic football is a 'land of opportunity' for investors. Nothing seems to have changed in his mind; instead, he suggested that 'People can go in, bring players in, push up through the leagues, tap into TV money and work the transfer market. Bringing in young players and selling them is not a difficult thing to do'. No mention of the club, its identity or its fans – it is just about the money.

You have to ask the question, with community ownership now so well established, when it comes to planning why would you not consider the fans as your first option? They are always there, will always spend money with you and only leave the brand when they die. Players, managers and coaches come and go but following our clubs is, for many of us, stronger than any religious devotion. I know, I stopped going to church 45 years ago, but I can't stop going to Firhill no matter how badly they are playing.

A few years back, with my fellow co-founder of the SFSA, Simon Barrow, I led a series of presentations at Holyrood and at Westminster where we took the opportunity to explain the work that we were doing to support community ownership. One of our members, Ian Blackford, the then Leader of the SNP at Westminster, posed an interesting question, 'Will Scottish football now change to become more democratic through community ownership?' Of course, in simple terms, the answer is yes and in the fullness of time there should be a cascade of information down through the supporter-owned clubs to allow a new level of democracy.

There is no doubt that one of the obvious key benefits of community ownership is better and more considered engagement from the club management towards the supporters. Almost without exception, we have seen clubs either owned or on the pathway to community ownership become more open, transparent and accountable, demonstrating just how it changes the supporter landscape.

As we discussed earlier, a few years back certain individuals could not see the opportunity and decided to circle the wagons as soon as any approaches from fans were made. Now, as the positive experiences at these clubs grow, football fans will have more confidence that community ownership is a viable proposition for their clubs. This has been shown by the results of recent surveys.

While the recent fans' submission to a Parliamentary poll saw over 2,000 fans expressing an interest in supporter ownership for their clubs, we can also see that The SFA's National Football Supporters' Survey (nearly 4,000 fans), revealed a strong majority of fans (91 per cent) believe that the community ownership model can work in Scotland and should be on the football agenda. Over the past ten years, there has been a consistent groundswell of support for community ownership in all the research conducted by the SFSA with support for the model never dropping below 90 per cent. In many respects, moving in this direction is revisiting the history as the senior, junior and amateur clubs in Scotland were without exception founded and created by local people to serve their own tight knit communities.

## Reasons Why Clubs Would Consider a Community Ownership Model

The key ones include:

- Owner(s) needs to exit and recoup some of their 'investment' – Motherwell, St Mirren, now St Johnstone
- Owner needs to exit – retirement or runs out of funds – Stirling Albion, Morton
- Philanthropic donation to community share transfer – Partick Thistle, Clyde, East Stirlingshire
- Liquidation/Administration – best option for long-term sustainable future – Dunfermline Athletic, Heart of Midlothian, Edinburgh City
- Owners bought club thinking they could make a profit and obviously they will not – Hibernian, Dundee, Dundee Utd?
- Revive the club where it has been lost to the community but the fans refuse to let it die – Gretna 2008, Clydebank, FC United, AFC Wimbledon
- Strategic community plan to move to be a Social Enterprise – East Stirlingshire, Clyde, Stenhousemuir
- A new club – FC United of Manchester

## The Success of Community Ownership

I used to believe that, if given the chance, community ownership could work at all the clubs in the United Kingdom. However, the divergence of the markets has probably ended any real chance for most middle-sized teams in England and Wales. Whilst the lure of climbing into the land of milk and honey of the Premier League exists, then most league clubs could in theory be used as tools to drive a business or ego that has the right level of investment in that direction. As a result of this, community ownership that was an aspiration of Andy Burnham and his early adopters way back in 2010, is a model that is likely to only be that for these smaller, non-league clubs or clubs such as Bury FC who have simply run out of any other conceivable options. It might be wrong, but it is unlikely that the two exemplar models at Exeter City or AFC Wimbledon will be repeated anytime soon.

As we have seen in earlier chapters, there are countries like Argentina, Germany and Sweden where they have the structural pathways in place that allow clubs to do this. The size or scale of the clubs involved is no barrier to being community-owned. In England, as the influx of foreign billionaire investment has arrived, it seems an unlikely scenario that there will be many more league clubs converting from the conventional structures to community ownership. New entrants are only likely to emerge from the non-league arena where there is less attraction for investors to get involved. There may be hope that the likes of Bury could come back as a phoenix club in the years ahead but having had a difficult experience of failing to go for community ownership during their first administration, it is hard to predict what might happen at Gigg Lane. We can but hope that the fans have the confidence to fly solo, or they have better luck in finding a benefactor that they can work with.

In Scotland, we have had a few bumps along the way, mostly notably at Dundee, however we can now see a successful model that is working from the non-league to the Premiership. The concept has now got real credibility, despite the best efforts of some in the world of football who feared the changes that it might bring. Openness, transparency, accountability and wider community participation have never been significant areas where the football authorities have been interested in investing time or energy. Maybe it should be no surprise to see that there was real fear from the football authorities of this new way of doing business.

As someone who has been working with fans for over a decade, the reasons that fans want to consider these options are fairly straightforward:

- There is a 'disconnect' between clubs and their local stakeholders

leading to a lack of accountability and transparency and causing damage to the social value of clubs in their communities. So many times the heart has been ripped out of the clubs by individuals who have used the teams for their own financial or egotistical desires.
- With every administration or liquidation event that has occurred in the UK the only people who have been around to pick up the pieces when clubs are in crisis are the supporters.
- As football has become more corporate, the value to the wider society has tended to decline and individual ownership at clubs generally serves the interests of owners and shareholders, over the interests of supporters and the local communities that they serve. It was this facet in particular that attracted the Scottish Green Party to the debate in Scotland.
- Corporate, group and individual ownership at clubs generally serves the interests of owners and shareholders, over the interests of supporters and local communities.
- A lack of involvement and representation of supporters has led to a democratic deficit for the most loyal customers – the ordinary fan. As social media and fans' networks have now brought fans understanding of what might be on offer in countries like Germany, Spain and Sweden there is a feeling that fans in the UK have been somewhat short-changed by our game. We can bank on your cash; we like the atmosphere you create and we know your love for the game means that your loyalty can never be questioned but we really don't want you involved in running the game.

## What are the Benefits of Community Ownership?

Before any fans consider campaigning, they do need to really appreciate if the prize is worth the considerable effort that they will have to go through to achieve their goal. Bringing the supporters with you during that campaign is vital and explaining what the benefits are of converting to this model is a good starting point for any fans' group. The trick when you are successful is then delivering on the promises that you made during the campaign.

There has been a rapid development of supporter and community-owned sports clubs in the United Kingdom in the past 15 years or so, which has been driven by supporters having a better understanding of ownership. This development fits into a wider context in which community ownership is being promoted and developed, which includes:

- The Localism Act of 2011 that operates in England and Wales which encourages communities to own and run assets and services in their area.
- UK Government funding to support this through the My Community Rights funding run by Locality and Social Investment Business.
- The development of the Social Enterprise business model that is now known and understood more widely in the UK.
- The huge increase in community shares schemes to support local facility development and businesses run by Community Benefit Societies have helped promote the co-operative nature of the platforms.
- In Scotland through the work around the Community Empowerment (Scotland) Act 2015 followed the Land Reform (Scotland) Act of 2003; this gave a greater understanding of how shared community empowerment might be beneficial. In simple terms, it was now recognised as a viable option for football clubs.

Part of the reason for this has been a growing recognition of the benefits of community ownership of facilities and services for communities in the area in which they are situated – employees, beneficiaries and local residents. This suggests that community-owned enterprises:

- Engage a wider range of local stakeholders in their ownership, governance and activities of the organisation.
- Provide different ways for communities to integrate with those organisations – such as through a coordinated approach to volunteering and providing related services or unique offers.
- Have an approach that prioritises longer-term sustainability over short-term profit, with higher levels of reinvestment in the business as it is now a business with a longer-term perspective.
- Are a positive contributor to the local economy where in the past these were often looked at as having less economic value. There is no doubt that the third sector was previously seen as being less valuable, probably through ignorance and an element of snobbery. A great example of changed attitudes we have seen at the SFSA has been with two of our affiliate partners; Social Bite with what they have done by campaigning for successful outcomes from homelessness has been world leading. Likewise, Brewgooder who create superb craft beers and all the profits that are generated go

to building clean water provisions in countries like Malawi. As companies like these become more successful the more the third sector's reputation is enhanced. If you have the correct structure, it opens up other opportunities to you that simply might not otherwise exist.

We have in previous chapters discussed the ongoing industry-wide issues and the serious deficits in good governance and financial probity in sport – especially football – so securing these benefits for more sports clubs should be something that is seen as a new and important part of a new mixed football economy.

## Wider Benefits of Community Ownership in Sport

Most football clubs deliver 'community benefit' through outreach work (sports development, education, provision of health and well-being etc) and often this is work undertaken by their community foundations, which are arm's length charities that sit outside of the club itself. Many of these deliver excellent work and have a significant impact on their communities. However, increasing evidence suggests there are added community benefits when sports clubs are community-owned as it drives the message deeper that this is by the football community for the wider community.

The Social Value of Football research was completed in 2008 by Substance, a social research co-operative, who compared the activities of supporter-owned and non-supporter-owned clubs and concluded that there was an 'added value' to the social value delivered with supporter-owned clubs. This included:

- A priority given to sustainable finance – not spending more than is earned – meaning that their engagement with their communities was long term and sustainable; a horizontal integration of community interests across the club, rather than it being the preserve of an arms' length charity.
- Company objects that specify the club's (as opposed to its charity's) obligations to deliver community benefit.
- Benefits felt by supporters as co-owners of the clubs, including roles in governance and volunteering.
- Better and more extensive relationships with local authorities and other local partners delivering social impacts.

Research into the Business Advantages of Supporter Ownership also highlighted that community-owned clubs:

- Had long-term sustainable partnerships as a result of their community ownership.
- Generated sponsor support through a desire to be associated with the principles of community ownership and the engagement with a wider, more engaged audience.
- Were able to embrace community involvement in finance-raising – by the fans for the community.
- Created more opportunities to use the appeal of the sport to enhance volunteer participation.
- Have greater levels of supporter satisfaction as involvement was less remote.
- Have sustainable finances and are less likely to suffer boom and bust.
- Build/repair reputational damage done by failed previous regimes that has seen the brand name suffer locally and nationally.

## Longer-term Strategic Alliances are Easier to Form

- Community ownership allows clubs to develop deeper and more long term strategic partnerships with the local community and businesses.
- Developing a greater sense of shared agendas and partnerships between local authorities, clubs and business at a time where there is significant focus on community projects and activities.
- When a club is supporter-owned with a structure that means it needs to report to its members this builds a level of trust and responsibility.
- A community-owned structure means that there is automatically increased transparency, which helps build trust between organisations.
- It is far easier for community-owned clubs to align agendas with public or private strategic partners, meeting strategic objectives that can help the wider community.
- As we see in countries like Sweden and Germany the local politicians have embraced the role of football in society and in the local communities. It makes the opportunity for partnerships more compelling. As I mentioned elsewhere, when the fans

bought Stirling Albion we had a debt of over £200,000 but due to Stirling Council that debt was looked on favourably and we were able to come to a community partnership agreement where we paid it back in kind over the next few years.

## Financial Information is More Accessible

- Community ownership creates a greater sense of financial responsibility; an increased recognition for clubs to live within their means.
- It allows fan-owned clubs to raise finance in other, less conventional ways, such as through 'Community Shares' or through longer-term funding initiatives and membership schemes.
- Fans often complain that clubs have kept them in the dark; with community-owned clubs, it allows more transparency in terms of clubs' finances and makes relevant information more accessible to fans.
- Fans who generate income through their membership schemes will have a direct influence on where that money goes. In the first years of partial fan ownership, the £120,000 a year that is targeted at Dunfermline Athletic goes to the youth academy; at Hearts they directed the money originally destined to buy shares from Ann Budge to build a new stand and even at St Mirren who have completed the pathway to community ownership the fans are able to direct a percentage of their funds to specific projects.

## Sponsorship Opportunities Are Enhanced

Sponsors are attracted to community-owned clubs due to the more complete buy-in that supporters have to these clubs. It has added a new level of loyalty and responsibility when the stakeholders own the club. In England, attendance figures increased when compared with competitors at the same level, eg FC United of Manchester and AFC Wimbledon have had higher crowd attendances than their leagues would normally attract. In Scotland, both Stirling Albion and Dunfermline Athletic increased the level of season ticket sales after community ownership and had significant uplifts in sponsorship revenue. In the first year of fans owning Stirling Albion the sponsorship revenue increased by 75 per cent although as personnel changed it failed to retain that level. The second year it reduced to a sizeable 10 per cent growth before it plateaued. It can also add value to a certain cache or enhance the reputational value of sponsors being associated with a club owned by its supporters.

Community reputational value can help to forge longer-term relationships between club and sponsor. We saw at Stirling Albion, where the sponsor was intending to leave the club, they recommitted for an additional four years making it – Prudential – the longest running sponsorship in Scottish football. The wider community benefit opportunities are open to exploration in ways that a standard limited company structure can't hope to replicate. Even although they are in the early stages of moving to community ownership, St Mirren have seen significant investment and innovation through the Kibble organisation. Having a flexible, innovative, community-focused approach can be hugely beneficial.

## Transparency, Openness and Trust

- All supporter-owned clubs have to publish annual accounts that have to be approved by members at their AGM.
- Provides a level of scrutiny and recourse for supporters, as well as a level of public transparency that is often lacking at other clubs, where benefactors can choose what they wish to tell the stakeholders.
- At community clubs there is a level of openness and transparency not seen at conventional clubs. This is a key factor in developing and maintaining relationships across all areas of the business.
- Offers the ordinary member the opportunity to scrutinise the club as they have never done before and to put themselves or any other suitably qualified person forward for election to either the fans' group board or the club board.
- There is a situation at a club that I have dealt with where the club was for sale and some *interesting* parties had shown an interest in buying the club. The decision was made by the exiting owners that a fans' group was the preferable option. Having the safety of the fans on your side is something that should not be overlooked or taken for granted. In previous times before the model was understood there was no chance that a football club board would have had faith in the fans.

## Concerns About Having Supporter-owned Clubs

It will come as no surprise to readers of this book that as an advocate for community ownership I don't see too many problems with it working for most clubs. However, as we have seen from some of the examples that I have highlighted it is certainly not something that everyone will embrace. There are challenges and concerns, and it is only right that we highlight them here.

### Timing Pressures

It may well be that it is not the right time to take the club on. In the previous example, the fans had heard rumours of someone trying to buy their club and in dialogue with the club they organised accordingly to offer a fan-centric alternative exit strategy for the existing owners.

The biggest timing issue remains the problems when clubs have gone into administration or liquidation. Unless fans have been prepared for such eventualities, there is often an issue being able to galvanise fans and get a long-term strategy in place quickly enough. Part of the problem is that after the initial surge in the development of supporters' trusts, many just became organisations that were either talking shops or small cabals of disgruntled supporters without any long-term objectives. Some were able to reform, modernise and campaign whereas others had to be replaced by other bespoke organisations such as the Foundation of Hearts or Thistle for Ever (now The Jags Foundation).

### Financial Pressures

There is always financial pressure at clubs no matter who is in charge. One of the biggest mistakes I made when at Stirling Albion was delegating the task of communicating with the 2,346 members who had contributed £40 each. Many of these advocates had been acquired worldwide and could have opened up a whole new market for us. With no benefactor present it is essential that your members step into the role to replace the benefactor in times of need. Stirling Albion failed to generate any income from these members and in the following years started to look inward rather than fully embrace the financial opportunities that it offered. Hearts of course have led the way by converting the initial 8,500 pledgers into providing a substantial revenue stream for the club. Even allowing for the natural churn, they still have around 7,500 members contributing monthly. Others such as Motherwell and St Mirren have followed suit.

## Political Pressures

The politics of running a fan-owned club can be difficult in some situations. A good example is with key decisions and who should take them. In the recent debates about league reconstruction, the community-owned clubs should have opened the debate up to their members to allow them to have a say. I am not sure they even thought about doing so. They need to start doing things differently. There will be internal political pressure points and, in some respects, those are also brought to bear with the football authorities. Certainly, in the early days of community ownership, the clubs were regarded as some form of dangerous trade union with an alternative agenda and different objectives. Fortunately, with critical mass this perception has moved and softened but there is still a general antipathy towards supporters. Indeed a very senior operator in the game when speaking to the SFSA CEO in October 2024 about me was still complaining that people don't like me for what I did at Stirling Albion. Not only did I find that incredulous but also concerning about the level of deep rooted contempt for community ownership.

### Structural pressures abound and a natural leader beyond reproach is essential

Few fans' groups are likely to be properly constituted right at the time when they are to be called into action. Even those such as trusts tend to have had little traction over the years and have become minority interest groups and non-inclusive, eg Hearts Trust only had around 30 members and little credibility and rather than use them, the Hearts fans created the Foundation of Hearts which grew to have 8,500 members. At Hibs, the trust had around 60 members but when the Buy Hibs CIC was launched it attracted over 4,000 members. Recently at Morton a new group, Morton Club Together, emerged again ignoring the existing trust who were not regarded as having the personnel or the capacity to drive change. At Partick Thistle before the emergence of Thistle for Ever as the community ownership vehicle the incumbent fans' organisation the Jags Trust actually ignored the community principles on which it was founded and decided to support selling the club to foreign investors. Any semblance of creditability it might have had went when it failed to even consult its members before doing so – hardly democratic. To put icing on this particular cake, the chair of the Jags Trust is also the chair of Supporters Direct Scotland which claims to still be in favour of community ownership.

While trusts have the capacity to facilitate a deal as Community Benefit Societies, having converted from being Industrial and Provident Societies, the more inclusive and modern route is a CIC, Community Interest Company. This offers added benefits such as an asset lock that can be important to protect the club. Again, the bill needs to be cognisant of the fact that it will take time to get fans' groups together. One practical solution to this would be to allow the SFSA to set up a CIC for every club that can almost be brought down out of cold storage when required to speed up the process.

I really had high hopes that something positive for fans would come out of the Rangers crash. So many decent Gers fans came forward and, working alongside the Rangers Supporters Trust there emerged a new group. After many months of negotiating between different individuals the new group was christened at the Louden Tavern and called Rangers First. I had great assistance from Richard Aitchison, a volunteer colleague, in bringing the concept forward where a CIC was created, and fans would purchase shares in Rangers. In no time at all it really took off and as the independent advisor I met both Charles Green and Dave King a few times as they wanted to explore their options and see how it might fit into their own strategy. In what seemed like the blink of an eye, Rangers First became the largest fan group in Britain with over 13,000 members, or 'membears' as they liked to call themselves, all raising money to buy as much of the club as they could. The financial demise of such a major club has shown that any club can be blighted by financial problems and that the support for fan ownership is really growing. Whereas some current owners might see such a robust fans' group as a threat, the new owners at Rangers appreciated what a powerful ally it can be and what a useful tool it might provide. Sadly, with political infighting at the club over the continued Green consortium ownership and the change of direction under Dave King, Rangers First was folded into one of its sub-brands Club 1872 and the momentum for a Hearts-style community ownership was lost.

Internal divisions can also cause a whole range of problems. This is probably one of the hardest areas to manage in fans' affairs. I had many difficult moments at Dundee where, as seen earlier, we failed to keep the community ownership dream alive as the faction I was supporting did not have the credibility to deliver for the fans. At Hearts, I was in a very tricky situation trying to get a credible plan together in the hope that we could get a fans' group in place that could be ready to carry the community ownership banner forward. I worked closely with the then MD David Southern, the departing Lithuanians and the Scottish Government, before working with Bryan Jackson. The problem was that my starting point had been the Hearts Trust as they were members of Supporters Direct Scotland. The main issues were that they were like many trusts set up a long time ago and had failed to deliver anything significant for the fans (so I was told) and there had been infighting and some issues around financial irregularities in previous years.

It took many months of negotiations with all seven or eight representative groups around the table to eventually get a consensus to back the FoH as the vehicle to take this forward. Initially, we asked former Hearts Commercial Manager Lawrence Brodie to help as a Jambo to chair the meetings, which he kindly did. It became pretty obvious that unless we had a long-term leader then the concept would implode as some of the organisations wanted to look backwards rather than forwards. Having spoken to Lord George Foulkes who I had been consulting with all through the process, he suggested Ian Murray MP. I met Ian at the City Chambers, went through the whole story and convinced him to do what I couldn't do and be the Hearts leader. If that hadn't happened, I really don't think Hearts would currently be in community ownership as having a strong considered leader is an essential part of this process. Success of the project at Hearts owes so much to the fans but equally Ann Budge and Ian Murray both had to believe that it could be done. There was also a unique set of circumstances at play which allowed us to have the superb support of the CEO David Southern. There is no doubt that Hearts was the first opportunity to build on what we did that worked or didn't work at Stirling Albion. That initial Save the Albion campaign and eventual purchase really did act as a catalyst for how the model emerged elsewhere. In the case of Hearts you had a much larger support and many more talented volunteers, with it the model improved significantly.

I would also point out that whilst social media is a huge benefit for campaigning it is also a huge problem to try to manage. In the Hearts situation, I was right front and centre of the daily dialogue and interactions at the club. However, most of the work I did involved behind the scenes activity with the owners and with the Scottish Government, other interested parties such as politicians, the media and then the fans' group. Little could be communicated at this sensitive time and that allowed some fans to decide to have a personal narrative against me. I probably worked harder and gave more to Hearts than any other club, yet the negative narrative some 'fans' fed into the social media channels has meant that much of that muck is still floating about the message boards. I am incredibly proud of what I helped achieve at Hearts and people like David Southern, Bryan Jackson, Ian Murray and Ann Budge know what I did but the masses thought I was a chancer due to the false narrative painted on Twitter. Much of that from just one fan who got it in his head that I was only interested in being the next Chairman of Hearts, not in actually working for the greater good.

## What Does Success Look Like?

Community ownership is not right for every club or for every group of fans but where the opportunities exist then it really is worth taking to embracing it. Here we will look at some of the most successful transitions into community ownership.

### Exeter City – The Pride of Devon

Like so many of the clubs that will be featured on our journey, Exeter City only considered radical change out of adversity. In fact, the whole concept of supporters owning clubs was so far removed from normal sight that it was never really considered as an option. The plight of the Grecians came into focus in the 1990s when, along with many other clubs, they had an inability to stay solvent. Like many other football clubs who chased the on-field dream, there became issues when the revenue generated by what is a fairly modest-sized club like Exeter City was stretched to pay the growing wages bill. So many clubs had cosy relationships with banks, often thanks to the joys of Saturday afternoons in corporate hospitality. Football clubs were different from other real businesses. In these heady days of spending, few banks and even fewer football administrators ever thought to stop and ask to see the wages to turnover of these local clubs. They also had fairly loose arrangements when it came to the valuation of football stadiums considering their restricted use.

Fortunately for the fans of City, they had the foresight to set up a supporters' trust ahead of what became the start of an interesting journey. The Exeter City Supporters' Trust was formed on 6 May 2000, following the club's 2–1 home defeat to Shrewsbury Town. The fans had insight from the pioneering work of the Northampton Town Supporters Trust. It was led by the legendary Brain Lomax who sadly passed away in 2015. When he passed, David Conn of the *Guardian* said of him:

> Brian Lomax, who has died aged 67, was the visionary pioneer for the idea that football clubs rightfully belong to their supporters, and he became the founding father of the modern movement to form supporters' trusts at almost every club in Britain. Lomax inspired a generation of activism with his remarkably open and generous manner, and with practical expertise, having himself formed an original supporters' trust at then troubled Northampton Town in 1992.

So, taking notice of what Northampton Town had been through made perfect sense for Exeter City fans.

Whilst the creation of supporters' trusts across the country was at that time a very positive development for fans, it took many years for them to bed in and to get to a point where they had credibility with ordinary fans (who previously only had supporters' clubs or supporters' bus organisations working on their behalf, with very limited impact. In these early days, it was about building capacity and credibility with supporters and the clubs; the whole notion of fans actually buying a club was way off the radar at that time. More often than not the way to the club's door was for trusts to raise funds for the club. In many cases, this route was often abused by clubs. At St James' Park, it soon became obvious that the directors of the club only saw the trust as a 'cash cow' and had no intention of giving up any real power or allowing any insight into how the club was being run. This led to a change of the trust's constitution in February 2003 from supporting the club financially to owning it.

On 14 May 2003, John Russell and Mike Lewis were arrested over allegations of financial irregularities at the club. Just to add a bit of tabloid sensationalism, it later emerged that Uri Geller was one of the people who had contacted the police to report them for their financial indiscretions. Uri, of course, famously brought Michael Jackson along to the club to proclaim love and world peace in 2002 in what can only be described as one of the most surreal events ever to be held at a football stadium. Of course, as we know in life, hindsight is a wonderful thing.

Following Russell and Lewis' arrest, some fans decided to act. Ian Huxham, Terry Pavey and Julian Tagg, all of whom were prominent members of the Exeter City Supporters' Trust at the time, were appointed as directors of the club. Shortly after, Ivor Doble, who was an elderly gentleman and majority shareholder, asked the trust to take over the day-to-day running of the club. Complex legal arguments with both Inland Revenue and football authorities meant that City's first season of non-league football was plagued by off-the-field uncertainty. On 5 September 2003, the supporters' trust purchased the club from Doble for £20,000 which, according to then trust chairman Dr David Treharne, was 'Pretty much everything the trust had at the time'.

The trust's purchase of the club was announced on 5 September. In October 2003, the club entered a Company Voluntary Arrangement, which was accepted by 88 per cent of the creditors, in order to reduce the £4.5 million debt Russell and Lewis had left behind. In April 2007, Russell and Lewis pled guilty to various criminal offences related to their time in charge of the club. Russell was sentenced to 21 months in prison, whilst Lewis was ordered to complete 200 hours of community service. In February 2008, both Russell and Lewis were permanently suspended from football by the FA. Uri Gellar seemed to perform a vanishing act and as for Michael Jackson, well, that as they say is another story entirely.

On 8 January 2005, Exeter City drew 0–0 against Manchester United at Old Trafford in the third round of the FA Cup proving that miracles sometimes do actually happen for wee clubs. Sadly, City eventually fell to a 2–0 defeat in the televised replay at St James' Park a few weeks later, with world superstars Cristiano Ronaldo and Wayne Rooney scoring the goals that took the Red Devils through to the fourth round. However, as the TV commentators mentioned several times that night, the replay was probably the best financial outcome that the Grecians could ever have wished for. The income from these two games was estimated at just under £1 million, which led to the club's debts being successfully wiped out.

In June 2008, the trust's membership surpassed the 2,500 mark following the club's return to the Football League. In 2012, the trust membership reached its peak at over 4,000 members, but it has since dropped to just over 3,000. It is the majority shareholder of Exeter City, controlling 53.6 per cent of the voting shares in the club. Since taking control, the trust has handed over more than £1.75 million to the club. Given its stability and longevity as a community-owned club, Exeter City are looked at lovingly by those who work in this area. Any fans' groups who are interested in hearing everything there is to know about community ownership should look no further as the folks at Exeter City are always very willing to help. Their knowledge and expertise is something I really enjoyed learning from when I discussed what we were doing with Thistle for Ever.

### Portsmouth FC – In and Out

As we have seen in Chapter 5, one of the most compelling, yet distressing, football stories of the last 20 years has been the long and winding road for Pompey to fan ownership. It is fair to say that the supporters of this iconic club have been taken to hell and back by a succession of unscrupulous investors and it was no surprise that they took to community ownership as an alternative solution. Following the financial shambles that took the club to the very brink and back, Portsmouth became the biggest fan-owned club in the United Kingdom.

To get a better understanding of how it evolved and what happened next, I spoke at length to long-term SFSA follower Colin Farmery who was the Communications Director and a member of the supporters' trust and then the club board. I was particularly interested in why after a few years they decided to sell the club to an investor. Colin explained,

> Given the circumstances there is no doubt that community ownership was a huge success at Pompey. The heart and soul had been ripped out of the club by people who didn't care about anything other than making money and having the power of owning a football club. Putting Portsmouth FC back in the community with its supporters made perfect sense as it allowed everyone to love and cherish this special club again. There was a fantastic spirit of everyone working together for the greater good of the club we all love.

So the question I then posed was: Was community ownership a success or a failure? Colin suggested it was very much a success.

> I would suggest that there will be few people who feel that community ownership at Portsmouth didn't work. One of the shining lights in this experience was in seeing that, for the first time in decades, there was openness and transparency at the club after seasons of turmoil and distress. It was a huge success that over four years the club operated debt-free on a breakeven basis. It brought us back onto an even keel and reconnected the club with the city. It was not without its challenges, one of which was that the initial stance of the trust was that it did not want to dilute its 51 per cent shareholding, so attracting inward investment was a challenge, however it was important that the club operated debt-free on a breakeven basis throughout this period.
> The trust never managed to create a sustainable financial model so the opportunities to do what Hearts went on to do or to replicate some of the membership schemes in the likes of Germany or Spain were missed. Despite a promotion, there was a belief that to get to the next level (the Championship) that further investment would be needed given the changing financial dynamics in the Premiership and the Championship. We were competing against some massive budgets.
> Given the size of the club, there was always a stream of suitors calling at Fratton Park. Michael Eisner started talking in late 2016 and by 2017 he put a proposal to buy the club. There was a healthy debate at the time and the two unique parts of the ownership – the Community Shareholders with £1,000 of shares and the Presidents

who had invested up to £50k – both had to agree to the sale. The vote was passed, and ownership changed. However, many of the facets of community ownership remain in place and the club and owner have a respectful partnership. The view from the Pompey faithful is that Eisner is as good an owner as they could hope for. Of course, what the story can't say is what might happen after Eisner. For the sake of the Portsmouth fans, we do hope for a positive outcome from that scenario.

### Heart of Midlothian and the Foundation of Hearts

Foundation of Hearts (FoH) membership numbers remain around the 8,000 mark, ensuring it remains the biggest fan-driven movement in Scottish football history. They will own the club on behalf of supporters in the not-too-distant future. In June 2020, the club had just dismissed an approach from Foster Gillett, son of the former Liverpool owner George, who was interested in 'investing' in Hearts. This came at the time when the club was in the final throes of seeing the transfer of shares from the FoH benefactor Ann Budge only halted due to the impact of the pandemic. The approach in itself was not a surprise as 'investors' are always looking for a project, however it showed so little respect for the amazing work done by Hearts fans over the past five years. Having done so much to secure and stabilise the club, why would they just give control away to someone who is just passing through? Hearts, like so many of the community-owned clubs, have set a pretty high threshold where 75 per cent of the owners would need to agree to any sale. They, as many others, have found out that the grass is not necessarily any greener when someone with no connection with the club or the city rolls up offering investment.

The FoH have done superbly well by raising £10m of donations to date of which £3m has gone towards the cost of Tynecastle's £22m redevelopment project which includes the new main stand. Another £2.5m was used to repay Budge's initial investment to gain control of the Edinburgh club, and the remaining £4.5m has been used as working capital by Hearts.

Hearts fans so loved Budge that she has become a feature on the Board at Tynecastle and her decision to retire late in 2025 was greeted with a resounding outpouring of thanks from the vast majority of fans who recognised just what Ann did for the club.

## St Mirren – At The Second Time of Asking

My first involvement with St Mirren fans was when I was at Supporters Direct (SD). St Mirren Independent Supporters Association (SMISA), the Saints Trust, had backed a breakaway movement from the organisation called Fans First as several members of the SD Scottish Council decided that an independent fans' organisation was preferred to what the English-run SD could offer. After I was appointed, I met with Wullie Bell of SMISA on several occasions to try and bring them back into membership at SD. Wullie was adamant that his members would have nothing to do with SD due to the governance structure that it had and the fact that we had Richard Atkinson acting as an advisor for us on community ownership. It is fair to say that Wullie was no fan of Richard, who he saw as an outsider, sitting on his club board. I understood where he was coming from on the SD structural position but there was little I could do to alter that. However, I was confused by his disapproval of Richard who I knew was a huge supporter of the community-driven concept.

Richard had called me not long after my appointment at SD to have a chat about community ownership and to explain his background in football. He explained that he ended up on the board of St Mirren FC and prior to this the closest he had ever been to the club was the long stay car park at Glasgow Airport. He got involved with the idea of community ownership having helped look at the transfer of assets for some minority sports clubs and he firmly believed that these 'assets' should in fact be community-owned. So, when he offered to help me at SD, his motivation had nothing to do with football, it was to do with the belief that actually, the community should control its own destiny. Football was this great big 'thing' loved by the community it is based in and would it not make much more sense if the people who are providing all the money through the door, either in season tickets, on sales or hospitality or paying their TV companies subscription, be part of its management? Richard really had the community ownership bug and was a vital ally during my tenure at SD. His belief was that the whole game would benefit if supporters actually had transparent access and proper engagement with the club that they love.

Richard was well connected through his business at the Maxi Group of companies which allowed him the opportunity to indulge his passion. St Mirren were, like many of Scotland's clubs, a club in which a group of wealthier fans had invested. In this instance, the club was debt-free and had sold the decaying park at Love Street and managed to relocate to a modern new stadium just along the road. At St Mirren, he started a process which lasted three years and saw him convince a sceptical board led by Stewart

Gilmour towards community ownership and eventually Richard joined the board of the club. He said he gave himself six months to step in and see if this worked and it led to the creation of a campaign called '10,000 Hours'.

I remember at a Rangers First meeting when we were talking about Richard's background he pre-warned the rammed audience at the Louden Tavern that if they were Googling him and 10,000 Hours, they would find all sorts of good stuff and all sorts of bad stuff because that is just the 'internet' for you. There is no doubt that 10,000 Hours was significant, and it undoubtedly paved the way to the more recent success that has seen the club move towards a guarantee of community ownership; indeed, both Gordon Scott and Tony Fitzpatrick were on board right from the start. The difficulty that Richard faced was that he had agreed the deal to buy the club, in principle, at around £2 million, which probably overvalued the club given that the majority shareholding had been available for sale for several years with very few credible buyers in sight. There was also a political issue in that SMISA just didn't take to Richard. I don't know if it was his Equestrian and Bible Society background or if it was just not steeped in black and white. There is no doubt that Richard was an innovator, but he was not helped by pursuing a path where he felt that a Community Interest Company (CIC) would be able to easily get grants to fund the purchase. Trawling through the archives you will also find that the fans were sceptical and that was partly due to the complex financial structures, taking on debt to buy the club and probably more than anything not having any input prior to the launch of the scheme. As a marketer, I have always believed that the best campaigns are the simplest and are helped if it 'does what it says on the tin'. Sadly for this campaign, the 10,000 Hours name needed an explanation before you even started; in fact, to this day I am still in the dark as to why it was chosen. If it had been called Buy the Buddies or Buy the Saints, it would have helped. Despite that, what Richard did achieve was significant as it was the first step to developing a monthly membership levy from fans and in looking to utilise a CIC to lock in the assets of the club.

When it launched, the target to be reached was £2m so, in other words, the deal they had done to buy the clubs was going to cost £2m and there was little wriggle room. At that Rangers First meeting, he explained:

There was then a long series of problems, it was myself and another guy, none of us had any relationship with the club or the supporter base which, to be honest, was always going to be a problem. I kept getting questions put to me about 'what was in it for me'. That is, however, just football fans. Someone stands up who thinks he knows and states 'wait a minute, you have an agenda'. No matter how I described myself, stating that I did not have an agenda, I did not want to run the club, I didn't even want to be on the board. I think in the nearly three years I was on the board of a football club, I think I went to 20 games or so.

He was always getting abuse about never being at football matches because his main job was of course during the week trying to raise capital and raise interest for a fans' subscription scheme.

The old adage about having to break eggs to make a omelette came to mind as Richard walked a tightrope between the boardroom and the supporters' clubs. Yet despite that challenge, there were enough Buddies willing to go for it, in fact, 1,007 people pledged £13.50 per month. What was remarkable was, despite Wullie Bell and SMISA not backing it, 1,007 people engaged with the project enough to pledge money to the team they loved. It was significant as there was no underlying issue at the club. The board were popular, they had no debt, a brand-new stadium and were doing well enough on the park. There was no crisis, no Pars or Jambos implosion. Yet Richard and his colleagues came from the 'outside', came together and managed to persuade 1,007 people to give an average of £13.50 per month to buy the club. There were of course significant humps and bumps but an offer of £1.25m was eventually made to buy the club. At the end of the day, that offer was rejected. It was their club to sell, and they wanted a bit more than that. Offering the £2m in the first place hindered the campaign, failing to find social enterprise funds that would provide a loan restricted the income as did the failure to engage the majority of the fan base in having a unifying leader at the helm of an easy-to-understand campaign. But not all was lost, and I jousted with Stewart Gilmour on several occasions over the years about whether the model could ever work, and I always reminded him that 1,007 St Mirren fans could generate significant revenue that would allow him to exit secure in the knowledge that he had left it in the hands of the people of Paisley who love the club more than anyone else.

Having started something significant by opening the door to the concept, Stewart set in motion a chain of events that sees the Buddies well on the way to becoming one of our next fully community-owned clubs. Again, as we have seen across these chapters, the joy of community ownership is the flexibility and scope to adapt to different situations at different times at different clubs. In the first instance, a former Saints Director Gordon Scott stepped in to pay off Stewart Gilmour and his fellow shareholders who wanted an exit strategy. The plans mirrored Ann Budge at Hearts and Les Hutcheon at Motherwell where they put the money up and ran the club until the fans could pay them back. In the Saints' case, it was meant to be ten years, until another unique development occurred in early 2020 when it was announced that St Mirren could become Scotland's latest fan-owned football club as soon as next year if new plans were announced.

Under the plans, the St Mirren Independent Supporters Trust (SMISA) would enter a unique partnership with a local social care charity called Kibble, which will eventually transform how the club is owned and run. SMISA is already on track for majority fan ownership of the club but is not due to buy out current owner Gordon Scott until 2026. Under the new plans, Kibble would buy 27.5 per cent of Scott's shares, with SMISA then taking its own stake to 51 per cent before the end of 2021. It was believed that no league team in the UK was owned and run in partnership with a major charity in the way that this deal was structured. This was a hugely significant step forward taking community ownership into a completely new territory with this compelling partnership. It was the type of development that Richard Atkinson had been looking for in his campaign but could not find due to the market not being that well developed or understood.

Kibble, based in Paisley since 1840, brought its commercial experience to St Mirren, helping bring in new income to be reinvested in the team, while working with the club to create new training and employment options for the young people in their care. It was a no-brainer for the fans' organisation and SMISA's 1,200 members were asked to vote on whether to accept the new proposals. At the launch of the proposal, SMISA chair and Paisley MSP George Adam said: 'St Mirren's place at the heart of life in the town is precious. We created the Buy The Buds campaign back in 2016 because we knew there could be no one better to safeguard that than the people who will care for it most – the fans.'

Of course, fan ownership is not as easy as running a club as a dictatorship and it often leads to issues on committees and boards and there has been a fair bit of churn at SMISA over the past few years with lots of resignations. Most recently, that old warrior Stewart Gilmour emerged as an unlikely candidate who I do hope can bring it some well-deserved stability. It certainly is a unique proposition and as far as we know they are the only professional football club in Europe that has a partnership between the team supporters and a charity. I am sure it will prove a success and others will look at the benefits of having a well respected charity that has shared values with the club offering an alternative ownership model.

# COMMUNITY OWNERSHIP AS A VIABLE OPTION

### *Motherwell FC – A Club Induced Plan Needed Fixed*

When I first encountered the Motherwell attempts at community ownership, I have to admit that I was confused and disappointed at what I was seeing. I am very proud of having played a small part in changing the direction at Motherwell who, I can now say, are in my opinion the exemplar of the best that community ownership can offer. It was certainly not always the case.

Having been funded by the Scottish Government to help clubs in distress and to help fans' groups, I introduced myself to the club then run by Leeann Dempster in later 2012 or early 2013. I had anticipated that The Well would have been very interested in picking my brains given the high-profile nature of what I had achieved at Stirling Albion and was starting to do elsewhere. I was of course curious to find out what the Well Society was about and what its aims and objectives were. I had found the initial web offering and prospectus confusing and lacking the thing that fans needed to see which was an end game. I was pushed to have the meeting by my brother-in-law who lectured in economics for many a year and was a Well fan. He had at that stage not committed as he couldn't understand what the plan was, so maybe I could find out.

As an advisor in this new landscape, it was not my place to criticise but in the first couple of meetings the club were very defensive as I started to deconstruct the offer that was being made. I did eventually leave happy in the knowledge that John Boyle was *gifting* the club to the fans once he was happy that they had £1m in the bank and thus would be secure and sustainable. Of course, it turned out that the initial Well Society was a bit of a mess as it was created by the club to facilitate the sale of the club to the fans. It was never to be a gift. It never said this anywhere in the documentation and was a very different concept than the club being gifted to the fans.

The Well Society went through the wringer as Dempster departed to oversee another failed fans' buy-out at Hibs and Boyle threatened to withdraw his support to sell to the fans. The Well Society had a cracking team of fans drawn from the very top of business and knew they had to get rid of Boyle as soon as they could or risk the last three or four years of work being in vain. They also had a fear of who might buy the club given that Boyle was seemingly getting more desperate for the cash. They did see Boyle exit by paying him off with funds from another benefactor Les Hutcheon and set about reforming the society and creating a pathway to community ownership. The Well Society was reformed and as it set about representing fans and delivering the ownership mission it got to the point that Les Hutcheon was able to be paid off and regular monthly payments and a growing membership eventually derived democracy. The two main lessons for community ownership to be learned from this was that it is far better if the fans' organisation is created by the fans for the fans and not by the clubs, as in doing so it will always be conflicted. Secondly, if a benefactor wants to sell to the fans, be honest open and transparent and work with the fans and don't threaten them.

My brother-in-law Pat did eventually join the Well Society and still contributes to this day. For me, it was a privilege to help and be a small part of that story and I am always welcomed at the club which is a really nice feeling.

In later 2023 the club board went on a fishing expedition, even asking Taylor Swift on social media to consider The Well. They were looking for inward investment but when another American suitor in the shape of Erik Barmack came calling, they withdrew their offer of investment in Motherwell, citing fears over the proposal creating 'significant divisions within the fanbase'. Members of the Well Society, the club's majority shareholder, were midway through a two-week voting period on the proposal, with the board of the fans' group opposing the move. However, the board of the Fir Park club had endorsed working with the former Netflix vice-president and his wife. The US-based couple had proposed spending £1.95m over a six-year period, with the offer contingent on the Well Society contributing £1.85m over the same time. Inward investement in a fan-owned club can be achieved but in this case the dilution of the fans' ownership failed to deliver a compelling argument as it seriously undervalued the club which was in real danger of ceding control for some cash and a promise.

## Stenhousemuir FC and the Community Interest Company

Stenhousemuir Football Club has adopted a new approach to running a football club and became a Community Interest Company (CIC). It is the first football club in the main leagues of Scotland and England to do this. The main reason for the club going down this route was to ensure that through the asset lock that they protected the club for future generations. As we have seen across the football world there are many opportunists who are only too happy to prey on vulnerable clubs and those in the know in Larbert wanted to ensure The Warriors were there for future generations.

Stenhousemuir Football Club plays in the Second Division of the Scottish leagues and was established in 1884. It started as a club for members but like many football clubs, it eventually converted to a limited liability company with a wide spread of owners. Over the years there became a wide spread of passive or deceased shareholders with no dominant force. This position left it exposed to being taken over by people who did not have the best interests of the club at heart and could cause problems of the type well known in modern-day football in the UK. The action to move to become the first CIC was inspired and ahead of its time.

Stenhousemuir has always considered itself to be a community club and has built its community work up over recent years. It provides facilities for community activities such as football coaching to the schools in the area, midnight leagues for youngsters on Friday and Saturday evenings, soccer camps during the school holidays, etc. They have 16 youth teams with two full-time and about 40 volunteer coaches to coach them. The use of two five-a-side pitches and the installation of a FIFA-recommended synthetic turf on the main pitch has allowed large numbers of the community to hire and use these top-class football facilities.

In recent years it has had a successful membership drive where shares in the CIC were purchased, taking the current shareholders to over 500. In simple terms, the club is a Community Enterprise that operates as a football club. To become a shareholder it costs £37.50 and the person's name will be entered in the Companies House (Scotland) register of shareholders. A share is for life and can be transferred to another person any time you specify. The directors of the club proactively encourage supporters to purchase a share or shares, as they genuinely believe that that is the best way forward for the club, enabling it to thrive and prosper now and in the future, knowing that it is in the safe hands of its supporters.

Since the club became a CIC, more and more supporters have taken the opportunity to become shareholders, and now have a voice in how the club is run. If you own a share or shares in the club, you can have your say in how it's run, and in addition also have access to the club's AGM and a pathway to the boardroom.

## Protest Clubs Prove a Point

### *AFC Wimbledon – Nobody Cared About Them*

The story of AFC Wimbledon is both one of the most horrifying and inspiring in British football history. Wimbledon FC spent the majority of their history in English non-league, before an incredible rise up the footballing leagues during the late 20th century. They originally joined the Football League before the pyramid was established. They were elected, in preference to Workington and the journey climaxed in them beating a world-class Liverpool side at

Wembley to win the 1988 FA Cup. It was the archetypal David and Goliath story on the back of the rags to riches climb from nowhere.

However, they would never reach the same heights again. The club was forced out of their historical home Plough Lane as the redevelopment required by law was unviable. This caused the club to ground share with Crystal Palace, seeing a fall in attendances and subsequently financial difficulties as the owners were looking at an exit strategy. In 2002, it was announced that the club was being moved 60 miles away from Wimbledon to Milton Keynes to become part of the newly built town's continuing development. Outraged that their club was being taken from them, Wimbledon FC's supporters decided the only option was to start a new club from scratch, which would follow in the original club's footsteps in working its way up the ladder from non-league. The fact they managed to do so is a huge testament to the resolve and commitment of the fans. If you want to read about the love of football, then I do recommend you read some more about this fantastic journey; it really is inspiring.

The new club, named AFC Wimbledon is majority-owned by The Dons Trust who are committed to own at least 75 per cent of the club. The Dons Trust, which is fully democratic, operated a one member one vote policy and had over 750 members by the time AFC Wimbledon played their first game. The club has been a real success story since then. Between February 2003 and December 2004, they went an English record 78 league games unbeaten. The success continued and their membership has grown to over 4,000, with the club rising from the ninth tier of English football to the third tier – the same division as the old Wimbledon, now named MK Dons. AFC Wimbledon's rise has been incredibly remarkable, however, it is far from over. The club have now moved into their own newly built 9,000-seater stadium, with an option to extend to 20,000. The new ground is located 250 yards from the old Plough Lane – after almost three decades away from Wimbledon, the Dons are heading home, and football is all the better for having them back.

### FC United of Manchester – An Anti-Glazer Movement

FC United of Manchester were founded in 2005 by disgruntled Manchester United fans who were unhappy with the club's increasing commercialism. There had been talk of starting a 'new Manchester United' since the '90s, however for many the Glazers takeover proved the final straw. Although Manchester United still exists, FC United supporters will still claim to be a phoenix club on the belief that their version of Manchester United died some time ago.

After suggestions by a leading Manchester United fanzine called *Red*

*Issue*, public meetings were held regarding the formation of a new club and FC United of Manchester quickly became a reality. After one day, the new club had over 4,000 individual pledgers and £100,000 in the bank. The club now has over 5,000 paying and voting members, that makes them one of the UK's largest fan-owned clubs at the time of writing, by measure of number of individual members.

After ground sharing with nearby Bury, the club finally opened their new stadium in 2015, after receiving charitable and governmental grants as well as significant investment from members. They currently play in the seventh tier of English football, despite having made a fleeting appearance in the national league. Operating as a Community Benefit Society, the club's constitution commits them to democracy, being a non-profit and avoiding 'outright commercialism'. This is encapsulated nicely by their slogan 'our club, our rules'. Members are required to pay only a minimum of £15 for adults and £3 for children. Even if a member wishes to contribute more financially, the constitution still only allows one share and one vote per individual. The story has not been without its controversy. In 2016, the board called an EGM and offered to resign, all prompted by claims by members that the club was no longer being run as a members' organisation. Key founding figures like Adam Brown and Andy Walsh stepped down. Many felt that the board had been left to their own devices and that a rebalancing had to take place. The good news is that the club emerged from the crisis and is now back on an even keel. They won promotion to Step 3 (top division of the Northern Premier League) in 2008. Since then, they have spent just four seasons at Step 2 (National League North). Given their large crowds, there is an argument to say that they have significantly underachieved in playing terms.

### FC City of Liverpool – Different from the Expensive Corporate World

FC City of Liverpool were formed in 2015 by disgruntled supporters from both Everton and Liverpool. They were tired of what watching Premier League football had become and wanted to support a team that expressed their Liverpudlian identity, while also encapsulating what they believed football should be like – football for the community by the community.

The club is not a protest club as such but was designed to provide a footballing alternative to the city's two topflight clubs. This is shown in their choice to wear the colour purple – what you get if you mix red and blue. A registered Community Benefit Society, they are committed to having strong community ties and grassroots football. After their formation but before they had signed any players or even a manager, the club had over 500 paying members at their launch showing that there was a real appetite for what they were offering. Despite having yet to settle at a permanent home, the club has won numerous promotions as they continue their quest to reach the national league, the top division in English non-league football. The club has grown to having around 1,500 members, with memberships now costing £60 annually for adults and £1 for under 16s. Regardless of financial contribution, each individual is limited to one share and one vote, to ensure democracy.

## Moving On

What has been exciting for me to watch is to see how, despite the best efforts of some of the people who thought they knew best or were politically motivated, Scottish football has embraced community ownership. There are developments at a whole range of football clubs that are changing the football landscape. Now we have started to see a return to the clubs being owned by communities rather than corporations or wealthy benefactors – who can have a very different level of benevolence based on their own objectives. The movement has got such traction that we no longer have to wait to have a crisis at a club to see it become supporter-owned, now boards are looking at using the biggest asset they have – the supporters – to provide a long-term sustainable future for the club. Long may that continue.

CHAPTER 12

# Community Ownership in Scotland – the Inside Story

*There is no power for change greater than a community discovering what it cares about. – Margaret J Wheatley*

## The Implosion Gives Fans a Voice That Is Soon Silenced

### The fans revolt

IT IS HARD to recall all the ins and outs of what actually happened during the Rangers crash in early 2012 but what we do know is that there was a five-way agreement called between the SFA, SPL, SFL, Rangers FC in administration and Sevco, the new entity that was designed to allow Rangers to receive a slap on the wrist and be invited back into the Premiership almost as if nothing had happened. An immediate PR campaign was developed by the SPL and the SFA which claimed that the topflight without Rangers would spell Armageddon for our game. If you opened the front door at Hampden Park at this time, a river of negativity seeped from under just about every door on the sixth floor. It was a strategy that came back to haunt them. Self-interest is, of course, one of the main drivers of these members' organisations.

In a typical approach to the problem, Stewart Milne at Aberdeen suggested that a sensible way out of the crisis was a Premier League of ten clubs, guaranteeing his team four games against Celtic and Rangers. The fans had other ideas and the influential Dons Supporters Together responded by countering his suggestion and giving a different perspective. They said:

> The overwhelming opinion of supporters in Scotland is that any newcomer should enter senior football by applying to the SFL for admission to the bottom tier of Scottish football and working their way up in an honest way. Rangers, like all other clubs must be seen to comply with the rules and honour their debts otherwise why

should fans ever bother to turn up again knowing that the league is permanently rigged in their favour.

It was a powerful message. If it was any other club then they would have to start at the bottom so why should Rangers be treated any differently? If a club is deemed to have 'cheated' by spending money they didn't have, ends up in liquidation, then is replaced by a phoenix side, the only place for it to start again is at the bottom. That message that was delivered to Milne was accompanied by the threat to boycott purchasing season tickets. With over 50 per cent of revenue coming from the supporters coming through the turnstiles, Milne had to take the threat seriously. What happened at Aberdeen was repeated across the country with fans at most clubs threatening a season ticket boycott. The timing of the demise of Rangers was perfect in the sense that it happened just before the sale of season ticket books started. For the first time in history, the ordinary supporter wielded some power and the campaigns at individual clubs had a collective purpose. One of the reasons this had never happened before was that fans operate in individual silos and, like the teams that they follow, they are really competing against each other. And remember there was no national fans' organisation to help them at that stage.

The whole scenario led to the biggest implosion that Scottish football had ever seen with clubs and fans calling for the heads of Mr Doncaster and Mr Regan. They totally misjudged the situation that they faced and built up the myth that without Rangers in the topflight Scottish football would face a 'slow lingering death'. Even at the 11th hour it was reported that Regan was working on a plan for Rangers, by then under the command of Charles Green, to start in the First Division (Championship) rather than sending them to start at the very bottom of the pile. Many of the clubs were furious and Livingston called for vote of no confidence in Regan and Cowdenbeath, Dunfermline Athletic and Queen of the South all came out with strong comments disapproving of their leaders. What they misjudged was that Scottish football wanted sporting integrity more than it wanted to exploit the economic value of Rangers fans that had already been taken to hell and faced a long climb back.

*Time to call the Government*

When asked by the SFA and SPFL to help secure much needed commercial revenue the Scottish Government released a statement that suggested that 'Once the Scottish football authorities decide on a course of action, and demonstrate a willingness for reform, the government aims to influence the process to ensure favourable outcomes for sponsors.'

The Government had full inboxes and sacks full of letters from frustrated fans (voters), as had most of the MSPs, calling for reform of our game and for some action. These were unique times and one of the aspects that Donnie Jack, the senior civil servant responsible for Sport and his team were starting to understand was that there was no one organisation that represented the ordinary football supporter. By coincidence, I was consulting for a company he was talking to as part of his remit with Sports Scotland. The London-based Supporters Direct had departed the scene in Scotland as nobody would pay for them doing what little they did. They were sniffing around the Scottish football car crash hoping for some financial crumbs from Holyrood that might bring them back. There was genuine interest in my working with the Scottish Government to help the 'fan problem'. Unable to employ me directly as a consultant they decided to utilise the SD structure to get things moving fast. It wasn't really the response that Hampden Park had anticipated from the Scottish Government as they were used to the silence of fans rather than them being enabled.

Right from the start I saw this as a real opportunity to build something of substance for Scottish football fans. Football fans had, for the first time in history, united to get a message across to football that they were not to be ignored. This was a moment of opportunity to build on that momentum. To me, the movement started by The Dons Supporters Together was inspiring and gave hope that a proper national fans' organisation could emerge to give fans a voice. Given that we had funding from the Scottish Government to do it, how could we fail?

*A less than warm welcome at Hampden Park*

The football authorities saw it differently. This was a fall out from the Armageddon period and Scottish football had 140 years of no supporter voice but the Scottish Government had funded me via Supporters Direct Scotland so they had to be seen to go along with it. Of course, having been the face of fan-owned Stirling Albion for nearly two years, they knew who I was and that I wanted Scottish football to do things differently. At my first meeting at Hampden Park, the three CEOs of the SFA, SPL and SFL were gathered at the request of the Scottish Government. David Longmuir had sat down during the presentation but Messrs Doncaster and Regan stood leaning against the window sill in the SFA boardroom for the whole presentation. Only David Longmuir showed any real interest. It felt like they really resented having to give up their time to be there. When I finished, I asked for questions and was a bit surprised to hear a CEO say quite brazenly 'So why should I ever listen to fans?' I retorted that if he were the CEO of any other business organisation on the planet and decided to ignore his customers he would get the sack.

For me it was about making them realise that they could not get away with ignoring the fans. At that time I still had the confidence and the belief that I could make them see things differently, after all, I was backed by our Government so what could go wrong?

Of course, as I was to find out later on this journey, they had all the power and I had virtually no support from either SD in London or from the Scottish Government. Instead, it was like having to step into the ring to face a rather agitated Tyson Fury with your hands tied behind your back and no trainer in your corner. My face was going to get bloodied.

## A game of politics

I started work in July 2012 and quickly discovered that what I had inherited at SDS was an organisation that had closed its doors for two reasons. Firstly, there was no money, no sponsors and no brand equity to talk of and what I had not known was there had been a massive split in the organisation. SDS was made up of supporters' trusts who all paid £50 a year to be part of the co-operative. There were no individual members, just the trusts. At the time that SDS had closed its doors, apart from a lack of funding, supporters' groups at Clydebank, Dumbarton, Berwick Rangers, Aberdeen and Rangers and a few others had tried to make the organisation a properly constituted Scottish body run from Scotland by Scots. In the London HQ, this was not very popular as SD wanted to expand and have lots of different European fans' organisations all feeding back into the mother ship. They had created SD Europe for this purpose and losing Scotland from the empire was not part of the plan. Neither SD in London nor the Scottish Government had, at any stage, understood the growing antagonism towards us not having an independent supporters' organisation that was actually Scottish!

I was very comfortable using my experience and voice in the media that I had built upon from my Stirling Albion days to get us a say on everything that was going on. It started with the merger of the leagues and through our PR agency's hard efforts we ensured that as soon as the word fan was mentioned in football we got a say on issues, large and small. Invariably, it caused conflict as I was trying to run a fans' organisation with teeth and the football authorities and the Government wanted a passive nod to fans' affairs, just like the way SDS continues to be today. Within the first six months, I had been warned three times by the civil servants that the football authorities were not happy as I was being too critical. It could be anything as simple as making a comment on the timings of cup fixtures or ticket prices for a Scotland International, where I would gauge public opinion and raise concerns. The role of the organisation was meant to be positioned as a 'critical friend' to the football authorities but sadly, from day one it was only allowed to be a friend. I of course refused to play that game as I firmly believed that if you are going to do things you have to do it right.

The Scottish Government made it quite clear after the Rangers crisis that football clubs going into administration was the last thing they wanted to see. They found football and its inability to look after its own financial affairs embarrassing to Scotland and wanted to avoid any further clubs crashing. Sadly they could do no more than hope.

Over the course of the next two years, I worked as a Scottish Government *insider* successfully at Heart of Midlothian, Dunfermline Athletic and Motherwell, and unsuccessfully at Ayr United, Dundee, Kilmarnock, Hibs and a few others. With no support from Hampden Park and a role that had never been explained to the wider public, it was always going to be a challenge to do the best for fans. None of these jobs were without incident or difficulty, but that is probably another book. Here is just a glimpse of the action.

## That Sinking Feeling

### *Dunfermline Athletic FC – 'Masterton OUT'*

My first major threat came at the Pars where the former Governor of the Bank of Scotland, Gavin Masterton, had over 90 per cent shares in the club and was running out of money. He needed a share issue to raise £500,000 to keep the club afloat. Masterton was incredibly well connected politically and having adapted the Heart of Midlothian share prospectus that cost the Hearts fans £1m he wanted me and of course the Government-backed SDS to endorse his scheme. By this time I had already spoken out a couple of times at fans' events warning about the dangers of such an offer. The club was on virtually the last throw of the dice and they made the offer of giving fans 5 per cent of the club and a couple of seats on the board.

Mr Masterton was holding an investors seminar and I was to be the star speaker to support and endorse his offer. I refused to do so and was immediately called to East End Park the next day, where I was to meet with Masterton, Before the meeting a Senior Civil Servant told me, before the owner appeared in the boardroom, that unless I backed the plan it could threaten my funding, i.e. my job. This was a level of politics that I have never experienced before and was a very concerning development. However, I stood firm and refused to be bullied, believing in what I was doing.

I refused to see the Pars fans be turned over. I was proud to help Ross McArthur and his team and the fans out of administration. I am so proud to say that even to this day I am welcomed at East End Park with open arms anytime I visit.

### Kilmarnock FC – 'Johnston OUT'

Michael Johnston bought the club for £1 and it had around £10m of debt attached to it. He was attracted to what I had been involved in at Dunfermline Athletic as, through the administration event, the Bank of Scotland wrote off many millions of pounds of debt on East End Park (partly due to the club being saved for the community). I was summoned down to Rugby Park and had several meetings with Mr Johnston who had created a vision for what he called a Community Engagement Board. It had no power, no shares and no purpose that I could see. At this time the main Killie board only had him on it and the fans were rebelling against him. I of course refused to back his scheme (he also wanted me to provide the confidential documents pertaining to the Dunfermline Athletic deal). I refused, but unlike Mr Masterton at Dunfermline, Mr Johnston went public on the fact I was backing his scheme. When I demanded a retraction he eventually did so but leaned over the table and told me that I should worry for my job. A few weeks later one of his MSP allies contacted Shona Robison the Sports Minister and I was called in for a kicking. In fairness, unless you were a Killie or Pars fan you wouldn't have got the nuances of what was going on. It was just a gentle kicking and, despite the complaints stacking up, I was not too worried as I felt that the Scottish Government would see I was doing the right thing for the fans. Wouldn't they? How wrong I was.

### Hibernian FC – 'Petrie OUT'

If there was ever a competition to find the least popular club chairman, the most recent President of the SFA would be right up there. The fans had had enough of his management over many years and had started a Petrie Out campaign which was led by former journalist Simon Pia and former club midfielder Paul Kane. I was not involved in the campaign but was asked to come and talk about the prospect of community ownership at Hibs. Given what had happened at Hearts it seemed a real prospect. There was a real appetite for this and in no time the BuyHibs campaign had nearly 6,000 fans doing surveys and pledging funds to the fledgling organisation. Unfortunately, Mr Petrie did not like this as it didn't suit his agenda. Leeann Dempster was brought in as chief executive and the Hibs Supporters Limited (HSL) was originated to kill off the fans' scheme. I and many Hibs fans were sceptical about the scheme which was not a 'by fans for fans' development; instead, it was given to them as a club plan. Of course, history has shown that Mr Farmer had no intention of selling the club to the fans anyway but what it did do was get the troops back in order and gave Mr Petrie control of the fan ownership narrative.

### SDS – 'Goodwin OUT'

Sitting in my office in Stirling, I got a joint letter from Mr Doncaster and Mr Regan telling me that they were advising my Head Office in London and the Scottish Government that they were withdrawing support for the organisation (me), which they obviously knew would kill my funding and of course put me out of work. There were about six or seven 'concerns'. With the help of my trusted PR Guru, I sent a robust response giving my version of events to what I would call trumped-up charges about nothing. I also went to see the senior civil servant who I was sure would back me (they had detailed monthly reports on every meeting I had attended). By now, fans, and me in particular, were just becoming a problem. With no accountability, no transparency and someone who had previously run a fan-owned club and believed in fans having a say, it was getting worse than awkward. The only solution they saw was for me to apologise to the SFA and SPFL and tell them I wouldn't upset club chairmen again.

Obviously that was never going to happen as you can't protect fans' rights and be subservient. I was also being put under pressure from the London HQ of SD. Their CEO (a new fellow who when I asked him a few months previously who he supported had told me football was not really his thing as he was into choirs – a stonking appointment obviously) made his way to Hampden to listen to the concerns. It was quite clear that the plan was to get me out of the way and SDS would have a nice comfortable relationship at Hampden. It is a relationship built on a complete lack of integrity that endures to this day, as SDS love proclaiming that they are the official recognised organisation endorsed by the SFA and SPFL. Apart from clinging on to that Hampden Park relationship, the organisation has not done much at all since I departed.

I thought about staying to fight it but with no resources and being backed into a corner there was only one way I could see a victory and that was to get clear of what my lawyer called corporate bullying and set up an independent fans' organisation that didn't think money was more important than integrity.

I had to accept golden handcuffs just to claim the four months' salary that would have taken me to the end of my contract. What I couldn't get my head around was that the SFA/SPFL were now funding a London-based fans' organisation and over the next two years the money flew into the Supporters Direct coffers. I have been and shared coffees and chats with all those involved over the years as it was 'just politics and you have to move on'. Whilst the SFA spin doctor Darryl Broadfoot was saying positive things to me, press were getting some bizarre stories about my departure. Even in late 2023 one of my SFSA colleagues, who was new to the organisation, was told to sit away from me by some club representatives because I was 'toxic'. When asked why I was toxic there were no examples given.

However, I will never forgive those at Supporters Direct who were supposed to be a fans' organisation. Everything I did was professional and documented and my reward was that they met with the Hampden Park crew once and decided that the correct course of action was to threaten me with disciplinary action rather than sticking up for all the fans that I had helped along the way. To this day they have stuck to the narrative that I was the problem and even the new Scottish version of the organisation never dares criticise Hampden Park about anything. Hang your heads in shame.

## What Is It Really All About? – Community Ownership

The day after I got the letter telling me that the SFA/SPFL were withdrawing support for me, I sent Stewart Regan a text message appealing to him to meet and work a way through it. I felt I was being hung out to dry and had a robust defence for all that was being said. In his response, he told me,

> I have tried to maintain a supportive position over the last few months. However the feeling is that your agenda of fan ownership has been pushed without the involvement or support of the clubs and league body. This has caused real dissatisfaction and has led to the issue of the letter. You are aware of the PGB concerns and regrettably the feeling is that you are leading the organisation down this route.

We had always seemed to have an excellent working relationship with the SFA, so this was deeply disappointing to hear.

As we have seen in previous chapters, there were people in positions of power in our game who saw any structural change in the game as dangerous. Fans running clubs means a different type of person in charge and that has the potential to impact the whole game. As former Head of Communications at the SFA Darryl Broadfoot said to me after my departure from Supporters Direct, 'It's just politics and you are collateral damage, they don't want change, they don't want community ownership and they don't want fans like you trying to change things'. Not much comfort when you have been forced out of your job when trying to help fans at Kilmarnock and Hibernian buy their club or prevent fans at Dunfermline from being sold a pup.

## What Do the SFA and SPFL Really Think About Community Ownership?

As we saw in Chapter 9, the Scottish Government when pressed by the Scottish Green Party decided to ask for consultations on the subject of community ownership and the right for football supporters to buy their clubs. As part of the consultation process, the SFA and SPFL made their objections to community ownership known. Having dispensed with the community ownership champion, the next task they had was to make sure the model was stymied.

The specific concerns they raised were:
- Members (clubs) don't want it
- How do you value a football club?
- Most clubs only have an emotional value not an economic one
- This legislation will reduce the potential inward investment in clubs
- This is interference in the industry that is unjustified and unacceptable

## Down But Not Out – a new fans' organisation is created to work for community ownership and fight for fans' rights

The Scottish Football Supporters Association was established in April 2015 to be an independent voice for fans in Scotland. At the initial meetings with Neil Doncaster of the SPFL and Stewart Regan of the SFA it was said that if the SFSA was to promote and support community ownership then they would be unable to have a relationship with the organisation.

The reality was that it was only six months after they had pushed me out the door, seeing me back again was not really part of their plan. Let's be honest what type of nutter gets pushed out the door and then bounces back to do the same job less the £50k salary six months later. As Mrs G says, I must be mad, or maybe it is a drive to do the right thing for fans? They firmly believed that there was no need to change the industry and where the established conventions were threatened, they wanted to use all their power/influence to try to talk down any proposals. The message was clear in 2015: if your organisation supports community ownership, we can't have a relationship with you. Of course, what made it all the more remarkable to us was that they were funding SDS and the origins of that organisation in England had been community ownership. They had been silenced and if we at the SFSA wanted to have cordial relationships with the SFA and the SPFL we had to withdraw support for the community ownership agenda. All it did was strengthen our resolve to support fans. There were decades that the Kremlin believed that the Berlin Wall would never come down but down it came eventually with a significant crash and the world was never the same again. The same was happening in the football landscape yet football just did not want to see it. Nor did Supporters Direct who took the money, did virtually nothing apart from what they were told to do and decided to go along with the narrative that they still carry today – 'being close to the SFA and SPFL is important to us and Goodwin is a baddie'.

## The Political Map

I remember doing an interview with Gordon Waddell of the *Sunday Mail* who asked me to look ahead and guess how many community-owned clubs there would be in ten years. I predicted that it could be between 15 and 20 by 2025 and nothing I have seen since then has given me any reason to change my mind. In the rest of this chapter we will take a look at just what clubs might be ready for community ownership in the coming years.

Despite all the challenges or hurdles that have been laid in the path of community ownership in Scotland, we have seen the concept grow and become an accepted alternative to the conventional benefactor model. The middle ground of multiple ownership of club shares spread widely was partly historical and intergenerational with the important paper passed down the family line. There is no doubt that a piece of the club is still very important to people to hold and important to have on display on the family wall. Whilst that should always be encouraged so should other seismic changes that have emerged that have made community ownership of football clubs credible.

Of course with every yin there is a yang and it seems to be a very interesting period ahead of us in Scottish football, where opposite but interconnected forces are pulling together.

If we look at it in rather simplistic terms, on a political sphere, at the very same time as the rising left-wing of fans owning and running clubs, we have seen the emergence of the American-led millionaires coming into our clubs and looking to change the market. Let us not forget that these market disturbers led the charge to review the game through the development of the much-anticipated Deloittes report that never saw the light of day. Maybe the early assertions that it would seek to protect their investment and abolish promotion and relegation helped send a torpedo that hit it below the waterline before serious discussions could even start. Certainly, with a more right-wing ownership *in situ*, bringing different concepts and ideas to the game, mostly from the USA, we have to be open to change if it enhances the longer-term health of the game.

The problems I see are that with little or no attachment to the club, its history and its values, there are dangers that a purchase is seen purely as an investment. However, just as football has had to accept the growth of community ownership, so too we must accept these millionaire owners as Scottish football operates as a robust multicultural pluralistic landscape where all people's values and aspirations are respected.

As we saw with the 2019 bid for Partick Thistle, it was partly blocked by the rules that we have in Scotland regarding cross-border ownership. This is a level of protectionism that is held in high regard by some as it protects our clubs and is seen as a very real block to potential predators. I think in the future that is a position that will be seriously challenged to allow future inward investment. It depends on where you sit on the ownership spectrum – will it be great for our game or very dangerous?

It could mean that an organisation such as The City Football Group Limited (CFG) becomes a holding company that administers association football clubs at our clubs. The group is owned by three organisations; of which 81 per cent is majority owned by Newton Investment and Development LLC, 18 per cent by the American firm Silver Lake and 1 per cent by Chinese firms China Media Capital and CITIC Capital.

The group derives its name from Manchester City FC, its flagship football club, and acts as the club's parent company. CFG also owns stakes in clubs in the United States, Australia, India, Japan, Spain, Brazil, Uruguay, China, Belgium, France and Italy.

This, probably more than anything, could be the biggest challenge to the continued growth of community ownership in Scotland.

## Senior Clubs in Community Ownership – Where We Stand

I have defined this as clubs where, through an organisational structure, the supporters' groups have a majority shareholding with articles that protect the shareholding being sold without supporter consent.

- Annan Athletic
- Clyde
- Clydebank
- East Stirlingshire
- Greenock Morton
- Gretna 2008
- Heart of Midlothian
- Motherwell
- Partick Thistle
- St Mirren
- Stenhousemuir
- Stirling Albion

## A Secured Pathway to Community Ownership

I have defined this as clubs where there is an agreement in place that the shares will eventually be transferred over and secured as detailed above. In the case of Greenock Morton or St Mirren, this was when payments had been made by supporters to benefactors. In the case of Partick Thistle, it is when the agreement is accepted by the company that was set up by Colin Weir to buy the club. There will be others who come into this transition phase prior to community ownership. The watchword in these circumstances is patience. It took St Mirren five years to get there and Hearts was of a similar length and for others it can be even longer!

- Partick Thistle *(finally completed August 2023)*

## Unincorporated Clubs Needing an Incentive to Convert to Community Ownership

These are defined as clubs who have origins closer to a bygone era that makes them an easy conversion to community ownership if they so wished. These are clubs that are more akin to a Bowling Club or a Golf Club where members have a say through a voting structure. So, in that sense, are closer to community-owned clubs than clubs who left this model over a hundred years ago to become limited companies. If there are members who are interested in modernising and becoming officially community-owned, they will be easy to convert. The most recent conversion from this type of club was Annan Athletic.

- Brechin City
- Queen's Park
- Stranraer

## Limited Companies with a Wide Shareholding and a Pathway

- Aberdeen – *converted from being a public limited company to a private limited company in late 2019*
- Airdrieonians
- Albion Rovers
- Alloa Athletic
- Arbroath
- Ayr United
- Cove Rangers
- Cowdenbeath
- Dumbarton
- Dundee
- Dundee United
- East Fife – *majority shareholder 53 per cent*
- Edinburgh City
- Elgin City
- Falkirk
- Forfar Athletic
- Hamilton Accies
- Inverness Caledonian Thistle
- Kilmarnock
- Livingston
- Montrose

- Peterhead
- Queen of the South
- Raith Rovers
- Rangers
- Ross County
- St Johnstone – *now a question of a longer-term strategy for when the recent American owner Adam Webb might move on*

## Public Limited Companies

Celtic – wide spread of shares following the Fergus McCann floatation with key majority shares held by Dermot Desmond. Celtic are the only club in Scotland that are listed on the Stock Exchange.

## Exploring the Options for a Range of Scottish Clubs

If we go back to my Gordon Waddell interview in the *Sunday Mail* a few years back, I suggested that a significant number of clubs could end up under community ownership in the years ahead. Below we will select a few of the clubs mentioned above and see how the community ownership prospects might apply to them. Interestingly, from the original article the fans' groups that I was working with at Ayr United, Dundee United and Hibernian were ultimately not to get community ownership but that is not to say that when these owners are looking for a different route to plan an exit, community ownership could again be viable.

## Coming Soon to a Stadium Near You

### *East Fife FC – it takes time*

I have been working with the supporters for about eight years and in March 2024 with the support of the Fans Bank we are now in the position to hopefully conclude a deal with the current owner that would see the club get to a position where it holds around 56 per cent of the shares. We hoped to conclude this deal in the September but sadly we were unable to access any funding from the Fans Bank which currently has no money.

*See Appendix 2 for an example of the fans' business plan.*

## Partick Thistle FC – it takes time

We have reflected on the unique situation that emerged at Partick Thistle elsewhere in this book in what can only be described as a significant game changer for community ownership, not just in Scotland but worldwide. With Thistle embroiled in a boardroom coup and the threat of a sale to a foreign investor, the Euro Millions winner Colin Weir did what nearly every football fan on the planet dreams of – buying the team that you love. The big difference in this case was that Colin didn't want a seat on the board or to run the team; he decided that the fans' group Thistle for Ever who had started a campaign to buy the club for the fans should hold the shares. The story became world news and got mentioned in the USA, South America and in Germany where a fans' group gave Colin Weir an award for his gesture on behalf of all football fans. It appeared as the perfect antidote to the mad world that has seen once loved ordinary clubs such as PSG and Manchester City become the playthings of the rich and famous.

Sadly, the good news story was dramatically stopped in its tracks with the untimely and unexpected passing of Colin. Thistle CEO Gerry Britton said at the time that Partick Thistle will 'build on' the legacy left by Colin Weir after the death of the club owner. Weir acquired a majority shareholding in November 2019 with the intention of gifting that to the fans in March. His death and the COVID-19 pandemic threw the timetable out as did the subsequent battles that Thistle had to try and stay in the Championship after they were harshly dealt a relegation blow.

'He has left us with a hell of a legacy to build on. That's a challenge for everyone involved to take that on and build it in a way to make Colin proud,' Britton went on to tell the BBC at the time of Colin Weir's death. The sad thing is that legacy was just the start of the story and I firmly believe that other benefactors who love their clubs may also consider this option in the future by gifting their shares to the clubs that they love. Maybe Colin's generosity had an impact on the decision of the Rae family at Morton who wrote off £2 million of debt and provided a pathway for fans to take the club forward. By the time that you read this chapter Partick Thistle should be owned by Thistle for Ever following the likes of the Well Society and the Foundation of Hearts into history. As we know it has taken nearly three years for the correct pathway to community ownership to be established and I am sure that the sterling work of the renamed Jags Foundation ensured that in September 2023 Partick Thistle became firmly established as supporter-owned.

### Greenock Morton FC – getting across the line

I was asked to come and present to a group of fans who were in the early stages of formation. The Morton Club Together group was led by Graham McLennan and we quickly set about meeting at Gourock Golf Club. Over the next few hours, I gave background information to the group and discussed the various strategies that had been deployed at clubs in the past. The MCT were ahead of the game and like many other groups going down this route had decided to bypass the existing supporters' trust which they explained had failed to properly engage with fans and the club over the years. A new fresh organisation was the preferred option, and I was pleasantly surprised at just how well they were already making progress. What was hugely encouraging for me was from a standing start they had attracted members who now saw community ownership as a viable option. Having commenced operations in April 2019, as I write this in July 2020 they had just announced that a deal had been struck with the club where debt (estimated to be around £2 million) was written off by Golden Casket, the Rae family confectionary business, and the shares were to be transferred to the fans' group. One of the things that struck me at that first meeting was the breadth and quality of the composition of the interim Fans' Group Management team. From senior legal figures to project managers and business owners all wanting to hear about the trials and tribulations and to put their own stamp on it with Morton colours. I was really impressed by what I saw and reported the same back to David MacKinnon.

It is interesting to me as an observer of the model to see how the knowledge and understanding of the concept is growing within the different dynamics at each club. At Hearts the fans got a loan from Ann Budge, at St Mirren likewise from Gordon Scott and now a new element has been added with the involvement of Kibble. At Morton, we have seen a move closer to what Colin Weir did at Thistle where the fans are having a debt write off to benefit the community. It is exciting times at the tail of the bank with a new pathway being put in place to drive the old club forward in these changing times. I am delighted to see the progress having been made at Morton who are now community-owned.

### Aberdeen FC – privately held main investor Dave Cormack

It might seem a far-fetched notion at this early stage in the tenure of new majority shareholder Dave Cormack to suggest that one day soon the Dons might become a community-owned club. However, as we have seen elsewhere, where Colin Weir moved the dial from benefactor to philanthropist, community ownership could become the perfect exit strategy for himself in the years to come. Otherwise, he could get stuck in the benefactor trap that Stewart Milne saw where you have to find a new Stewart Milne with equally deep pockets and the same passion for the club as you have. Early indications are that Cormack likes to do things differently and if Hearts fans can pump over £1m a year to the club and build a new stand then why not the Dons fans?

### *Dundee FC – privately held by American Tim Keyes and his Football Partners Scotland group*

As we have seen elsewhere in this book, Dundee were early adopters of the community ownership model and sadly it did not work out for them. They had too many fans' groups, not enough experience and a model that had only really been road-tested at Stirling Albion. The American dream of the owners to build a transatlantic relationship with a Premiership club that could sell on talent to the Premiership and Championship in England seems to be long gone and the rumours are that the club is back for sale again but knowing what the long-term strategy is for Dundee FC is often difficult to say. Keyes and Nelms currently hold 75 per cent of the club equity but little has changed over the years and the club continues to bounce between the Premiership and the Championship.

The pain is probably still too raw for the last generation that tried and failed with community ownership but who is to say that in a generation's time, maybe with a new fans' organisation in place, supporters might want to increase their current share in the club to become majority owners again.

### *Dundee United FC – privately held by Mark Ogren*

This club has consistently been an example of burning cash as well as generating cash from player sales over a prolonged period. It seemed as fast as the big deals for star players were coming in that the cries of 'we are skint' were being heard across Tannadice. When Stephen Thompson sold the club that he and his sister inherited from their father Eddie, he seemed like a man who had really had a hard shift. He needed cash as soon as he could get it. Maybe it was that or having seen the less than impressive stab that Dundee had at community ownership that meant that there was little enthusiasm for community ownership with a long-term payback as we saw at Hearts, St Mirren or Motherwell. Instead, inward investment came from the USA and significant sums have been spent not just in buying the club but in moving it forward. What any foreign investor does not seem to see is that whilst the Premiership in Scotland offers significantly more in earning potential than the Championship, it is nothing compared to the opportunities for success in England. What the new American business model is that has been in place since 2018 is hard to see. However, what history tells us is that the opportunity to consistently make profit in Scotland from a provincial club is virtually impossible to do. If I were a United fan, I would be starting an Arabs community ownership model and be ready for what might be coming down the tracks in a few years' time.

### Falkirk FC – on a pathway to community ownership

Part of the problem that the club had was that there was a big engagement gap between the board and the fans. This has been going on for many years. From the fans' perspective, the Falkirk Trust had done a sterling job when the club had come out of provisional liquidation having been sold to the Colin Liddell consortium, which became known as the Major Shareholder Group (MSG). The Back the Bairns fans' group contributed well over £300,000 and was rewarded with shares in the newly restructured company and a place on the board through the Bairns Trust, who were given the shares but it was nowhere near the value of the cash raised. Whilst it made perfect sense to give the share to the trust as the recognised Industrial and Provident Society, many felt that the Back the Bairns campaign had a far wider reach than the narrow group that ran the trust.

The trust, despite attracting many good people over the years, failed to ignite the support and kick on from getting that initial shareholding. Many good things were achieved with a new stadium, a productive academy and an award-winning community programme. Sadly, the fans' place on the board disappeared as the on-field performance declined in a period of angst for fans and board alike. I had spent a lot of time working with the club and members of the trust to see if a new fans' organisation could be created by merging the trust and the creation of a new organisation from season ticket holders. It always felt that, despite their best efforts, there was a fear or lack of trust from the boardroom of the fans, partly due to some of the criticism that had been levelled at them over the years. I had around a dozen meetings with board members and fans between 2014 and 2018 to talk about better representation and community ownership. In December of that year, it was announced at the AGM that a joint venture, between the MSG/board, minor shareholders and supporters, was given unanimous approval.

So, at long last it seemed that the new group called Back the Bairns, in recognition of the previous campaign, emerged under the expert guidance of David White and Kenny Jamieson to work with the club and a new share issue would bring in £800,000 of fresh investment from over 1,000 fans who had pledged to participate. It would dilute the MSG's shareholding from 62 per cent to 31 per cent and it would allow for the new fans' group to follow the pathway to community ownership that had been so successful at Hearts and Motherwell. It would bring new, democratic governance structures that would reflect the broader ownership base. In March 2019 having previously endorsed it and with no obvious reasons being stated, the board announced that they were talking to other interested parties. It looked like a real slap in the face for fans who got no explanation as to why the MSG had changed its mind. But, unperturbed, the fans' group were marshalled to ensure that it could meet the deadline that had been set. Back the Bairns worked as a consortium of over 40 local businesspeople, including current shareholders and club sponsors. It looked like they would certainly gain the confidence of the board, but alas the deadline that they had set was extended and both of the bids they received from interested parties were withdrawn as they stipulated that they were wanting more time to get fresh bids in.

It looked like the fans' bid had been used as a way to maximise the earning potential for those departing directors. Unsurprisingly an EGM was called proposing no confidence in the board. In what was a huge slap in the face, around 90 per cent of shareholders supported the motion but, in these situations, it is a numbers game and the motion was defeated by the MSG who held more shares. It was described by an SFSA member who attended the meeting as volatile, embarrassing and depressing as the MSG accepted that valuable offers were lost, in part due to them being dysfunctional. It seemed that the club had reached a low point with directors who had overstayed their welcome but who wanted to maximise their earnings and had shown poor judgement when dealing with the supporters. However, a new low point was just around the corner when it was announced that they would host a pitch which considered further offers.

The Back the Bairns scheme was also on the table but given the history was hardly going to suddenly move into pole position. Lo and behold Mark Campbell was announced as the preferred bidder for the club on a Friday and by the next Monday was meeting the fans to talk about his plans for the club. Campbell had been sniffing around Sunderland AFC and makes a non-speaking cameo in the fantastic Netflix series *Sunderland 'Til I Die*. Using the success of former Celtic chief scout John Park as his lure and his offer to invest £8m to £10m of his own wealth, promising fans a fourth stand, a hotel, a new youth academy and even a grass pitch, as well as significant investment in the playing squad seemed incredible and too good to be true. Supporters heard straight from Campbell's mouth just what his plans were, and the MSG felt they had done their job. Fans couldn't wait for the due diligence to happen and to get on with a new era in the land of milk and honey. However, they were a bit concerned and indeed sceptical when rumours started to emerge that when Sunderland asked to see the cash there was none there. More concerning was when simple investigations were conducted that the 'low profile but highly successful businessman', seemed to be devoid of any successful businesses at all. This book has dozens of examples of folk wanting to take over clubs to feather their own nest or to massage an ego.

Even when the *Sunday Mail* told us that Kenny Rodger lookalike Campbell was being sued in the US by a former employee for alleged sex discrimination and sexual harassment, it failed to derail his bid. Supporters sent the club a dossier that showed that there was no evidence of his claimed success in real estate or a coffee empire on the other side of the Atlantic. The fans' fear of a Walter Mitty or Craig Whyte scenario fell on deaf ears, even when evidence showed a list of failed companies in Campbell's wake. It was a storyline you could not make up, yet the board working for the MSG went ahead and unveiled Campbell to supporters. Months passed and the board did its due diligence and where there was a problem, they got some sort of woolly answer that contradicted the evidence that had been gathered by the fans' group and he remained the preferred bidder despite flashing warning lights. There was a formal announcement from the club and Mark Campbell in November 2019 confirming that the deal was not going ahead. At the December club AGM, no satisfactory reason was given to the shareholders as to why the Back the Bairns activity could not proceed or as to why the Campbell deal had not proceeded. The club rumbled on until a fateful night in October 2021.

The Q&A that beats all others saw the Falkirk board implode after the most famous Question and Answer session ever. Now seen by over 30,000 folks worldwide, it is the perfect example of how not to treat fans!

The fall out was immediate and within weeks the team that brought together the fans and the patrons under the guidance of Kenny Jamieson and Stuart Adam came into power. Now there is a growing fans' organisation heading for 700 members contributing funds every month and a pathway to community ownership in place that we are working with to ease the transition as the club became the first recipient of funds from the Fans Bank. They now own over 25 per cent of the club.

### Hibernian FC – a Gordon family exit strategy?

Hibs had a benefactor in Sir Tom Farmer who sold to new American owners rather than to the Hibernian Supporters Limited scheme that had been set up to sell shares to the fans. I have no idea why he did not look across the city to the success at Hearts where fans had raised significant funds and pursued a fan-centric solution. Given the efforts that it made to neutralise the www.BuyHibs.org movement by creating a new in-house fan organisation, HSL, we have to assume that getting fast money was more appealing, or was it that fans could not be trusted? Given that there is no money to be made in Scottish football it remains to be seen whether the cost to sadly deceased Ron Gordon's family is something that can be maintained for a significant period of time. It would be good if HSL could become an independent fans' body but that seems unlikely, so maybe a new group like the BuyHibs team should ready itself for future action. The potential alliance with AFC Bournemouth's owner Bill Foley might however show a different strategy.

### Kilmarnock FC – will Billy sell to the fans?

As we saw earlier in the book when I worked really closely with the excellent Killie Trust during the Michael Johnston era, there was a growing appetite for community ownership and a very strong trust in place with an excellent committed team. Mr Johnston was never interested in any form of community ownership and his objective was always to maximise his returns. Billy Bowie is a very different kettle of fish and in my meetings, as he made tentative steps onto the board, he was always mindful of the support and wanted to know and understand community ownership. Since he bought out Michael Johnston, crowds have increased, engagement with supporters is excellent and the trust are now contributing funds and buying shares in the club. Billy has also strengthened his board with Cathy Jamieson the ex-MP and SFSA Director who is a proud advocate of community ownership. I would not be surprised if that strong fan–board relationship continues to grow and lead to what could be an opportunity for the supporters to eventually buy the club in the future.

### Ross County FC – what happens after Roy?

In several places throughout this book I have made positive references to the Ross County owner Roy MacGregor. He really is Mr Ross County having taken the club from the Highland League to the Premiership as well as winning the League Cup along the way. It is a fairy tale story given that Dingwall has a population of around 3,000. In my time running Stirling Albion, despite us creating a whole new structure that was the complete opposite of Roy's ownership of the Staggies, he was open, welcoming and very keen to help by offering any advice to us new boys on how to run our club. It was fantastic to see behind the scenes just how the club was structured and how Roy had helped sell the *Club of the Highlands* concept far and wide to anyone who would listen. It was great to see on match days kids arriving from the far-flung reaches of the Highlands, getting coaching in the morning and then watching the first team play in the afternoon. It is a huge investment in football in the area that for many years had been deprived of the type of attention that it deserved.

Roy is charming, clever and, of course, very rich, which has allowed him to devote the necessary resources to make all this happen under his watch. It would be a very different Ross County if Roy was not there to guide it along. The nearest parallel to the Staggies story is with Brookes Mileson at Gretna who had an equally strong community spirit and took Gretna, with a population of 2,750 according to the last census, to a Cup Final and the Premiership. County of course have been around far longer and have had the chance to build a structure around the club that is more robust. Who is to say that Brookes Mileson would not have worked to put a similar strategy in place at Gretna if he had survived? The strategy of being a focal point as a professional team in the Borders, another often ignored geographical area, is not dissimilar to what Ross County have achieved in the Highlands. The tragedy that unfolded at Gretna was the death of the wealthy benefactor which left the club burdened by players' salaries that it could not afford and playing in a league that was beyond their natural position. I am sure Roy MacGregor will have reflected on this when he is planning the future for Ross County once his energy, enthusiasm and his wealth are no longer available to the club. I have no idea what his thoughts are on developing a legacy or having an exit strategy. What I do know is that he loves his club and will want the best outcome for it going forward. There seem to be three options: a) he passes it on to family or fellow directors, b) he sets up a trust or foundation with an income to maintain the club, c) he gives the club to the community. The fourth option of selling the club to an outsider does not seem to be likely given what we know about white knights that lurk about in football. The truth of the matter is that each option brings different challenges.

*St Johnstone FC – club sold but what about the longer term prospects?*

Before the season went into pandemic lockdown, we started to see behind the curtains at one of our most reserved and successful provincial sides. In several interviews, chairman of St Johnstone, Steve Brown, accepted that the club had 'over-egged' their spending on players and are unable to sustain what is a top six wage bill. This was not really a news story, more a confirmation to the press that the Saints' miracle of top six finishes over a sustained period had come at a cost that the provincial side with a small support of around 3,000 fans could not sustain. What did cause surprise in the following months was to see the highly successful architect of the on-field performance Tommy Wright, walk away from the job he loved. Brown confirmed that heavy losses had forced the hand of the Perth outfit and that they could simply not be sustained indefinitely.

As part of his interview with *The Courier*, Steve, who succeeded his dad Geoff in the role eight years ago, has revealed he has warned his sons to steer clear of the McDiarmid Park boardroom. Despite the many good times and the significance of the first-ever Scottish Cup win and taking this team to Europe, he describes it as a thankless task. He said:

> I don't want my family to come into it. They have promised me they won't. People who are in football know it is seven days a week, every week. It is a lot of sacrifices. It is the nature of the beast. But I wouldn't wish it on my kids. As much as you still get the buzz it is a burden at times.

Given the direction of travel with the interview, it was no surprise that in December 2022 the Browns were selling up and that the revenue generated would be reinvested in Saints in the Community projects. Eventually the club was sold to an American businessman Adam Webb who has come in and made a very positive impression. But, as we have seen elsewhere, with no chance of turning a profit it might well be that in the years ahead he will be minded to seeing the Saint Johnstone fans take over the strain at the club given his health issues and the long distances involved between Atlanta and Perth.

*Albion Rovers FC*

The 'Project Phoenix' consortium attempted to seize control of Rovers in 2023 with a bold bid to rebrand the club 'Shamrock Rovers Coatbridge', but that was immediately kicked out by the board of directors at Cliftonhill and ridiculed by fans. But in early 2025 they were back at the table trying once again to build an interest in the project. I have attended a few meetings and the fans have great leadership under a former Rovers Director Ronnie Boyd. There is a very long way to go but Community Ownership is now very much on the agenda.

### Dumbarton FC

This proud old club fell into liquidation after ten years of ownership by an offshore shell company in Belize. For over a decade they did nothing for the club as they sought a way to get planning permission to use land that the club owned to build houses. Eventually they ran out of money and The Sons went into liquidation.

What happened next shocked the football world, when a new owner appeared from left field. The new Dumbarton owner, Mario Lapointe, believes he can get the club on a stable financial footing within the next two years. A big part of his plan involves installing an artificial surface at The Rock and having the stadium in use all year round, including music and comedy festivals.

The League Two side is one of the oldest in the country, and twice national champions, having won the top-flight title in 1891 and 1892. Now that they have a Canadian businessman/singer-songwriter at the helm it remains to be seen what the next chapter in the story will look like. They are now at the bottom of the SPFL pyramid, having suffered relegation from League One last season. And Lapointe pinpointed that history, as well as a passion for football in the country, as one of the main reasons why he chose to come to Scotland.

## Exploring Options for Celtic and Rangers: Could They Be Game-Changers?

Seeing clubs in Scotland go on the opposite trajectory than those in England sees them head towards the arms of community and the certainty that it brings. Recent history tells us that the alternative to community ownership is a far riskier strategy.

### Celtic FC – could they be community-owned?

The Fergus McCann era regenerated the club, and the incoming owners had a strong stable club that would allow them to further prosper. This period of growth and dominance had further assistance through the demise of Rangers and their long struggle back to the top of the league. With solid foundations, economic benefits from strong performances in Europe, a stunning performance in the transfer market where players such as Wanyama, Forster, Van Dyke, Armstrong, Dembele and Tierney all enhanced the team before being sold for a significant profit, the club was prospering. Much of the frustration came from the Resolution 12 campaign that wanted to establish whether Celtic were denied access to the UEFA Champions League in 2011, when Rangers clearly owed tax to HMRC from prior years which could be a reason for the SFA to refuse them a UEFA Licence.

Many fans felt that the club were ignoring shareholders' pleas for action. For those of us who watch fans' affairs, it seems that the Celtic AGMs of the past few years have become an annual event where the fan shareholders ask questions that never get answered to their satisfaction. There seems to be a general feeling that Celtic fans, whilst appreciating that the club is generally in rude health, want more accountability from their board whom they fear have lost sight of the club's original raison d'etre which was founded in the community, that although now global, still has a strong sense of community. There seems to be a democratic deficit where supporters have very little influence or say at the club. Many fans want more than just being able to obtain an answer to a single question at the AGM. Clubs like Celtic will point to the fact that they have a Supporter Liaison Officer (SLO) as a result of a UEFA Financial Fair Play requirement who can give fans a voice. Whilst having an SLO is an important role for clubs to have, the reality is they are club employees and can't offer more than a link to the club command and control system, becoming more of a filter than a communication channel no matter how good they are.

A few years ago I was asked by a Celtic website to write an article about community ownership, and whether it could work for a club like Celtic. As I have expressed elsewhere in this book, I firmly believe that the size of the club is no barrier to having a club move to a community ownership structure. We know that things would need to be done differently at Celtic but if approached sensibly it could provide little worry as governance and communications would be improved and the connections with the support enhanced. The fear that any club board would have is that the lunatics would take over the asylum. In reality fans with the right skill sets do emerge through a community structure and there are usually enough checks and balances in place to ensure this does not happen. Having the right controls and processes in place would ensure that Celtic could become a beacon for supporter democracy and more importantly for them to have the financial support that could enhance their business.

Fergus McCann had his share issue in 1995 to provide the income that would regenerate the club through a one-off share issue that raised funds and put shares into the hands of those folk who loved the club, to prevent one person, or a small group of people, running the club as had happened under the previous regime. This aim was diluted in 1999 when Fergus sold his shares on leaving Celtic and Dermott Desmond snapped up enough to become the largest shareholder. The share, as we know, gave small shareholders little input and the purchase was a one-off payment. I could easily imagine a future where, in return for providing supporters with a range of appropriate skills and meaningful input at board level via a membership scheme, a pathway to fans owning the club could emerge. A membership scheme utilising the ongoing resources that exists within the Celtic support is also the source of potentially a huge income stream.

In 2019, it was reported that Celtic had sold 52,000 season tickets. In the same period Hearts had sold 11,500. So looking at a few dynamics that might interest Celtic... if they captured the same percentage of fans as Hearts with a 65.2 per cent uptake they would generate an additional income of £6.1 million per season. That is the equivalent of asking Dermot Desmond to write a cheque for that amount every single year. The huge benefit to Celtic would be that it gives them an income stream that their biggest rivals can't access and allows the members to decide every year how the money is spent.

### Rangers FC

Rangers FC – community-owned – could it still happen? Of course the landscape and the route to it happening are very different in 2025 than what we were looking at in previous years.

I have had many interesting times working with the Rangers support, stretching back to my time at SDS. For the most part, the Gers fans I met were superb. More than a few friendships were formed during that period, just as I had found at other clubs I had worked with around the country. Of course, I dare not think what was being said about me online by some folks. My role in the first instance was to try and get a new fans' operation up and running that could contemplate the opportunity for fans' ownership. The challenge was one I regularly faced in the world of fandom that, devoid of power or influence, many of the trust fans' groups had turned inward and relations were strained between the various groups. The anger the fans had for what had happened at the club was significant. There were further challenges in that the bigger the club, the more fans' groups you have to work with. I started with the Rangers Supporters Trust which was the obvious vehicle for a tilt at community ownership. I liked a few of the folks on the board and we got the local MP involved and launched www.BuyRangers.org to start the process. However, many of the other groups had issues with this and it became obvious that a bigger solution would be required to get traction. Months of negotiation with many meetings saw me meet with Charles Green and Dave King over the period as community ownership became a real possibility for the Ibrox club. Eventually, assisted by Richard Atkinson and many Rangers playing legends, the Louden Tavern witnessed the launch of Rangers First. In record time, the support that had been devoid of anything positive to talk about for an eternity got on board and in no time we had the largest fan group in Britain with over 13,000 members, or 'membears'. The financial demise of such a major club has shown that any club can be blighted by financial problems and that the support for fan ownership was really growing.

Sadly, there were many factions and the then owners saw such a robust fans' group as a threat, even though they should have appreciated what a powerful ally it can be in having the fans with you as owners/custodians. It was an opportunity lost that might never return.

The Rangers First identity was parked and the Club 1872, a Community Interest Company, emerged as its replacement vehicle, merging with the activities of Buy Rangers, which now holds 10.7 per cent of the shares in the club and is one of the largest shareholders. It was designed to ensure that future decisions about the club would have fans involved in the process and in doing so gives the ordinary supporters a huge opportunity to buy up shares as they become available.

The board wrangling over ownership and control of the club continued into 2023, with Dave King agreeing to sell his shareholding to Club 1872. This could have dramatically increased the fans' ownership of the club in the years ahead if the deal had gone forward. Rangers are not listed on a main stock exchange. Instead, JP Jenkins, Europe's largest platform exchange for unlisted securities, offers a matched bargain platform. In other words, it matches individual sellers with individual buyers of Rangers shares. In early 2025, the King sale eventually proceeded, and it allowed the San Francisco 49ers consortium to get 51 per cent of the club and with it the fans' stake in the club shrank to the lowest level since the Murray era.

I have always believed that if either of the Glasgow giants wanted to look at ownership in a different way, then the opportunity for the club could be huge. A membership scheme brought into play could see up to 50,000 fans contributing every month. Maybe in the future it could be a race to the top to see which of the Old Firm clubs decides that this is a route to be exploited. Of course, what has happened at Rangers in the past six months with them becoming part of the San Francisco 49ers group of companies makes the likelihood of any community ownership more pie in the sky than ever before, but maybe 20 years from now it might be very different

## So What Happens Next?

The Community Ownership story is a long and winding one that started when the clubs were formed and has continued to evolve in these recent times. What happens next depends on many factors and, of course, many factors remain unpredictable or unknown.

### The Scottish Government: Funding is in Sight

We have already explored the opportunities that the Scottish Green Party brought to the table in 2014 where significant support was called for the supporters of clubs to have the right to buy their club. Having shied away a few years back when the pressure came from the football authorities, what did emerge from that process was the Scottish Government Community Sports Empowerment Fund where community bodies and clubs can have access to up to £5 million to allow them to buy their club and facilities. This is a fantastic step forward and the SFSA will be right at the heart of it having suggested the concept years ago!

The first deal was completed at Falkirk FC and the SFSA are working on several more options in 2024 including what we hope will be a successful conclusion at East Fife too. As we all know, there is a spending crisis across the UK and this sadly has had an impact on the SFSA-created Fans Bank where funding is now on ice. We do hope to bring this game-changer opportunity for fans back soon!

We asked the Scottish Government for a comment as we have a couple of fans' groups that we have been working with over the past six months who are now disappointed.

> The Scottish Government remains committed to the Fans Bank and fully supports the aims and objectives of the policy. While the financial challenges facing the Scottish Government mean we are not able to provide further investment at the current time, it is our intention to be able to consider further bids in the future.

### Look at Community Clubs Differently

There is a real opportunity to see what is happening in the marketplace and how further support could be given to clubs who convert to community ownership. As these entities are social enterprises, it could be that there is further recognition given to clubs as an incentive to convert to community ownership. With no profit motive and driven by a community spirit, it could be concessions on areas such as rates or VAT that could help secure the longer-term aims of the clubs.

## What Can the SFSA Do?

- Offer advice – we have been there and done it and have helped fans across Europe.
- We continue to research this topic and more in-depth academic-led research is now needed to help further policy decisions. The SFSA partnership announced in early 2024 with the Dundee University School of Business will ensure that this important work continues to evolve with the times.
- Continue to educate the fans as to the benefits and challenges of community ownership.
- Continue to provide a platform that allows for cross-fertilisation of ideas between the various fans' groups and individuals.
- Develop a group of representative members under the SFSA banner that can reward and recognise community ownership (badge scheme) and look to monitor the progress of all our community-owned clubs, to raise standards and to help manage fan expectations.
- Work with the Scottish Government on the development of the Community Sports Empowerment Fund 'Fans Bank' providing a team of professionals who can evaluate loan applications. Look to develop the fund to give community-owned clubs access to seed capital for projects.
- Set up of an SFSA Community Ownership Advisory Group of members who are either in community ownership or are on the pathway to it has now progressed and will continue to grow.

## The Football Authorities

You would like to think that the continued growth of the new model will be accepted by the football authorities as a new way of doing business. Much has changed since those early days of community ownership when the Stirling Albion directors were called in to be quizzed on what their business plan was and what contingency funds they had in place. Clubs large and small have shown that the model has very strong credentials and can offer certainty, continuity of ownership and, of course, sustainable football clubs, thus avoiding the boom-and-bust cycle that has blighted the game we love. As more clubs become community-owned there is a huge opportunity to change the culture at Hampden Park to ensure that the wider supporter agenda is better reflected in the way the organisation operates.

### Football Supporters

Well, this is really where I pass the baton over to you, the ordinary football supporter. If you follow a team that is in community ownership or is on the pathway to being owned by the fans then it's over to you to play a bigger part in that process – we can never get enough willing volunteers at our clubs. It is so much more than just your financial contributions that are needed to make your club a success. It is essential that we build the clubs to become responsive to the individual communities that they represent.

If you follow a team that is not in community ownership, and you want that to change, then get in touch with your fans' organisations. It may well be that there is no organisation that is set up or in a position to take on such a challenge. If you need support in any of these matters, then get in touch with us at the Scottish Football Supporters Association and we will help you or any of your colleagues. We are always looking for volunteers too!

What is essential for community ownership to work as a democratic fans' movement is that members step forward for election and that they monitor and evaluate the progress of the members that they elect to ensure that it is not more of the same that they are paying for. It is so easy for some individuals to have their heads turned by a club tie and a little bit of power. Community ownership is not Fantasy Football or playing Football Manager, it is working for the long-term sustainability of the club you love. Make sure those in office are monitored, evaluated and know exactly what the members think – that is your job as an ordinary member.

## Caution: There, But Not Quite There Yet

As I have highlighted earlier in this book, I made more than a few mistakes in the various stages of community ownership and I am sure that there will be similar tales from across the many clubs that are moving in this direction. Some of the mistakes were strategic, some driven by financial restrictions and some were just political considerations. What is essential to appreciate is that it is impossible to get everything right and the pressures of football life are intense. Unless you have thick skin and a huge appetite for collaborative work then it is best not to apply.

Further caution is necessary as the model evolves too. It saddens me to this day that I left Stirling Albion without leaving a proper voting structure in place and a power vacuum resulted in a chairman assuming power and forming a dictator's clique. He has never faced any election and indeed has twice fought off attempts to get him out by many of the trust members that worked so hard with me all those years ago to save the club. Sadly many of them have not only dropped out of the trust but in going to watch the club they love. It took eight long painful years before this was resolved. I have a deep admiration for the fans who stuck with it and pressed the community ownership reset button at the club in early 2023. The early signs are showing great promise.

There is concern too that at a club like Motherwell who are looking for more investment, that they fall into the same traps that they had before under conventional ownership. The Video PR stunt might not have attracted Taylor Swift but what it did do was to bring in another 100 members to the Well Society. In the current weeks, the club board are getting all excited about new inward investment. Part of the problem is that the club board had not been running the club sustainably and had run up debt. The Well Society need to be very careful here and be mindful of what they might give away. If John Boyle, a lifelong Motherwell fan, couldn't make them more successful then how might someone from the USA? Of course, what they have successfully achieved over the past years is a good place to start with amazing fan engagement and a continued presence in the Premiership. Is it worth taking the risk of ceding control for a couple of places higher in the league? I don't think so.

Some of the concerns were: what is the investment for? Unless it is for structural purposes to help build the business then there would be a concern that the 'investment' is just about moving up the league. One of the fundamental facts in the football business is that you are what you are and you are the size that you are and it should dictate how you operate. Motherwell have been safe, secure and sustainable for years, so why the sudden cry for more investment? What can you realistically expect to achieve? Is it a message to other billionaires following the Hibs/AFC Bournemouth discussions that they might be interested? If so, shouldn't all of this have been discussed and debated with fans – the owners? It is a strange one, or maybe it achieved what it was meant to do – make a noise and get some more members involved.

I also have concerns that there needs to be more significant communication with the owners from the conventional board structures toward the fans' boards at clubs. Maybe I missed this because I am not a member of the various fans' organisations but did any of the fan-owned clubs consult with their wider membership on important issues at league reconstruction? We know that a significant majority of Scottish football fans (approx 85 per cent) have for ten years demanded larger leagues. Giving such a compelling argument, did the fans' boards at our community-owned clubs vote for reconstruction or did they even ask their owners (the fans) to reiterate the figures that we know to be true? There is an education job to do with fan-owned clubs having to be more responsive to their owners on key decisions. There cannot and should not be a democratic deficit in this department!

## In Conclusion

Over the last decade or so British football has changed beyond comprehension. In England, millionaires are being replaced by billionaires and the pathway for most of the clubs becoming community-owned has been blocked by the fixation of wealth and ego.

Much has changed in the ten years since I got involved in trying to save my local team from what was a very real threat of liquidation. In Scotland, that wee spark a decade ago has led to a change in the way that we look at our clubs and that is hugely positive. The myth that fans can support clubs but can't run them or heaven forbid actually own them has been put to rest once and for all. Fans are educated, articulate, knowledgeable and passionate. They also have a love that is so unique that it is part of their family DNA. These are our clubs, and we have every right to own and care for them for future generations. When I started writing this book in 2019, the Fans Bank was just a dream, there was no Expert Working Group, there was no game-changing research hub with a leading university. Much has changed for the better and with your efforts so much more can and will change for the better in the years ahead. I am sure community ownership is here to stay which just goes to show that despite what some of the powerful ex-chairmen wanted in 2014, you can't stop the fans once they have momentum.

So, good luck in your future football endeavours and remember, if you are not a member of Scotland's National Fans' Organisation – you should be! It is FREE and always will be.

CHAPTER 13

# Buying a Football Club for Your Community

*When you start supporting a football club you don't support it because of the trophies, or a player, or the history; you support it because you found yourself somewhere there: found a place where you belong.—*
Dennis Bergkamp

THE BASIC PREMISE of positive economic practice is that anyone can buy just about anything as long as what you are buying is legal. If the item is for sale and you have the right amount of money to meet the asking price, then you can proceed with the transaction and conclude a deal. This of course presumes that the seller is happy to sell to you. If so, then it is a simple task of getting the lawyers in to do the paperwork, pay the money and transfer the share certificates. As we have established elsewhere, football has other additional requirements that are meant to protect football clubs from unscrupulous or less desirable investors.

The 'fit and proper test' for ownership is the way that the football authorities *try* to ensure that the only people who come into their domain are folk they are comfortable with. It is about them trying to protect the integrity of the game. It is embarrassing for the football industry to have too many administrations and liquidations, many where it emerges that owners of dubious backgrounds have taken control of our clubs. The reality is that if there was a fit and proper test for the test itself it would fail miserably. For starters, they only look at who is fit and proper *after* the shares have been transferred – figure the logic out in that if you can.

### Establishing the Rules and Using Supporter Influence

As we have examined elsewhere, the whole UK football market has seen change from the top of the pyramid where the strength and money of the Premier League have dictated the ownership strategy with billionaires having replaced millionaires as the new order of the day. The knock-on effect is that the millionaires now operate in the lower leagues, still dreaming of pushing upwards to dine at the top table where, in theory, serious money can be made from football. The market change in England has resulted in the dream of community ownership for most supporters never being any more than that. Aside from lower league and non-league sides, the opportunity for community ownership in England has all but gone. With the strength of that market and the rewards it can offer there is no hope for fans owning clubs.

Yet in Ireland, Wales and Scotland where very different dynamics exist, we see community ownership thriving as there is less interest given that the rewards for getting to the top of the pyramid are so low. The best that fans' groups in larger clubs in England can hope to achieve is to exert as much influence on any potential sale. The reality is it can often be no more than a soundbite, although no existing or new owner wants to have a difficult relationship with their customers. Although, if your skin is as thick as Mike Ashley's then maybe that is not true.

Of course, as we saw in recent times, the much maligned Newcastle United owner did eventually sell the Magpies to oil-rich Saudi investors. Saudi has a dubious human rights record but does that matter to fans? Maybe it should matter to the reputation of the most successful league in the world. The Toon Army have been so marginalised from over a decade of the Ashley ownership that they would probably accept anyone to come in and replace Ashley as long as they have bucketloads of money to spend. Given that they can't do anything that impacts the sale anyway, maybe it is for others to consider. Football fans, it appears, are happy to park their conscience when it comes to the affairs of the club they love. That for me is sad but not surprising.

There has been precious little kickback from the fans. The club supporters have, as we know, little power but at a time when Crown Prince Mohammed bin Salman who heads Saudi Arabia's Public Investment Fund (PIF) has his human rights record scrutinised by the football authorities, all they can do is speak up. The football authorities are not known for looking beyond the most basic of requirements. In this case, do they have money, and will their involvement make the league bigger and better? Political storms usually always blow over anyway.

The BBC reports that in an online forum, which involved over 2,000 fans, Newcastle United Supporters Trust (NUST) chair Alex Hurst said: 'We exist to be a critical friend of the club, and hold them to account.' Of course, there is a wider public debate as to whether the Saudis' takeover passes Premier League tests. Will the football authorities consider the testimony of human rights groups and the fiancée of murdered journalist Jamal Khashoggi, Hatice

Cengiz, who have opposed the takeover? The desire to get rid of current owner Mike Ashley seems to override any of the negativity. As we know the vast majority of fans just want to be concerned with what happens on a Saturday afternoon on the park. So maybe it was no surprise that despite a statement by Khashoggi's fiancée being read out and contributions from fans, Amnesty International and local MPs, a survey published by NUST, which has more than 10,000 members, showed that 96.7 per cent of fans said they were in favour of the takeover; showing that in football nothing is ever black and white – even in Newcastle.

Supporter Greg Morrison said:

> I do feel quite conflicted. While we are not responsible for what goes on [in Saudi Arabia], we have to accept we are attached to Saudi Arabia and the issues attached to that. My plea is that fans don't resort to allowing our club to be used to justify or defend what goes on in Saudi Arabia, but accept and acknowledge that there are issues and encourage debate.

NUST board member Greg Tomlinson added: 'It's not impossible to be excited about Mike Ashley's departure and still feel concerned about the [human rights] issues.' Cengiz's statement said that fans should 'stand together and block' the takeover because the PIF was chaired by Crown Prince Mohammed bin Salman, who she said was responsible for her fiancée's murder in October 2018. By the time you have read this we will know what has happened as another chapter in the purchase of football assets is completed or Ashley is still hanging on to maximise his investment.

Buying a football club is slightly different from the normal economic rules that drive the world in which we live. Football is unique in that, depending on who is buying the club, the rules of supply and demand might not come into play. We have seen many stories emerge of entrepreneurs keen on a football 'investment' checking out the market to find the right fit for themselves. We had Vladimir Romanov be seriously interested in buying Dundee and Dundee United before finally settling for Hearts. After his less than successful spell at the helm at Livingston which ended with administration, Angelo Massoni expressed an interest in buying St Mirren, Motherwell and Heart of Midlothian, having believed that he had learned his lessons. Fans were not so forgiving. His first unsuccessful foray into Scottish football had failed to deter him and he wanted back to prove the point and to clear his name. If he had chosen to do so having driven Livingston to administration, he would still have passed the fit and proper test.

In theory, buying your local football club should not provide any major problems. However, much depends on the given circumstances at each specific club and how you go about finding a route to buying your club will depend on what you find when you knock on the door.

## Club Not for Sale – It's About Timing

Depending on when you were to approach the club there might be a quick rebuff if it is genuinely not for sale. Much of this will depend on the length of tenure of the existing majority shareholder(s), their own circumstances and what is happening on and off the park. Today, Manchester City is not for sale as the owners are building a worldwide group of football clubs, so it would be pointless trying. However, nothing in business lasts forever and football clubs have tended to outlive many worldwide brands and ownership regimes so the door might well open again in the future.

There are times when a football club is not for sale, but the reality is that with the right offer to the right shareholders then that position can easily change. In the 2013/14 season, Dundee FC started life in community ownership and was definitely not for sale. By the end of the season, they had been sold to a Texan consortium who had a business plan to make the club a regular top six finisher and to also sell players to English clubs. Neither has happened and as I write this in January 2024 the latest plan is a partnership with Burnley and, of course, the new stadium. Where the money is coming from for a new stadium is anybody's guess. A different example is in their Tayside rivals St Johnstone who have not been for sale for a generation, having been very secure in the Brown family ownership. Now it seems that the family don't see that tenure lasting to the next generation. To me, it seemed like it was the perfect time for Saints' fans to start planning a community-owned future with Stuart Cosgrove as the new chairman. Sadly, the Browns saw it differently and sold out to yet another American group of investors headed by Adam Webb who claimed to be interested due to the groundswell of interest in UK leagues in the USA. It remains to be seen what this means for the longer term.

## The Club is Not for Sale... To You!

As we have seen in previous chapters, there are many who remain unconvinced that anything other than the conventional benefactor model will work in football. As the knowledge and understanding of the benefits of this wider club support is promoted, this fear and often loathing for a new way of doing things will dissipate and it will be far easier for community ownership to emerge. I remember having a conversation with the delightful Douglas Rae, the owner and chairman at Morton, when we played them when I was at Stirling Albion. Douglas just couldn't get his head around the idea that fans could be running and owning the club. He was inquisitive but dismissive as it just did not fit into the conventional football business model he knew and understood. He has sadly passed away now and it is a shame that he was not able to see his son Crawford work with the Morton supporters to establish a new group, the Morton Club Together (MCT), as they seek to develop a long-term community-owned pathway for the club just eight years later.

Another dynamic is that the club could be for sale but only to certain people. We saw this in the scenario at Hibs where it was quite obvious that Sir Tom Farmer was looking for a financially beneficial exit strategy for himself rather than having any wider philanthropic mission. Rather than embrace the growing fans' interest in community ownership through www.BuyHibs.org the club decided to seek an alternative sale. During this period, the creation of Hibernian Supporters Limited, a vehicle by the club for fans to buy into a company that would buy shares in Hibs, was conceived supposedly to mirror Hearts and for the fans to own the club. That strategy, along with bringing in Leeann Dempster to shield the under-attack Petrie from fans, saw an anti-fan strategy plan come into play. When push came to shove, HSL was a toothless, club-run fans' organisation that was never even considered as a serious option as a pathway to community ownership. HSL still exists but was never given any opportunity to propose a purchase of the Sir Tom Farmer shares. If it had been an independent, properly constituted representative body like the FoH, it might have at the very least provided an alternative offer, but being controlled by the club that was never going to happen. However, all is not lost as foreign investors might not stay forever and if HSL learns the lessons from elsewhere then it could be in a place to take the club to community ownership in the future. However, to do so it has to be run as an independent organisation that lives and breathes for the fans. That seems an unlikely scenario.

## Other Interested Parties Causing Concern Creates a Blockage

We live in a competitive world where there is always the chance that other parties are seen as a more attractive package to the sellers. Much depends on the state of the club at that given time and the mindset of the owner. David

Murray accepted £1 for one of the biggest clubs in the UK when a few years before he was trying to sell it for £50 million. Until recently, the perception was that businesspeople were a better option to run a football club. The dozens of disasters and failures at clubs are often ignored. Up against it, we have community ownership being an untried model which is always going to work against fans being preferred bidders. The fact that businesspeople who ran clubs had caused 150-plus administration events at football clubs in years gone by is politely ignored. What was also ignored was the fact that when these new fans' organisations sprung up, they had boards that were being populated by highly qualified people such as lawyers, accountants, marketers and the like, bringing skillsets often better than what was on club boards. As we saw in the case at Stirling Albion, the club was for sale, the owner saw the other conventional parties as being more desirable and, as a result, the bid from the fans was regarded as less worthy of consideration. In that case, the suitors Dr Gordon McKay and a bid from Rod Petrie were eventually eliminated because the fans had built a credible alternative solution over a sustained period of campaigning.

In early 2020 at Falkirk, we saw a professional and well-constructed fans' offer from Falkirk fans' group Back the Bairns secure an agreement with the Falkirk board to galvanise the fans and move towards community ownership. Having been involved in the process many times over the years at the club and with fans, I was delighted at the outcome. However, despite the fact that the Bairns had accumulated over £800k in pledges from ordinary fans and from businesses, the club board put a halt to the proposals. It looked for all intents and purposes that the fans' bid was being used as a stalking horse when two other consortia emerged from the shadows to show an interest in buying the club. It appears that the only thing that is holding back a successful partnership here is for the existing shareholders to trust their own fans. Maybe the lure of getting a higher price elsewhere overrides the love of the club that they undoubtedly have. Letting go can sometimes be hard. Fast forward to 2023 and that credible alternate 'The Fans' were very much back in the driving seat following a board implosion at the club in early 2022.

At Partick Thistle, a boardroom coup d'état came in July 2019, sparked when interest emerged from a Chinese/American consortium who also owned Barnsley. The opportunity to recoup money invested previously, drove the implosion and resulted in a hugely divided support. Some were excited by the *Moneyball* game plan put forward (when I was in a meeting with Gerry Britton CEO and David Beattie the chairman, I said that the fans were asking to see the bidder's business plan and we were told to watch *Moneyball*) but the vast majority were concerned that the club was being sold down the

Clyde. From those fears Thistle for Ever emerged to take on the challenge of providing an alternative vision, which caught the imagination of Colin Weir who believed that community ownership was a better option for his team. Sadly, what should have been a simple process was complicated by his death and business advisors not wanting real community ownership.

## A Club is in Administration or Liquidation

As Bryan Jackson always says, 'Fans are the bank of last resort', when clubs are in a financial crisis. In many cases, this is the easiest time to have engagement and dialogue about supporters providing an alternative pathway. At every club in crisis fans are there to ensure the club they love is saved from oblivion. Very often it is difficult for fans to be prepared for the eventualities at the club they love, as football is very much a week-to-week business. Yet, our clubs outlive us all and if fans plan ahead then they will get their rewards. At Hearts, the FoH was a year in the making, learning and preparing as they knew that Romanov would have to be replaced at some time in the future. You could argue that a crisis was always looming but having the foresight to plan ahead and to build capacity gave community ownership a chance. At Stirling Albion, we likewise had over a year of campaigning to get us to a position where we had credibility and funds.

In July 2020, we saw the latest in a long line of casualties with Wigan Athletic going into administration, partly due to the COVID-19 pandemic. It is hard to imagine that a club that is struggling as a going concern might not consider selling. However, the scenario that many face is thinking that they can find a solution that will let them escape from the hole that they are in by continuing to dig. Where community ownership at clubs has failed in England, it has tended to be at clubs where fans had to step forward and save the club. More often than not, as we saw at Bury, Derby County, Chester City and many others, the initial efforts are very much about keeping the concern going and a huge amount of effort and fundraising goes towards that aim. In many instances, the debts that the supporters have inherited mean that they are running at 100 miles per hour just to stand still. In most of these cases too, the fans are no more than a stop gap as they simply do not have the resources to develop any future plans.

Already it has emerged that Wigan Athletic has had around 15 expressions of interest from parties willing to take over the club. The best that the fans hoped for was that their contribution would be recognised and that a benefactor who is community-minded steps forward. Fast forward to 2021 and the club is sold to Talal al Hammad from Bahrain. Yet little seems to have changed, as the BBC reported in late October 2022:

> Wigan Athletic Chief Executive Malachy Brannigan says the club is not up for sale amid speculation over the Latics' financial situation. The statement comes after the club were late paying players' salaries, the second time this has happened in 2022.

## The Steps on the Journey – With Partick Thistle as an Example

### Preparation: Be Ready to Act

If we look back at the history of community ownership in the UK, the introduction of supporters' trusts was undoubtedly a key foundation in the development of the model. This Government intervention was a real positive step in giving supporters' groups an understanding, belief and a structured legal fans' framework. Sadly, by the time I worked at Supporters Direct, many of the organisation's staff had a very prescribed way of looking at things and were close-minded, doing things the way it had been done when SD was established. In simple terms, it had failed to recognise the changing landscape and their thinking had not evolved to reflect the way the market was changing. I remember arguing the case for FoH and the Well Society who were not deemed to be worthy as members because they had ignored the existing trusts and had chosen to be something other than an Industrial and Provident Society (or soon to be a CBS – Community Benefit Society).

One of the factors that needs consideration is deciding what vehicle to use to develop the plan. As mentioned above, in the 1990s there was a huge push for SD to create fans' trusts which would give the fans the right legal framework to conduct business. Sadly, many of the trusts, with little opportunity to influence things at their clubs, became a place where a small niche of activists gathered and often became politically difficult for mainstream fans who didn't understand why they were there and what they were doing. Likewise, many of these trusts failed to connect with the club they represented. What follows in this, and the succeeding sessions, are the lessons at Partick Thistle.

I had always believed that Partick Thistle would be the perfect community-owned club. I had observed that since the Save the Jags campaign, the shareholding was diverse with no large block of owners in place to drive the club forward. Until July 2019, the board just got on with doing what was best for the Jags. It was strange, shareholding set up with the vast majority of key shares held by a group of individuals or families with Jags connections but who had either been involved in the past or who had no real desire to get involved in driving the club forward. Since 2010, on the field the club was on an upwards trajectory which culminated in a top six finish in the Premier League in season 2017/18. Off the field, there was little to note until the board, by then with chairman Jacqui Low having replaced David Beattie, was approached by a group headed by Paul Conway and his Chinese-American backer Chen Lee. They were interested in adding Thistle to a portfolio of clubs which at that stage had Barnsley as the only other partner. They had previously bought and sold Nice FC for a handsome profit. The Thistle board rejected the approach as it was felt it offered very little for Partick Thistle apart from the promises of future investment and to be part of a worldwide network of clubs that had yet to be established.

What happened next will be written in the annals of Jags history as the former chairman David Beattie gathered a majority of 55 per cent shareholders to orchestrate a coup to get back on the board to make the deal happen. Alarm bells were ringing across the Jags fanbase and at the SFSA we had regular contact with Barnsley fans who were warning us that they had no time for their owners as they had no time for the ordinary fans. On the park, it was no better as they were heading for relegation. It might have been a different reaction if the Jags were being asked to be part of a group with Chelsea or Manchester City, but Barnsley offered far less appeal.

## Be Part of a Group

If you want to progress a plan for fan ownership, then having a properly constituted fans' organisation will be key to your success. That either means convincing an existing trust or supporters' group to endorse and run with the plan or to establish a new entity to carry the plan forward. There is no doubt the political infighting did not help fans' affairs at Dundee with so many factions involved. If it had a FoH equivalent in the wings it might well still be in community ownership today. Experience tells us that a new clean and fresh approach is desirable where possible as it can sideline all the previous history.

For a new organisation, an interim board is a good way to approach the launch phase. It will be essential to align the skill sets that you have available to you, to ensure that all the key areas are covered. In the case at Thistle, we had a lawyer, accountant, communications experts, a political guru, a fantastic administrator/project manager and a digital/social media planner. They were in essence a campaign board who had all the necessary experience and, most importantly, good connections with the fanbase to deliver a campaign. If you are starting from scratch, recruiting these key players as a new group is an important first step as it gives you credibility and a strong working group that sellers, the media and the fans can have faith in. At Stirling Albion, there was no need to create a new group as these positions were filled by the supporters' trust that had been established many years before, so it was simply a case of co-opting key players onto their board to ensure there was the right level of skills. At smaller clubs such as Stirling Albion, it can be a challenge as there are simply not the numbers of key people that are available compared to clubs the size of Hearts, Motherwell or Partick Thistle. One way around this is to co-opt ordinary (non-fan) people; it could be friends, family or even business associates who might be able to help. If they are football fans it could be you will be able to get them to help. At Stirling Albion, at the crucial time of the negotiations we had nobody to conduct financial due diligence. I called on a friend Alan Ramsay, a Hibs fan and former Stirling University graduate who was a CFO at a blue chip firm. He gladly gave his time to help us at a crucial time when we had to do financial due diligence on the limited company. He was able to do it quickly, professionally and for free (ok we bought him lunch) which gave us the confidence to move forward with the project... Without his support we simply would not have had the confidence to take the club on at a time when we were told it was virtually bankrupt!

It is important not to get too carried away with the details of what type of structure you need as this will depend on how the purchase will be completed and what legal and financial considerations are in place at the time of any deal. There are many ways that different structures can be used to facilitate a purchase. At Stirling Albion, the most cost-effective way to buy the club quickly was for the trust, a Community Benefit Scheme, just to buy the shares of the limited company. I would not get too prescriptive in making recommendations here as each group will have their own legal teams to advise them. However, acknowledged as probably the most attractive model for community-owned football clubs is in having a Community Interest Company or a CIC, as it is known. This legal structure was designed for community entities and comes with the provision of having an asset lock which means that it can protect things like a stadium or training facility. In essence, it means that if the club is owned by a CIC, when the CIC is dissolved the only place the assets can go is back into another CIC, thus ensuring that the community is protected accordingly. There is flexibility in that the fans' group who owns the shares can be a CIC or indeed the whole club might convert to being a CIC as is the case at Stenhousemuir, who became the first club in the UK to adopt this structure.

To create a group you will need to get together like-minded individuals who are interested in your aims and objectives, who you trust and are all willing to work for the cause. Once you have your campaign name it is essential that it is registered at Companies House and that will allow you to open up a community bank account. Experience tells me that the quickest and easiest bank to deal with in this area is RBS/Nat West who are well versed in this sector and are fast, which can often be beneficial.

With a boardroom coup taking Thistle in a very dangerous direction, I contacted David Beattie who I had known for many years to suggest that if he and the other shareholders wanted to sell then why not let me get the fans organised and we could make an alternative bid. David never properly responded to my text apart from saying that he could not talk to me which I guess was a polite way of saying no thanks. The most bizarre situation that emerged in all of this was the actions or lack of action of the Jags Trust. If ever there was an example of a rogue fans' organisation not representing what it stood for then this was it. The Jags Trust was the vehicle that emerged from the shadows of the Save the Jags campaign and held 13 per cent of the shares in the club for ordinary supporters who had raised over £100,000 to stop the club going into administration in 1997. It was the first fans' organisation in the UK to get a fan on the board at the club after the Save the Jags campaign. However, that privilege had long gone, and its membership had shrunk to a small rump. Like many trusts, it had converted to become a Community Benefit Society from its original status as an Industrial and Provident Society. Over the years, little had happened at the trust; many fans had joined (like me) and departed as the organisation was constantly in a battle with the club and had a leader who seemed to be perpetually elected in Morag McHaffie. Many believed it was not fit for purpose, but few could have expected what was going to happen next.

Having constantly battled David Beattie for years it came as a huge shock to me and to many others that the Jags Trust, without any consultation with its members, came out in support of the *Moneyball* takeover that David Beattie was orchestrating. In fact, without the 13 per cent pledge of the Jags Trust the coup would not have happened as David Beattie's consortium could not get over 50 per cent of the shareholders to back him. Apart from failing to consult with its members on such a huge issue, it was also a disgraceful disregard of the trust's own origins and its supposed purpose to look towards community ownership for fans. It had bought the *Moneyball* lure, hook, line and sinker and produced a staggeringly biased document in favour of the takeover by faceless individuals and, of course, lent its shareholding to allow the coup to happen.

What is all the more remarkable in this story is that Morag McHaffie is also the chairperson of the newly reformed SDS which claims to represent ordinary fans across Scotland and to promote community ownership. To someone like me, this is a sackable offence, both from the Jags Trust and from SDS; but I had been there before with Morag. When I was being thrown under the bus by the SFA/SPFL (see Chapter 13) Morag was one of the SDS Scottish Council members who was supposedly right behind me. Sadly, that support was then withdrawn when the SFA/SPFL offered money for a silence pact to get a passive SDS to be in their camp. To make that acceptable to them they had to construct a story. I don't know what that story read like, but I do know that I am portrayed as a bogeyman. In the Jags Trust, we had a fans' organisation that was meant to be open and democratic, to be for community ownership yet it was induced to help facilitate a coup that would sell the club to outside interests without any consultation with fans.

What was obvious was that if I wanted to pursue community ownership at Partick Thistle it would have to be done amidst a coup, a dysfunctional fans' group in the background and a support divided between the lure of wealth and great things to come or the long hard road to community ownership.

## Create an Identity That Connects with Your Audience

Fans are, of course, unique customers and in any of the communication that you will have with them in the times ahead you will need to cut through all the clutter and noise that surrounds the club. No matter whether they are social media experts or just readers of the local paper, it is essential that a campaign can help support your concept. At Stirling Albion, we went down the route of saying what it does on the tin with Save the Albion. In cases at Rangers and Hibs, where the weight of media around the club meant more significant stand out was required, we went with www.BuyRangers.org and www.BuyHibs.org as these we felt would help drive the really important call to action. At Rangers, they already had an organisation that had been around for a while but it had challenges with some fans which given the size of the club and the fanbase there was always going to be. So, rather than have the trust name front and centre of things we chose a campaign title that did exactly what it said on the tin. We chose BuyRangers.org as the campaign to buy shares in the club, with the trust that has all the organisational structures to support it very much in the background.

With Hibs, the campaign came at the same time as the highly emotive

PETRIE OUT campaign where the vast majority of Hibs fans wanted the departure of Tom Farmer's man but also to move above the benevolent dictator model to something more akin to what was happening with their city rivals Hearts. If Ann Budge could be paid back over a period of years then what would stop Farmer from selling the club to the fans? A new organisation grew organically under the BuyHibs.org moniker powered by an Edinburgh financier Neil Wheelan who within weeks had brought 6,000 Hibs fans to the party all eager to play. However, the dark deeds from Hampden Park were soon to take me out of the picture and a pretend community ownership model was imposed by the Farmer/Petrie regime with its HSL scheme and the opportunity was missed.

At Hearts, where the organisation was designed for the long term, the fans were truly the foundation of the club and the Foundation of Hearts is a brilliant way to explore that concept. Probably the best example of a campaign that failed to develop an identity that connected with the fans was the 10,000 Hours campaign at St Mirren, which needed a level of explaining just about the name never mind the concept. It would also struggle badly on search engine optimisation which is important when you are looking for pledges and support. The rules are straightforward: make it memorable, make it simple and make sure it will work across all your communication mediums. It sometimes helps that in the case of the Foundation of Hearts it can also have a shorthand version such as the FoH that quickly gets established.

The first steps were made when I gathered around me a group of influential Jags fans who had the same fears as I had and believed our supporters could indeed provide an alternative to the *Moneyball* bid. Interestingly, all of them had at one stage or another been members of the Jags Trust but had long given up hope for the organisation. The SFSA is there to support any fans' organisation and my board agreed to help get the organisation set up, even if I had a role to play in both. We put out the creative brief to a highly respected brand expert and the name Thistle for Ever was universally accepted by around a dozen founding members who felt there was nothing better to drive us forward. It was a good campaign name and also a good, strong longer-term brand identity.

In this case, we got the team name (the original Thistle) in the title and referred to an old Jags song where we proclaimed that we as fans would follow Thistle 'for ever and ever'. Our clever marketing gurus also explained that when using the words FOR EVER rather than saying FOREVER, that this signified eternity which certainly floated our boat. The SFSA agreed with the dozen founding fathers that it would foot the bill for the legal cost and the design and website set-up, either until the organisation was financially on its own two feet or, if the campaign died, then the costs would be split between the founders with a £100 contribution per head. With that security agreed, Danny Sweeney of Total Brand created the logo, the design and the website that would facilitate the launch of the brand.

### Build a Knowledge Base

It is critical to any community ownership campaign to build a wide understanding of not only what the campaign is designed to do but also how the whole community ownership model works. Depending on the circumstances, there are opportunities to get experience and share knowledge. In early 2019 at the request of the then CEO, I organised an event at Falkirk FC where representatives from the Foundation of Hearts, St Mirren, Motherwell and I gathered to share our knowledge and experiences with the Bairns fans and the club. What I have also found through our work at the SFSA is that fans of all clubs are really happy to help and share with ordinary fans even if it means having to be nice to your nearest and dearest rivals. We all know deep down that it is just the colour of the scarves that makes us different and that underneath it all the loyalty and love we have for our club is no different from that of our fiercest rivals. It is really rewarding to see fans of all clubs work together. In this regard, the Foundation of Hearts and the Well Society have been superb, and it really has helped develop a wider understanding of the model.

One of the key things we did was to ensure that the founding members who would drive the initial campaign would gain as much knowledge as possible about the subject matter. This we were able to do through various SFSA documents, through discussions and through the members being able to refer to documents available online and through source materials supplied by directors at both the Foundation of Hearts and the Well Society.

Prior to launch it was essential that we would be able to answer (within reason) any question that fans would put to us about the campaign. We produced a Q&A that would appear on our website that we believed would answer most of the questions that would emerge. Post-launch we also gathered further questions and responded back to those who asked them. This process was obviously essential as the key attributes of community ownership are openness and transparency. The difficulty we had in the early stages of the Thistle for Ever campaign was that we had a divided support with many fans preferring to take the risk with a foreign *Moneyball* deal rather than putting the shoulder to the wheel and having the safety, security and sustainability that supporter ownership might bring. It is not ideal starting a campaign with a divided fan base.

Once the campaign got underway, we held our first public event at the club which was entitled 'The good, the bad and the ugly of Community Ownership', where Bryan Jackson and I presented many aspects from many of the examples we had come across in our careers. It was filmed and was available for anyone who could not attend the event that night.

To build a successful campaign it is essential that you can reach out to as many fans as possible and even after a successful campaign this role does not stop. In fact, it becomes even more important to continue building on the surge of support you have and to make the owners feel they are a vital part of the success of the club. This is something we failed miserably to do at Stirling Albion and is something that both Hearts and Motherwell have excelled at through the ongoing activities that the FoH and the Well Society have developed.

*Get your Organisation Launched – be creative!*

It is essential that you agree a plan with your team where the roles and responsibilities are set in place. Prior to the launch, you will need to get all your documentation in place and have your communication tools such as your website and social media platforms ready to be switched on. Until the moment you go live your team will be able to make amendments and adjustments without the full glare of the public looking at you. After the launch, it is never so easy and there will *always* be detractors wanting to trip you up or highlight something that you might have missed. All your team needs to be briefed and be ready as you are getting closer to the go-live moment.

How you best attract the attention of the media at this launch event will need to be considered as well as reviewing what other commitments the media might have. It would be pointless conducting a photoshoot or a press conference on a Friday when Sky Sports are more likely to be attending press conferences at Celtic and Rangers or holding your event during the international break when all the media attention is focused on the national team and their opponents. If you get this simple bit wrong, you can expect there to be very few members of the sports press turning up to your event no matter how exciting or fun you think that your activity might be. The press release should be factual, to the point and contain all the essential information you need to convey as well as having some key quotes from your campaign leader and their contact details.

With a small tight group of individuals behind TFE from locations across the country it was always going to be a challenge to get enough folk together for the launch. I was always going to be there given my history of community ownership and my role as CEO of the SFSA, but we didn't want it to just be me shouting about TFE. We developed a plan working our way back from what might be a good photograph. Fortunately, my two brothers-in-law are football fans, with Pat being a member of the Well Society and Gordon being a St Mirren fan. The idea was that they were supporting me as their two own clubs were heading for community ownership. In essence it was a family affair which is what community ownership was all about. A quick trip out to Fir Park got me a Motherwell top thanks to Craig Hughes at the Well Society and we all arranged to meet on a wet and windy day at Firhill on 9 September 2019. We had Sky Sport, STV, BBC and Radio Clyde in attendance as well as many of the Red Tops. TFE got the launch it needed and within hours fans who wanted something different to the *Moneyball* started to pledge on our website. Of course, once we were live what was essential was to communicate with the audience on a regular basis as it suddenly stopped being our campaign and became something for every Jags fan.

*Engage in Capacity Building*

Building your organisation comes in three simple stages:

STEP 1 – BUILD A TEAM

This, as described above, is where you build the team and work together on getting all your campaign activity ready prior to the launch. Gathering a team of dedicated, quality supporters who share the same objectives will be an essential part of the process. Think of it like a building site where a new house has to be built. The first and most important thing is ensuring that you have solid foundations in place to allow for a structure to be built that will last. It is pointless having a team of ten bricklayers when you really need a mix that can give you brickies, joiners, electricians etc. It might well be that some of the team in step one will only be involved in this initial stage, which is fine, but you will need some members who can give you continuity. The most important aspect is having a quality leader who can act as your site agent or conductor to get the best out of all the different skills that you have assembled. Without that leadership the process will be doomed.

STEP 2 – EXTEND THE TEAM

Post launch there will be others who will want to be involved in what your group is trying to achieve and to influence how you go about these tasks. This can be a tricky step as you don't really want to lose any of your key team members, but you also need to expand the operation after you have gone public. Getting to know the new members/advocates is important and making sure everyone knows who is coming on board. If you are building capacity through pledgers or through donations it is essential that your team communicates regularly to the wider audience. What usually happens is that when you have events other prospective members step forward to offer their services. Filtering out who can help drive things forward will be an important part of the process.

STEP 3 – FORM A BOARD

Getting to this position should be an organic process that will be based on how the campaign progresses. In the first instance your loose formation of volunteers will need to mould into a functioning Fans' Board. Having legal support in this process is important as it is the sign off on what the role of the new developing organisation will be. Once this is agreed then it is a matter of developing a constitution and a way of working that will ensure that it has people in place filling the essential key roles such as Chair, Treasurer, Secretary etc. What will also need to be established is how these roles will be filled on an interim basis and in the longer term when the democratic process steps in agreeing an election process for the board that allows all members the opportunity to vote.

At Partick Thistle these steps can be seen in action as follows:

STEP 1 – BUILD A TEAM

In some respects I was not best placed to run the Thistle campaign as I was so poorly connected with Thistle fans. Having spent 17 years down south in my career and being a passive member of the Jags Trust apart from family members, I didn't know a lot of Thistle fans. Much of the work that I had done for the club over the years was completed behind the scenes and didn't give me any profile. I did know a couple of influential Jags fans in Jonathan Kennedy and Erik Geddes who used their excellent networks to bring some sensational candidates forward to form our first Working Party. That Working Party suggested that as I had very specific knowledge and experience that I chair the operation.

STEP 2 – EXTEND THE TEAM

As we will see elsewhere this process for TfE was to a certain extent taken out of our own hands in that a deal was very quickly done where Three Black Cats, the company which Colin Weir owned, had purchased the shares in Partick Thistle. As part of the process TfE along with the existing vehicle that had been created to hold Colin's original donation to fans, the PTFC Trust, were given the task of developing a community ownership vehicle for the club. This process involved the setting up of working groups with various strands and tasks to report back with an overall solution that would allow the shareholding to be transferred to TfE in the future. The club asked for volunteers to be part of this process and around 40 fans stepped forward. Given the divisions that were around the club it made sense to try to consult and involve as many as possible. However, I would not ordinarily recommend so many folks be involved in a working group as giving them anything meaningful to achieve in a set timeframe makes it hard to manage. Each case will depend on its merits and the benefits for Thistle of doing it this way was in having the knowledge that we were looking after Colin Weir's legacy. Circumstances also got in the way when sadly Colin passed away and our four-month deadline to deliver things became less of an issue given the lockdown from the COVID-19 pandemic. The results of the season ending when it did and the impact on the club meant that the focus on delivering to a set timetable became less important.

STEP 3 – FORM THE BOARD

Ordinarily the original founding members would form the board of the fans' organisation usually on an interim basis until it is deemed the right time to have elections. It is important that you don't get hung up on trying to move to this stage too fast as there is a real danger that you over engineer things. Everyone has signed up for one member one vote and those who have followed your campaign will be indebted to the initial group for all the work that they have done to make things happen. What is critical is that there is enough time to let things settle down and for the organisation to form its own personality. In the situation at Thistle the circumstances allowed for this step to take a slightly different path with several members of the founding group stepping aside to allow the Working Group to become almost an interim board. Once pledgers become members and a timetable is agreed the interim board will be trimmed in size and there will be a clear pathway for elections. What will be important is that there remains a continuity within this framework to allow the TfE to prosper and develop its purpose.

## Ready for Action

Having a fans' organisation that is properly structured and capable of buying shares in the club or indeed being prepared to buy the club depends on how well you have become established and trusted. At Stirling Albion we knew that having that SAFC Trust was going to be a really important issue for us and given that there was no end point in sight we made the initial pledge that your initial donation of £40 would be returned to you, less the bank charges, if we failed in our objective. This was something that was missing from the original Well Society strategy that had been developed by the club to facilitate a sale to John Boyle. It took a few years after the departure of John Boyle from the scenes before the organisation had to be restructured and the trust that was missing re-established and built upon.

It is important to decide quickly whether there is a need to collect the cash or to simply get pledges for direct debits to be set up in the future. At Stirling there was a pressing chance that the club could go under, and we also felt that it was important to capitalise on the PR momentum that we were generating worldwide through the endorsement of the likes of Andy Murray, Cristiano Ronaldo, Usain Bolt etc. The big failure was that with 2,340 members signed up from around the world we never monetised this goodwill on an annual basis like the FoH and others have subsequently done. This was no more than not having the resources to do so. The FoH of course started with pledges and once Bryan Jackson had them in the driving seat and under the leadership of Ian Murray, they quickly converted the initial 8,500 members' direct debits into real cash. What is essential is that you have a community bank account set up and a system in place that can facilitate the management of your direct debits. Over the years I have recommended Go Cardless for this who I believe still do the same for both Hearts and Motherwell.

## Let the Show Begin With Your Campaign

There are two different aspects or stages to a fans' community ownership fundraising campaign. In the first instance you will have to work a lot harder if you are not yet working with the club. Once you become established with the club then the collaborative approach becomes so much easier as long as you are independent from them. It is essential that you build on your initial launch in being clear in what your objectives are. The more specific you can be the easier it will be to recruit and convert pledgers into full membership. So, your money will help us buy the club or fund the youth academy or build a new stand and in return you will get the following benefits. Offering benefits prior to getting in a position of buying or owning the club can be quite challenging. However, experience tells us that the more complex you make this the more you make a rod for your own back. Supporters love the team and want it to thrive, so the main thing is assuring them that their hard-earned cash is going to buy or grow the club and that they have a vote in how the process evolves. Additional benefits can be developed as and when it is necessary.

One perfect example of getting this wrong was in the original Well Society which was set up by the club. Having not been driven by a fans' movement and not having its own momentum it made the mistake of giving a complex range of club offers that eventually had to be stripped out when the society re-emerged cleaner and better managed by the fans several years later. The key is keeping it simple.

What is also essential is that there is a constant stream of activity and stories that will generate interest. Former players or staff endorsing the campaign or celebrity fans posing for pictures gives your communications team the opportunity to build momentum. Every time you create activity in the early phase of the campaign you should be looking at getting more pledgers signed up. Having a creative team working to generate ideas will give your campaign momentum. You should consider anything that might raise interest and capture the imagination. As the understanding of community ownership grows it becomes easier as you don't need to explain the concept to get support. There is also a huge role to be played by the local press who love the drama of a campaign with their local team. Nobody in the *Stirling Observer* ever thought that they would be talking about Ronaldo, Bolt, Murray, Meerkats in connection with Stirling Albion. It was good copy for them.

Once the stage emerges that the club and the fans are more closely linked it is so much easier for the fans' campaigns to be integrated and utilise the club resources. However, a distance is still needed between them, and the campaign can't interfere with any efforts that the club might be making in any particular area. Looking at the output from the Well Society and the Foundation of Hearts is a great way to see how this is balanced. What is also needed is for there to be regular presence from the fans' group at the ground on match days. The reality is that with this model of community ownership the campaign never ends, it just goes to a different stage.

The situation at all clubs is different and at Thistle the situation moved very quickly and was different to the campaigns at many of the other clubs we have mentioned in this book. With the input of Colin Weir three fans were put on the board and the working group was established to develop the plan to transfer the shareholding to TFE. It meant that the need for driving new memberships/pledgers was put on hold. The club promoted that fans can pledge a few times, but this was in tandem to the amazing response from the fans that raised £150,000 during the COVID-19 crisis to help keep the club afloat. The plan was that once the share transfer happened and TFE became properly established it would develop its own plans alongside the club to maximise the revenue it can make for the club as well as nurturing talent for the boardroom.

## Look for Allies

It goes without saying that a fans' collective that is potentially just emerging will be unlikely to have significant financial backing. However, if you are clear in your mission and have a focus on the prize then it should fill your group with confidence. The pathway and the understanding of what you are trying to achieve is now a far easier story to tell. From clubs who have been reborn such as Clydebank and Gretna through to FC United and AFC Wimbledon, each has a compelling story to tell that can be part of your campaign narrative as you educate on and promote what has gone before you.

At Stirling Albion eight individuals invested £200,000 to make the deal to save the club happen, trusting that they would get their money back. This was all done interest-free as a gift to the club. Benefactors such as Ann Budge at Hearts, Les Hutcheon at Motherwell, Gordon Scott at St Mirren and Ross McArthur and his colleagues at Dunfermline all saw the beauty and the opportunity of wider community ownership and decided that they would support the teams that they loved in this way. There is no doubt that despite the desperate efforts of the SPFL and the SFA to close community ownership down in Scotland all that has happened is that it has thrived. All of these individuals could have just bought these clubs outright but instead they chose to share their wealth and considerable business experiences with their fellow fans and secure the clubs on a pathway for a long sustainable future where openness and transparency will flourish. These are superb role models for others to follow and as a fans' group finding these individuals who might buy into the power of the many is something that is well worth thinking about.

When we set Thistle for Ever up, we were prepared in the first instance to become a legitimate fans' organisation that would champion the opportunity for community ownership and challenge the *Moneyball* bid to take over our club. At that stage there was always the chance or hope that Colin Weir, a huge figure at the club, might be interested in being involved. It was far from certain that this would ever happen, and it was to our delight that a few weeks later we were asked to meet his lawyers. We went through in detail how we would see community ownership working at Partick Thistle. We had no idea if Colin would consider giving us a loan to make it happen. Another few weeks later we were delighted when it was announced that Colin intended to work with the Thistle for Ever group to buy the club and gift it to the supporters. The excitement we felt was huge and the campaign kicked on to the next level where a deal could be done. We of course were soon brought down to earth with the awful news that Colin had unexpectedly passed away. His legacy at Partick Thistle will live on in future generation of Jags fans who will hear his story and celebrate what was achieved despite the near two-year detour due to his advisor Jacqui Low holding on to power for reasons that only she will ever understand.

### Start Negotiating and Overcoming Hurdles

As soon as the opportunity emerges to get a deal on the table then it is key that you have the support of your legal and financial team to ensure that your deal is properly positioned. Having internal resources is a huge benefit as it also brings a network of contacts. The larger the club the more skills you can call on, ideally on a volunteer or pro bono basis. Even in the case at Stirling Albion where we had no legal support internally, we managed to get a friend of mine from my university football team to give us mates rates to help us get the deal over the line. It was a necessary expense and several years later, when a consortium tried to buy the club, the work that the lawyer Jim McGinn had done in 2010/11 ensured that the door was closed to their plans to manage the club and saddle it with debt that had to be paid back in a five-year period. The main important point is that your group leaders delegate the task to professionals who can give you the best opportunity to get a deal over the line. Remembering the example above, it is not just the initial transaction but that provisions need to be put in place to protect all your hundreds or thousands of members. Of course, as I found at Partick Thistle, some of the hurdles you just don't expect and there are things that you can't plan for. However, if you have the fundamentals in place, you can and will succeed.

In this specific case, it started as a relatively easy process where Colin Weir's business and personal lawyers took charge of the affairs, and the deal was completed within a matter of weeks. Thistle for Ever was then in a place where we had delivered a proposal for the long-term development of community ownership at Partick Thistle.

Sadly when Colin died so did the simplicity of this campaign and his advisor Jacqui Low decided to take things in a very different direction. It became clear to me that the notion of community ownership was being side-lined despite everything being in place. I was being told that fans could not run football clubs and that Ann Budge said so. Of course, the context at Hearts was very different and some of the excellent fans who have stepped forward at Hearts over the years have disproven that assertion. Likewise, even if Ann did feel that the narrative was slightly different, it was her £4.2m that had saved the club in the first instance.

I was a very real threat to this new Not Really Fans' Ownership narrative that was coming from Jacqui, and she made it quite clear when the original TfE interim board had nominated John Penman and myself to be on the club board that she didn't want me there – having someone who had pioneered the concept in Scotland would have been impossible for her to work against. My consolation was that I was to chair a working group as it was deemed TfE was not inclusive enough. Within days, I was told I was not going to chair it after all. I toiled with this for several months and the final straw came for me when Jacqui decided the fans' organisation I had created in Thistle for Ever had baggage (I assume myself and my fellow creators) and that a new name/organisation was needed. It was just part of the delaying process and marginalising the person who had been around more community ownership campaigns than anyone in Scotland. I stepped aside gracefully as it was a battle I knew I couldn't win and from an SFSA perspective fighting with a club would not help us as an organisation. I supported the renamed Jags Foundation and despite them doing everything a fully-fledged democratic organisation should do, they were ignored. The Foundation Board resigned and a newly elected board replaced them, and they too were ignored. Eventually, the end game came into sight as the shares were given to a reformed Partick Thistle Trust which would allow Jacqui and her board to continue without the supporters' endorsement. The position was of course untenable and as soon as the fans started protesting the inevitable happened and the board resigned en masse to leave the 1,000 plus strong (now 1,600 members) Jags Foundation to engage with the PTFC Trust and take the next legitimate steps to the fan ownership I had always dreamed about.

Fortunately, under the steady leadership of Sandy Fyfe, chair of The Jags Foundation and one of my original go-to TfE members, the club eventually passed into fans' hands in September 2023.

## How Do You Manage the Club?

Once the structures are in place the main aspect that is different for a community-owned club is in how the club operates with its main owner/majority shareholder. These are not institutions or a long list of individuals who bought shares 40 years ago. The fans' organisation is the living, breathing place where fans who are the owners are represented, and their opinions are heard. The key thing is in making sure that the link that is established is robust and strong and functions properly. Again, one of the most important aspects is to ensure that what you develop is enshrined in your articles of association and are easily followed and understood by the owners. If you fail to do this it can lead to chaos or in the case at Stirling Albion, and to an extent at FC United of Manchester, significant infighting emerges that does not do the concept any favours. It is not to say that there is any more politics than happens at conventionally run clubs but with a fan-owned operation you can be guaranteed that the dirty washing will be in the public domain pretty quickly. In many places in this book, I have spoken about the many positive learnings from my time running the Stirling Albion campaign and running the club. However, the biggest mistake was the link between the owners (the trust) and the nomination board that was put in place when we took over the club. This was done on trust and never formally developed, which is my biggest ever mistake in football. It was meant to be a temporary situation for the first couple of years where the main investors worked on the board until they got their own money back. Sadly, it has allowed for a situation where the chairman of the club since those days has twice been asked to leave by the trust board and refused to go. The trust board resigned which was music to his ears as it allowed him to populate the trust with his own backers. Nearly ten years on there was still no proper democracy in place and neither the chairman nor anyone from his board had ever been elected. Fortunately, after having survived several scandals and fans' attempts to persuade him to depart, Stuart Brown and his unelected and unaccountable board left the building in August 2022 after historical social media posts were discovered that gave him no other choice but to go.

In my defence, running the club was my priority and this task was delegated to members of the trust, and nobody could have perhaps seen such a power grab happening. I do feel so sorry for all those real genuine Binos fans who worked tirelessly during the campaign that they have the ownership but not the openness, transparency or democracy that they deserve. For that, I can only apologise, and I am now enjoying seeing a properly elected fans' board run the club properly. The future is once again bright for the Binos.

To give you an indication of how things might work at Partick Thistle, in the appendices there is an early draft of our how our articles might look. We were inspired by the work already done by the Foundation of Hearts, the Well Society and the Exeter City Supporters' Trust (who are the original fan-owned club who have thrived for over 20 years). Anyone looking for the final versions of these documents or various other examples can contact me or visit the Scottish Football Supporters Association website.

# Appendices: The Community Ownership Tool Kit – Things You Need to Win

*I've never played for a draw in my life.*—Sir Alex Ferguson

THE PURPOSE OF these appendices is to give fans a summary of just some of the tools that you might need if you want to plan a community ownership campaign. Hopefully the guide of what you need for a successful campaign and the shared experiences from earlier chapters in this book will allow you to start the process. There will be further requirements that you will need once you have successfully gained ownership of the club. I have referenced these here and you can find so much more on the SFSA website where more detailed Word documents can be downloaded and used as templates.

Now that we have so many clubs in community ownership there are fans' groups and fans that are more than willing to give up their time and share their work, all for the common good. I would remind you that there is no right or wrong in this and that much of what will be created for your club will be tailored versions of these documents. My thanks again go to everyone who has contributed and shared so far. It is one of the most satisfying things to see fans of different clubs supporting each other.

Additional support is now available as the SFSA has just announced a partnership with Dundee University's School of Business to enhance the research options for future development. This includes the setting up of an Expert Working Group where fans who have experiences at many of the clubs mentioned in earlier chapters of this book can share best practice and support the overall concept of community ownership in Scottish football. Please get in touch if you want or need further advice or if your club feels it can contribute to what we are trying to do.

# APPENDIX 1
# Business Plan

AS A FANS' GROUP you need to develop a simple business plan that shows how you can work towards the clubs having a longer-term sustainable future. Once in the club you need to differentiate the role of the fans' organisation and the club. It is essential that once the fans' group has purchased the shares that they (the members) have the ability to decide where the money raised goes. Is it youth development, is it facilities or is it to enhance the first team squad? Here is a recent example of a simple plan (draft version) as used by the East Fife FC (EFFC) fans as they galvanised their campaign to buy the club in 2024. Printed here with their permission (thanks to our friends at East Fife for allowing us to share this).

## East Fife FC: A Fans' Business Plan DRAFT

EXECUTIVE SUMMARY (THE PLAN IN A NUTSHELL)

What you want to do, how you are going to do it, why it is important you do it and what the wider benefits are likely to be

ORGANISATION MISSION

Our mission is to move East Fife Football Club to community ownership to ensure its survival as a professional football club and that it leads and/or contributes to a range of community support projects relating to the health and prosperity of the Levenmouth community.

VISION

To create a viable community club run by the community which has its place in professional football leagues and addresses the wider health and material needs of the local community.

PRIORITIES

- To establish financial stability by May 2024.
- To involve fully community groups including Fifers for the Community, The Youth Academy, the Men's Shed and other relevant organisations by December 2023 and then ongoing.

- To identify a support group with relevant skills and knowledge to run the club by the end of 2023.
- To take advantage of the impending rail link to develop new income streams for the club when it opens March 2024.

## United club ethos

BACKGROUND

EFFC is a private limited Scottish company Number SC007902 incorporated in 1911 and now with a major shareholder with over 50 per cent of the shareholding. Since 2005 the supporters' trust has been acquiring a shareholding in the club and it is now the third largest shareholder.

The trust is a Community Benefit Society incorporated under the Industrial and Provident Societies Act and registered with the Financial Conduct Authority. It has adopted the model rules for a Supporters Community Mutual as laid down by Supporters Direct and seeks to benefit the Levenmouth community by:

- enhancing the social, cultural and economic value of the society by acting as a responsible custodian of its assets and the football club for future generations
- strengthening the bonds between the club and community
- promoting participation in football by all sectors of the population
- being an inclusive and representative organisation
- playing at the highest level compatible with financial stability

## How We Will Get There

ACTIVITIES & SERVICES

The main problem the club has is that it has a non-resident owner who controls over 50% of the club but who shows little interest in developing or investing in the club. The result is a constant financial struggle to survive and a constantly deteriorating physical structure.

In addition, the existing board while just maintaining financial survival with the help of Government Covid funding has been unable to make any significant commercial improvements.

A local registered SCIO, Fifers for the Community (FFTC), succeeded in gaining funding for an artificial pitch which is used by the football club for its matches with an agreement in place for the club to pay rent for the pitch while FFTC in turn rent the actual ground on which the pitch is installed. There are agreements in place to maintain and replace the pitch surface at five-year intervals but there are concerns about whether the football club will be able to meet its financial commitment to this.

Our community is not well off and lies about seventh in the Scottish Index of Multiple Deprivation and yet there are many flourishing community groups to help people and we see that EFFC should play a greater part in this.

Currently these groups include:

- Fifers for the Community which provides and maintains the artificial pitch and which also is involved in supporting facilities such as the Shed group which provides a mental health resource for local men and women.
- The East Fife Community Club, which incorporates four previous groups – East Fife Junior Supporters Club, East Fife Youths, East Fife Community and East Fife Girls and Women Football Club. The effect of this arrangement is that from the age of three children can play and continue through a well-structured path to whatever level is appropriate for the individual.
- Levenmouth Together, a well-established community support group aimed at combating poverty and other economic and social consequences of the impact of Covid, energy costs and other negative external factors.

Our intention is that by taking control of the club we will play a much greater part in helping our community deal with its issues through not only football but also by engaging in a wide range of support activities for health, economic and social development, issues in which the current owners have shown little interest other than deriving financial support.

One significant development will be the arrival of the railway line in March 2024. There are several sources of funding available to help local businesses prepare for and take advantage of this. We will exploit these by improving club facilities to make it an attractive venue for non-football activities and by adding to club infrastructure to improve operational efficiency.

## Initial Activity

FACILITIES

Create a secure parking area and resurface it to provide facilities for attendees at events; install appropriate PA and connectivity systems to provide technical support for concerts and other events; create a well-lit walkway to connect the ground to the new rail station and the promenade/bus station.

APPROACH TO IMPROVEMENT

Put together an entrepreneurial group as a subset of the new board to look for and develop both large and small scale improvements.

LOCAL PARTNERSHIPS

There is a strong network of community groups in the Levenmouth area and we would work to ensure the club played a central role within this network.

We will also seek to work closely with local and national business agencies and Fife Council to ensure our developments fit their strategies and thus benefit from support and possible funding.

Several of our support members have close links with these agencies and include local councillors, directors of economic development, Fife Tourism Partnership and Levenmouth Together.

## Diverse Sources of Income

Currently the club has done little to expand normal support let alone create other income streams. Opportunities to improve on this situation include:

Attracting more family support. Over 1,200 new homes have been built in the club catchment area over the last ten years and planning permission exists for a further 1,200. A planned campaign for the start of the season would contact these new families informing them of the existing opportunities for a wide range of age groups and offering incentives to come to a match and sign up for season tickets etc.

Developing hospitality. Like many clubs the hospitality facilities at Bayview are much underused. We would focus on areas like family events such as weddings, birthdays and funerals – the recent addition of a lift to the hospitality suites is an advantage here. Additionally, we are an ideal venue for community club events such as AGMs and fundraising activities.

Business use. Currently the area has limited facilities for business meetings and we feel there may be an opportunity for small business conferences.

While the area still lacks hotel accommodation (the provision of which on club ground may be something for the future) our parking facilities and near-future closeness to the railway station provides potential to take advantage of this market. Early discussion with Fife Council Economic Development Directorship suggests they would be willing to support this through research and promotion.

Event venue. The artificial surface, a south facing grandstand with capacity for 2,000, car parking and hospitality facilities along with the absence of a similar facility nearby offer the chance to provide a range of events including music performance, community celebrations, sports events and the like.

## People

Our first priority when successful is to reconstitute the existing board of directors of EFFC. A small working group is currently identifying possible additions to the board though there are three existing members we may invite to continue.

We would seek to strengthen the club by including representatives of local groups including Fifers for the Community and East Fife Community Club.

In staffing terms, while we would continue with the existing strong group of volunteers, we acknowledge that there is a need for proper commercial development and would seek to recruit for that role and for the associated financial activities.

## Club structure

The existing East Fife FC Ltd would become an asset of the East Fife Supporters' Trust and as such would require fitting into the governance structure of the trust. The intention is to change the limited company into a community-owned organisation using an appropriate legal format.

Operationally the professional football team would continue in much the same way as it does at present while over time the community groups referred to previously would be incorporated into a single structure.

An advisory board with representatives of significant local community groups would be set up.

## Marketing & communications

The club has to date suffered from a lack of investment in marketing and communications. The new board will create a senior marketing post and will ensure that continual two-way communication between the club and its stakeholders using a wide range of media. One simple addition will be to use the lists of season ticket holders and trust members as a means of marketing events and offers – in other words adding more value to the people concerned.

## Performance

MEASURING PROGRESS

Both the board and the advisory group will meet on a monthly basis to plan and review activity. The agendas will reflect the need to check performance by ensuring all actions have a named individual responsible for each action, a target date for completion and a brief reporting section. In addition to general business, each meeting will have a theme and focus on a particular area of activity – eg marketing, facilities, planning and so forth. Finance will be a standing item on all agendas and management accounts will be presented to ensure proper scrutiny at each meeting.

## APPENDIX 2
# Launching Your Campaign

IT IS ESSENTIAL that you create a memorable and highly impactful launch event that can get national (if you have an angle) and local media along.

See photos section for examples of two that I have personally delivered.

At Stirling Albion we chose to launch at Bannockburn as it was local, was another famous battle at Stirling (our battle was to save the club), it didn't cost anything and it provided a great backdrop for TV and photographers. Amazingly, we did even get the BBC and Sky Sports Scotland to come all the way to Stirling as the story and the visuals were strong enough.

At Partick Thistle many of the other key players in our initial Interim Management Group were for business or personal reasons less inclined to step in front of the cameras. I had to find an angle that was not just about me turning my attention to the Jags so I volunteered my two brothers-in-law to step forward as they both followed teams that were in community ownership.

Following up on the initial launch is just as important to keep the momentum going and the second hit at the Jags was a mention at Holyrood and a photo call with the local MP and MSP who were backing the community ownership campaign.

What is also important is that you have all the marketing tools including all your social media feeds ready to be switched on as soon as you go live. In both the Albion and Thistle cases we had a Press Call and followed that evening with a fans' event, where the campaign concept could be discussed. It is essential that you have a well-documented Q&A developed for the event and it can also be added to your website and allow your social media team to answer questions from it.

## Possible Questions for Press/Fans' Launch

It is essential that you have thought through all the potential questions that may get thrown at the panel by either the fans or the press. These can be used by your presentation team to ensure that they are well briefed for the launch. Given the power of social media these can also be lifted and directed back to anyone asking the questions on your social media channels. It really is worth using the exercise in developing the Q&A to ensure that your team are well briefed and that you have thought of everything. Some of the questions might be awkward, some not so. Either way you need to be prepared or have the answers tailored directly to your own clubs and to the specifics of your own campaign.

These are the questions that we used when we launched the campaign to buy Stirling Albion from an owner who was not keen on selling the club to us:

Q. Why are you doing this?

Q. How many people do you need to sign up to allow any realistic hopes of a buy-out?

Q. What level of local pick up are you hoping for?

Q. What exactly are you selling to people?

Q. What do they get for their money?

Q. Will they be shareholders?

Q. Will they own something for life?

Q. Do people who join need to pay any form of annual resubscription?

Q. Isn't this just a Scottish Ebbsfleet FC?

Q. With crowds so low at Forthbank is it realistic to expect the amount of people you require to give money to help Stirling Albion?

Q. Why should people outwith the local area be interested?

Q. Would you accept larger donations if it meant guaranteeing places on any new board?

Q. Will you continue to appeal for members to join the 'fund' even after any buy-out takes place or does the campaign end at this point?

Q. What do you think is wrong with the current boardroom set up at Stirling Albion?

Q. What happens if the campaign fails to raise enough money to buy the majority shareholding in the club?

Q. Why wouldn't people get all of their £40 back?

Q. Would the trust make any money out of an unsuccessful campaign? Ie would any of the unreturned money end up in the trust coffers?

Q. Will the trust continue to attempt to liaise with the club if all offers are rebuffed and the campaign fails?

Q. How long will the campaign run?

Q. If the campaign isn't successful in taking over the running of SAFC do you fear for the club's future?

Q. What does the campaign think the majority shareholding is worth?

Q. Would the campaign be prepared to go 'significantly' above their valuation to take control of the club?

Q. Would you be making any offers to existing shareholders to try and get complete ownership of SAFC?

Q. If the campaign raises just enough to buy the majority shareholding how do they propose running a club with an empty purse?

Q. Does the campaign team think they will have enough experience to run a football club?

Q. The current board seems to be struggling to make ends meet. How does a rookie collection of football club owners hope to do any better?

Q. Have you spoken to Stirling Council about your plans?

Q. Do you have any plans to buy Forthbank?

Q. Is Forthbank seen as the long-term home for SAFC or would you have any plans for a new ground?

Q. Would you like to see Stirling play full-time football?

Q. What are the ambitions of any new board?

## APPENDIX 2: LAUNCHING YOUR CAMPAIGN

Q. How will the new board be made up?

Q. Would all people who join the campaign be entitled to vote on club affairs?

Q. What sort of issues will the members be entitled to vote on?

Q. Will they be able to pick the team?

Q. How does the new board plan on re-engaging with the local community?

Q. Have the campaign had any meetings with other trusts who have attempted takeovers?

Q. Do you think it will be harder to be successful considering the economic climate?

## APPENDIX 3
## Press Release

Most of the fans' groups I have known attracted a range of skill sets from willing volunteer groups. There is usually expertise in legal, financial and communications among other things. You might even be fortunate enough to be able to call on the services of a dedicated PR agency.

Here below is the example of format that was developed for the BuytheAlbion campaign by Wave PR and once we got the club we just adapted and used the same format. If you have an agency they will be able to distribute a release for you, if you don't you need to build a press database and send the release out yourself.

It is essential that you check the story and if possible use your contacts in the press to make sure they are interested in the story/event/activity before you release it. Timing is one of the biggest challenges – you can't compete against a Celtic–Rangers or Scotland Press Conference or another major news story so don't try!

Have a headline and pick out a couple of headline points, ensure you have a date on the release and describe what is happening and why. It is useful to include a couple of quotes from key people and make sure that your release is coordinated with being uploaded to your website and social media. Make sure you have contact details on the release too!

### NEWS RELEASE (EXAMPLE)
**STIRLING ALBION PLAYERS OFFER TO 'PLAY FOR THE SHIRT'**

PLAYERS TO PLAY FOR FREE IN FEBRUARY TO SUPPORT CLUB'S 'FAN AID' FUNDRAISING CAMPAIGN

STIRLING COMMUNITY URGED TO TURN OUT FOR VISIT OF LEAGUE LEADER AND FOR JOCKY SCOTT'S FIRST GAME IN CHARGE

**4 February 2011**: Stirling Albion FC's 'FAN AID' fundraising campaign, launched just four days ago and has received a massive boost from right on its doorstep – its very own players.

And with the welcome and valuable boost received from its own playing squad, who have offered to forego their wages in February, the club hopes recover some financial ground lost over the last three months.

Following three months of match postponements due to the severe winter weather conditions resulting in no income coming into the club, 'FAN AID', a fundraising campaign to secure additional donations from fans on top of their admission price, has been launched.

Paul Goodwin, Club Spokesperson said:

'This is a fantastic gesture from the players and one that is most appreciated. Since the supporters' trust took control of the club just seven months ago we have managed the affairs of the club prudently and within an agreed financial structure. However, no business can cope without any income for three months and with every bill paid we are now operating at the bare minimum, which is why we started the FAN AID campaign.

Having the players come to us to say they appreciated our efforts and wanted to be part of the campaign just says how they feel about our club. The trust has neither overdraft nor any millionaire backers; but what we do have is 2,400 dedicated members and supporters and a team that we are now even more proud of.'

Club Captain Ross Forsyth said:

'The owners (the fans) have done a great job given the unique circumstances and the team appreciate just what they have achieved and wanted to support the FAN AID campaign. The boys just felt that as we are all in this together saying that we didn't want paid in February was a positive thing that we could all do.'

Fans will be able to make additional donations at the Doubletree Dunblane Stadium this Saturday, and at every future home game, where Stirling Albion will take on First Division leaders Raith Rovers.
Paul Goodwin added:

'Now is the time we really need the support of the Stirling community. Saturday is a perfect time to come to the Doubletree Dunblane Stadium if they haven't been for a while as we'll have the league leaders in town and our new manager Jocky Scott's first game in charge to enjoy.'

**For More Information Please Contact Paul Goodwin on 07702 252519.
Additional comments Ross Forsyth on 07xxx xxxxxx**

## APPENDIX 4
## Funding

AS WE HAVE explored elsewhere in this book funding will be required to buy shares in the club you want to buy. There are several ways this can be done:

- Donations and other ad hoc fundraising activities
- Regular monthly membership contributions
- Benefactors giving loans that have to be repaid to them (Ann Budge, Hearts; Gordon Scott, St Mirren)
- Through the new Scottish Government Community Ownership model (Fans Bank)
- Through another party – as we saw at St Mirren where the Kibble charity invested in the club by taking part of the shareholding. This was an unusual step but has opened the door to other potential funding streams for fan groups.

### The Fans Bank

The Fans Bank was a concept that I developed in 2014 and discussed with the then Scottish Government Sports Minster in early 2015. Having been through the whole process with Stirling Albion and been involved with Rangers, Heart of Midlothian and Dunfermline Athletic it became apparent to me that with a rock-solid fans' repayment scheme in place and unquestionable loyalty the only thing stopping the potential purchase of shares was the availability of instant money for fans' groups. My work had me consult with the Scottish Greens on the Land Reform and Community Empowerment Act. As my case work included Kilmarnock (Michael Johnston) and Hibernian (Rod Petrie) the SFA and SPFL made it quite clear to everyone involved that they did not approve of community ownership. Sadly as you will have read elsewhere it led to me losing my job.

Fortunately, just six months later myself and Simon Barrow set up the Scottish Football Supporters Association and one of our first tasks in April 2015 was to write a paper for the then new Sports Minister asking for a dedicated Fans Bank to be instigated that would facilitate such a process. Eventually, such a scheme was approved by the Scottish Parliament just as the Covid pandemic took hold.

As I write this in January 2024 we are in the final stages of completing the second deal, one that hopefully will take one of our iconic clubs into community ownership. The first deal that launched the scheme was facilitated at Falkirk FC who I had worked with for many years to get them closer to community ownership. Falkirk Supporters' Society was the first beneficiary of the Fans Bank after being awarded a £350,000 interest-free loan.

It will facilitate the purchase of 875,000 shares in Falkirk FC, giving supporters a stake of around 25 per cent of the club and small shareholders around one-third ownership, with medium and large shareholders also owning a third each.

### Banking

It sounds like a very obvious thing to say that on an operational basis both the club and the supporters' organisation will need banking facilities. The fans' group will also need to have a facility to collect fans' monthly contributions. Over the years we have found the company best suited to deliver these for fans' groups is Go Cardless who has a track record stretching back to us finding them and using them at Stirling Albion. They then went on to provide their services to many others including Hearts and Motherwell too.

## APPENDIX 5
# What a Fans' Organisation Needs

### Thistle for Ever – Key Elements for Articles of Association

Objectives:

- To promote the interests and objectives of Partick Thistle Football Club (PTFC).
- To hold shares in PTFC in trust for the supporters of PTFC.
- To acquire further shares in PTFC as and when they become available on the appropriate terms.
- To ensure that PTFC is properly and legally governed, taking into account the interests of members of TfE, supporters, the community and that PTFC continues to be a member of SPFL.
- To oversee the running of PTFC as a viable operation thus ensuring that professional football continues to be the main aim of PTFC.
- To raise funds for the benefit of PTFC.
- To communicate effectively with members.

Membership:

- One member one vote.
- Membership open to all PTFC fans.
- Minimum pledge (amount to be agreed).
- Under 16 years of age are non-voting members.
- Membership not transferable.
- All members entitled to attend AGM.
- Three months minimum membership to vote at AGM.
- Six months minimum membership to stand for election or put motions to AGM.
- Staff/management encouraged to become members.

Board Composition:

- Eight members elected by AGM.
- Chair, vice chair, treasurer and others.
- Board members will not be paid for their time on TfE business

- (any eligible expenses?)
- Chair elected by board, two-year term. Any extension ratified by AGM.
- Unless voted otherwise at AGM, chair may not stand for election until 12 months after end of term.
- Vice chair to stand in for chair as necessary.
- Minimum of two board members to be season ticket holders.
- Two-year term, half of board to stand down each year.
- Four members of TfE board will also sit on PTFC club board.
- Aim for gender balance through encouraging nominations.
- (PTFC representative non-voting position – this would be temporary until shares are handed over).

Board Roles and Responsibilities:

- Responsible for running all business of TfE.
- To hold in trust shares in PTFC allocated to TfE.
- To promote the success, financial security and operational security of PTFC.
- Come to majority decisions.
- Appoint representatives to PTFC board.
- Financial returns / accounts.
- Decision to wind up organisation to be remitted to General Meeting.
- Agree to separation of roles/responsibilities between PTFC board and TfE board.

Quorum and Casting Votes:

- Minimum of three board members to take decisions.
- If the numbers of votes for and against a proposal are equal, the chairman or other director chairing the meeting has a casting vote.

Decisions Requiring Unanimity:

- Sale of shares in PTFC.
- Others to be agreed.

Conflicts of Interest:

- If a proposed decision of the directors is concerned with an actual or proposed transaction or arrangement with the company in which a director is interested, that director is not to be counted as participating in the decision making process for quorum or voting purposes.
- Unless this is waived by an ordinary resolution for the specific decision in hand.

Annual General Meeting

- Each AGM to take place within six months of financial year-end.
- AGM date reminder sent with one month's notice by email (or post, to members not registering email address).
- Arrangements in place for postal/proxy voting.
- One month notice of motions/nominations for board.
- Board nominations must be with permission of nominee.
- Nominees to provide CV before AGM.
- Motions must be in writing/email.
- Proposer/seconder must have six months paid membership.
- Members proposing motions may present in person at the AGM.
- Attendance by non-members may be approved by the board.
- Arrangements to be in place for online attendance.
- Changes to TFE articles to be passed at AGM (see Resolutions, below).
- The AGM requires a quorum of 30 members or 10 per cent of members entitled to vote (whichever is lower) to do business.

AGM Voting:

- Votes to be decided by a combination of show of hands, postal votes and online voting.
- Proxies may be appointed subject to strict conditions (signed permission, name and address of member and proxy given).
- Proxy must vote in accordance with written instructions if given, otherwise at proxy's discretion.

# APPENDIX 5: WHAT A FANS' ORGANISATION NEEDS

Resolutions:

- Matters requiring special resolution (at least 75 per cent of votes cast at the AGM): Changes to TfE articles.
- Matters requiring extraordinary resolution (at least 90 per cent of votes cast at the AGM): Winding up of TfE.
- All other matters to be made by ordinary resolution (50 per cent plus one of votes cast).

Extraordinary General Meeting:

- EGM can be triggered by written application (email or letter) backed by at least 50 members or at least 5 per cent of the membership, whichever is higher.
- Request for EGM must state the purpose and that is the only business to be conducted at the EGM.
- EGM must be held within 28 days of the request being delivered to the TfE registered office (or registered email address).
- Notice of the EGM must be given with at least 14 days' notice to all members by email (or post, to members not registering email address) and to TfE's auditors, stating the business to be dealt with at the meeting.

Other:

- Any member is entitled to inspect any TfE annual accounts, AGM and board meeting minutes.
- Develop a joint TfE and club's Fans' Charter that is freely available and is updated annually.

The Co-operative Rules:

- Democratic member control
- Voluntary and open membership
- Member economic participation
- Autonomy and independence
- Education training and information for members
- Agreement to cooperate with our similar organisations
- Concern and participation in the community

## Club Mission Statement

*The shared vision*

The Club and Thistle for Ever have worked closely together in 2020 to develop a joint vision for the future of Partick Thistle Football Club.

Our shared vision is to make Partick Thistle an outstanding community-owned club, playing football at the highest sustainable level.

Underpinning this vision are six commitments:

- To grow the ownership model through the recruitment and development of a committed fans' organisation.
- To promote sporting excellence.
- To develop home-grown academy talent.
- To engage with our members, supporters and the wider community.
- To deliver viable financial performance as part of an integrated business plan.
- To develop first-class capabilities – people, premises, pitches, pride.

The club will achieve this by:

- Aspiring to excellence in all that it does.
- Working in consultation with supporters, customers and the community in order to maintain the highest standards of performance in an equal opportunities environment.
- Following a policy of prudent financial management in order to develop the club profitably over the medium to long term.
- Recognising that in the competitive world of professional football the club must be ambitious, creative and adaptive to change.
- Being actively involved with the local community to ensure that the club's resources are used to our mutual benefit.
- Continuing to recognise the importance of the club's youth development and standalone charity Community and Charitable Trust programmes – information on community activities are regularly published on the club and community platforms.

Partick Thistle Football Club is proud of its heritage and wishes to strengthen the good relationship that exists between the club and the local

## Supporter and Customer Charter

When fans take over the running of the club there is so much to do and so often so little time to do it. At Stirling Albion we had no continuity and had to learn everything on the job. There was very little support from the football authorities but fortunately there was fantastic cooperation from Falkirk FC the bigger near neighbours. In most circumstances there will be some degree of continuity and certainly at larger clubs there will be staff in place that should make the whole process fairly seamless.

One of the important developments is to deliver a high level of match day and overall club experience. One of the ways that this can be achieved is through having a Supporter Charter.

This is a natural next step for any fan-owned club to go beyond what conventional clubs offer and deliver the optimum customer experience for their members and visitors to the club.

### SUPPORTER AND CUSTOMER CHARTER
(developed for Partick Thistle with the assistance of Exeter City FC)

### Key Objectives

Our key objectives for the coming season in relation to customer service are to:

- Achieve excellence with regards to Family Excellence and Away Fan Experience activity.
- Continue to build and improve on our firm foundations for customer service for all fans customer groups.
- Increase the number of opportunities for fans to have their say on a variety of club matters.
- Ensure the match day experience for families with children and all supporters is excellent.
- Retain and progress the SFA Equality and Inclusion Code of Practice standards met by the club.

## 1. Customer Service

1.1 The club is committed to providing an excellent service for all its supporters, customers and stakeholders. We welcome constructive input from supporters regarding customer improvement, satisfaction and value customer feedback on both positive and negative aspects of our business and activities.

1.2 Any comments regarding aspects of customer service should be made to the club's Supporter Liaison Officer (SLO) or our Operations Manager who can be contacted by telephone on 0141 579 1971 during normal office hours, by email to customerservices@ptfc.co.uk or writing to them at Partick Thistle Football Club Firhill Stadium, 80 Firhill Road, Maryhill, Glasgow G20 8AL.

1.3 Once received, the club will make an initial response to any contact from a customer within five working days. If the initial contact from the supporter/customer is in a written format then a telephone call or email may be sent to acknowledge receipt and to establish any further facts required.

1.4 In the case of a written complaint an initial investigation will be carried out and a response issued in writing within a further ten working days from the date of acknowledgement. Whilst initial responses may be in the form of a telephone conversation or an email it will then be confirmed in writing by post/email.

1.5 Any complaints received from customers will be recorded in a register and reported to the relevant football authority as required together with any reports of investigations into the complaints.

1.6 The club sincerely hopes and expects that any complaint received regarding customer service can be resolved to the customer's satisfaction and the club will make every effort to do so.

1.7 The normal procedure for complaints to the club will be addressed in the first instance by the Operations Manager/SLO with the line manager. If this is not resolved satisfactorily an appeal should be made to the chair of the football club. The final appeal can be made to the board of directors. At every stage, the complainant and their representative will be given the opportunity to attend any appeal in person or by written submission.

# APPENDIX 5: WHAT A FANS' ORGANISATION NEEDS

## 2. Staff Conduct

2.1 Club staff will endeavour to be courteous and helpful to customers at all times, offering them the best possible service and information available. Partick Thistle Football Club is committed to briefing staff on key issues so that they are sufficiently knowledgeable to be able to directly answer the majority of supporter queries.

2.2 All members of staff will do their best to answer any queries or concerns. If they are individually unable to answer a query they will refer the matter to their supervisor or line manager and the customer will receive a response as quickly as possible, but no later than 21 days.

2.3 The club has the same expectations of its paid and unpaid staff (volunteers) as any other organisation and expects them to act as role models in all their activities.

## 3. Consultation and Information

3.1 This is a good opportunity to remind supporters that the club's majority shareholder is the Thistle for Ever a Supporters Society Limited (a Community Interest Company OR other ) with company number . Whilst the supporters of many other clubs strive to have a voice at Boardroom level, the TFE has four representatives on the Club Board and is represented on all major committees within the club. No new directors can be appointed to the Club Board without TFE approval. Governance is undertaken through a Club-TFE Agreement.

3.2 The trust is registered as a Community Interest Company (or is defined) and is a democratic organisation, existing for the benefit of the community. Each member has one share in the TFE, which entitles them to a vote in elections to the TFE Board. In turn the TFE Board elects members to the Club Board and other committees within the club. The TFE Board must also obtain the support of its members before it can make any decision which is of material importance to them.

3.3 The club actively consults supporters on a regular basis through a variety of forums. As an example, this charter was consulted via the website and open meeting. Both the club and TFE hold 'fans forums', during which question and answer sessions are a regular occurrence.

3.4 Meetings may be held outside Glasgow in order to ensure that our 'exiled' supporters are consulted and given an opportunity to express their views. Fans' forums and meetings with other supporters' groups provide additional opportunities for fans to raise issues and debate all matters regarding Partick Thistle Football Club.

3.5 The club publicises its position on major policy issues on the official club website, on the TFE website and in the matchday programme. The club also issues information via social media, local radio, newspapers and the Press Association.

3.6 TFE Trust has pledged consultation with its membership regarding matters requiring shareholder approval, for example on issues affecting the club's ownership and the stadium. This is actually outside of the club's responsibilities but one that is of course supported. TFE is committed to conduct an annual survey of members and publish the results in full.

3.7 Our stewards/matchday attendants/ambassadors provide a customer relations service and will be happy to answer questions or direct you as appropriate. Our matches are classified as "Steward Controlled" or "Police Controlled" in consultation with the appropriate authorities. CCTV is in operation at all points of the ground.

3.8 First aid is available by asking any steward or club official for assistance.

3.9 The club's process for banning supporters follows any court, police or legal directive and is sanctioned by the board who will write to individuals to inform them of the terms and conditions of their ban. Any supporter who is reprimanded by stewards or officers of the club might also be banned. The normal process will be for a formal warning in writing for a first offence clarifying the implications of any further breaches of behaviour. A formal ban will normally be the subject of an internal meeting with club management and the supporter(s) informed in writing within 10 days of the hearing. Any ban will be subject to a "back to support" meeting and signed agreement.

## 4. Ticketing

The club gives the earliest possible notice of any changes to its ticketing policy and the reasons for the changes. Tickets for Partick Thistle supporters can be purchased online via the club website, during the week in person at the

# APPENDIX 5: WHAT A FANS' ORGANISATION NEEDS

club shop and reception, over the phone on 0141 579 1971. On matchdays purchases can be made at the Ticket Booths at the Jackie Husband Stand and as directed elsewhere from time to time. Please note matchdays access to some parts of the stadium is by ticket only and they must be obtained in advance or from the Ticket Booth. Collections on the Matchday are held at the respective ticket booth. Note that advice for visiting fans may change based on the particular match and details will be available on the club website prior to the game.

Booking fees and postal charges may apply. Cheques must be supported by a valid bank card. Credit and debit cards are accepted online or for purchases at Main Reception or Ticket Booths or at the club shop.

### 4.1 Pricing

4.1.1 The club continues to strive for wider access to matches by offering a broad range of ticket prices and initiatives in order to attract new supporters or specific target groups. The club also operates a scheme whereby an early purchase of a season ticket is accompanied by a discount.

4.1.2 All people entering the ground must pay at the turnstile for admission or have a valid ticket purchased in advance or at a ticket booth at the ground on the day (where applicable).

4.1.3 Restricted view tickets are not generally on sale, but if requested may be sold at a discounted rate.

4.1.4 The club reserves the right to vary general admission charges at any point throughout the season.

### 4.2. Sales

4.2.1 In the case of an all-ticket game, the last opportunity for purchasing tickets, subject to availability, will be before the close of business, as publicised, the day prior to the game unless otherwise stated. Ticket office opening hours will be adjusted for increased accessibility for all-ticket fixtures and details of opening hours will be publicised on the official club website, matchday programme, social and local media. The club also has a facility for purchasing tickets by telephone or online and details are available on the official club website or from club reception.

4.2.2 The club reserves the right to charge an administration fee for processing telephone and online bookings for tickets for all fixtures. Tickets booked online will be posted out to customers, but may be left for collection by arrangement.

4.2.3 Tickets for 'all-ticket' matches will not be held for collection later than three clear working days before the date of the fixture without prior payment.

4.2.4 The club reserves the right to withdraw season tickets from supporters whose conduct is not in keeping with that stated in this Supporter/Customer Charter under the section 'Supporters' Conduct' or published in the Ground Regulations. The Ground Regulations are posted at entrances and on the website.

4.3. Allocation

4.3.1 For 'all-ticket' matches or games where it is expected that demand may exceed supply, the club operates an agreed priority system that ensures trust members and registered supporters get first access to tickets for big games both home and away. This system has been agreed by the majority shareholder, TFE, and is defined in the priority system rules.

4.3.3 The priority system is regularly reviewed to ensure that it is fit for purpose and can be found by clicking here.

## 4.4 Concessions

4.4.1 Concessionary prices are available to junior supporters (under 18 on August 31, of the current season), full-time students possessing a current and valid matriculation card or proof of full-time education and senior citizens (born before January 1, 1954). Please note our babes in arms policy now relates to children aged 4 and under who do not require a seat. As such, any child aged 0 to 4 years old will not require a ticket to enter a match at Firhill Stadium

4.4.2. The Junior Jags – Kids Go Free scheme

4.4.2 The club reserves the right to charge normal match day admission prices in the absence of proof of qualifying for a concessionary rate.

4.4.3 The club provides an area of the ground for the use of family groups and junior supporters and the club fully supports the Football League initiative, 'Enjoy the Match'.

# APPENDIX 5: WHAT A FANS' ORGANISATION NEEDS

4.4.4 Information regarding tickets for disabled supporters is detailed below.

4.5 Cup competitions

4.5.1 The club reserves the right to decrease or increase the price of admission to home cup fixtures.

4.5.2 Season ticket holders are guaranteed admission to home cup fixtures and will be given priority over the general public for ticket sales as set out above providing they have purchased tickets before the date advertised for those tickets to go on general sale.

## 4.6 Refunds

4.6.1 Refunds are issued on unwanted matchday tickets provided they are returned to the club at least 48 hours in advance of the advertised kick-off time of the game for which they have been issued. Any administrative charges are non-refundable.

## 4.7 Postponed or abandoned matches

4.7.1 If a match is postponed before kick-off and after entry to the stadium, tickets will be valid for the re-arranged fixture. For those supporters not issued with a ticket upon entry, vouchers will be issued on exiting the ground that will enable free admission to the re-arranged fixture.

4.7.2 If a match is abandoned after kick-off, but before half-time, spectators will be entitled to up to 50 per cent reduced-price admission to the rearranged match on production of an original ticket or voucher issued on exiting the ground. The club reserves the right to set the reduced price of admission.

4.7.3 If a match is abandoned during or after half-time, spectators may be entitled to reduced-price admission to the rearranged match on production of an original ticket or voucher issued on exiting the ground. The club reserves the right to set the reduced price of admission.

4.7.4 Tickets bought for the original fixture or vouchers issued on exiting the ground must be retained in order to qualify for the above concessions.

### 4.8 Accommodating away supporters

4.8.1 The club abides by SPFL and Scottish Football Association Regulations governing the allocation of tickets to visiting clubs. The club does not charge admission prices to supporters of a visiting club higher than those charged to our own supporters for comparable accommodation.

4.8.2 Concessionary rates offered to senior citizens, students and junior supporters also apply to supporters of a visiting club. The club reserves the right to charge normal match day admission prices to visiting supporters in the absence of proof of qualifying for a concessionary rate.

### 5. Merchandise, catering, bars, hospitality and car parking

5.1 The club endeavours to ensure that all reproduction strip designs shall have a minimum lifespan of two seasons, subject to the kit suppliers and shirt sponsors remaining unchanged.( this would be a change – this used to be standard practice at clubs and should be something that a community owned club should aspire too)

5.2 The club will display a sign, and detail on the website/social media, stating the launch date of replica kit sold in the club shop. Club staff are also expected to inform the customer of this information, especially in circumstances where the introduction of a new kit is imminent. The club carries out its obligations under current regulations to prevent price fixing in relation to the sale of replica kit.

5.3 The club shop refund policy is that a refund or exchange is offered on all full-priced items which are returned unworn with a receipt within 28 days of purchase (28 days from Christmas Day for Christmas presents). Sale items are not refundable but can be exchanged if returned unworn with receipt within 14 days of purchase.

5.4 The club catering on matchdays is provided in-house with an occasional franchise by special invitation and on a cash basis. This gives the club an opportunity to provide the range of products that supporters require. The catering manager will listen to suggestions regarding service or product range. Any suggestions should be sent to customerservices@ptfc.co.uk.

5.5 The club has two principal bars in the Jackie Husband stand( hospitality) and in the Aitken Suite in the main stand(Supporters Bar). Further bars are available in the private hospitality 1971 Lounge and Ambassadors Lounge. Alcohol will only be sold to persons who are over 18 and identification might be required to obtain service.

5.6 Hospitality is only available if booked in advance. Hospitality can be arranged for individuals and groups in The Jackie Husband Stand . All these areas are covered by an alcohol license. Season Ticket holders will enjoy hospitality at the advertised price minus the match entry price. ( or add discount details in here)

5.7 Our standalone charity City Community Trust also offer matchday experience packages which include refreshments( could be worth considering).

5.8 Car parking at the ground is extremely limited. On-street parking is also limited due to neighbourhood parking schemes. There are, however, convenient park & ride facilities and many local car parks available. Details of car parking arrangements can be found here. There is also a underground stations at Charing Cross and at Kelvinbridge which are walking distance of the ground. Glasgow International Airport is serviced by taxis and buses that run to the city centre.

## 6. Community Activities

6.1 Partick Thistle Football Club is proud of its long and increasingly developing role in the local community and there is a commitment to further this from all sections of the club, especially from the TFE, Partick Thistle Community Trust, The Weir Academy ( add others )officers, management and playing staff.

6.2 The club, and all its associates explore opportunities for increased community involvement and works across the following areas:
Education: helping young people realise their potential.
- Social Inclusion: promoting greater cohesion in communities and encouraging empowerment.
- Health & Wellbeing: promoting health and wellbeing in the community.
- Sports participation: promoting sports participation and physical activity. Activities that underpin the club's commitment to corporate social responsibility.

*Celebrating our heritage.*

6.3 As part of its matchday activities the club offers local and some national charities the option to make a half-time collection. Details of the half-time opportunity for charities can be obtained by emailing info@ptfc.co.uk. Running events are staged throughout the year where funds raised are split between the standalone PTFC Community Trust charity and nominated charities.

6.4 Events are also run in conjunction with or on behalf of local charities.

## 7. Supporters' Conduct

7.1 The club wants all supporters to be part of the pride and passion at Firhill Stadium in a safe, secure and enjoyable environment. We are, therefore, committed to preventing people from behaving in a manner likely to jeopardise the safety or enjoyment of others, or to bring discredit on the club or city of Glasgow. Please ensure you understand the Ground Regulations published on the website and displayed at entry points.

7.2 Anyone attending matches at Firhill stadium must abide by the regulations which are displayed on notice boards at all entrances to the stadium and at other high visibility positions. Ground Regulations can also be found on the club website by clicking here. A copy of the ground regulations can also be sent to anyone on request by telephoning club Reception on 0142 579 1971 or emailing info@ptfc.co.uk.

7.3 If the club becomes aware of any person having been convicted of or involved directly in a football-related offence (whether at the club's ground or otherwise) or having been in serious breach of any club's ground regulations, it will, in consultation with the Police Scotland in the case of an away game, and representatives of the club's Supporters' Group, make a decision as to whether that person should become subject to a club exclusion order. Each case will be judged on its own merits and the length of any ban will depend on guidelines and the severity of the offence and with regard to any breach of the club's Ground Regulations.

7.4 The normal procedure for appeals to the club will be addressed in the first instance by our Operations Manager or Supporter Liaison Officer with the line manager. If this is not resolved satisfactorily appeal should be made to the chair of the football club. The final appeal can be made to the board of directors. At every stage, the complainant and their representative will be given the opportunity to attend any appeal in person or by written submission.

7.5 The Sporting Events (Control of Alcohol etc.) Criminal Law (Consolidation) (Scotland) Act 1995: It is an offence for a person to enter or attempt to enter a football ground while in possession of a flare, smoke bomb or firework. The sentence for these offences can be as much as three months in prison, and in many cases, fans who have no previous convictions are being given prison sentences for attempting to enter a football ground with a smoke bomb in their pocket as the courts take these offences very seriously.

7.6 Flags, Drums and bagpipes are permitted at Firhill Stadium but may be restricted during capacity games. Visiting supporters are advised to contact info@ptfc.co.uk to pre-arrange access for drums, flags and/or bagpipes. The Club will then advise on the latest position. Please note that drums are only acceptable in standing areas of the stadium. Flags and banners must be inoffensive, non-political and be supported by a valid fire certificate.

### 8. Safeguarding children, young people and adults at risk

8.1 The club is committed to safeguarding and promoting the welfare of children, young people and adults at risk and expects all staff and volunteers to do the same. The club has a safeguarding policy which is available to view on request from club Reception and we take our responsibilities for the wellbeing of children, young people and adults at risk seriously. To make a report email info@ptfc.co.uk or ring 0141 579 1971. Children under the age of 14 must be accompanied when attending matches.

8.2 Where a child under the age of 16 breaches stadium regulations and would normally be asked to leave the ground if older, the child will be placed in the care of the matchday child protection officer who will endeavour to contact the child's parent, guardian or other family member if appropriate. In cases where this is not possible or practical, the child protection officer will keep the child in a place of safety until the end of the match. For serious breaches of ground regulations the club may deliver the child into the custody of the police. This decision will be made by the club's safety officer.

## 9. Disabled Supporters

9.1 The club is committed to ensuring that all those who wish to watch football matches are able to do so, subject to ticket availability but irrespective of disability. The club has a regular contact with the Scottish Disabled Supporters' Association and they can be contacted by visiting their website by emailing http://scottishdsa.co.uk/contact-us/

The club's SLO will try to ensure that the needs of all home and visiting supporters are met wherever possible.

9.2 The club provides accommodation and assistance for disabled spectators and their assistants. Tickets should be booked in advance, as availability cannot be guaranteed on the day of the game. Please contact club reception for details of our disabled facilities, admission prices and ticket allocation. The club has a written policy detailing its commitment to disabled supporters in accordance with the requirements of the Equality Act (2010).

9.3 The club provides exclusive commentary for blind and partially sighted supporters via radio headsets that can be used anywhere in the ground. Supporters wishing to use one of these headsets are advised to contact club reception in advance of a game to make a reservation.

9.4 Existing disabled area season ticket holders will have the opportunity to renew their disabled area season tickets at best possible prices and season tickets will be allocated as follows:

- First priority will be given to existing disabled area season ticket holders whose seats will be reserved until the final season ticket renewal deadline.
- Second priority goes to existing non-disabled area season ticket holders who wish to move to a disabled area.
- Third priority will be given to any current members of the TFE or an affiliated group who wish to upgrade to a season ticket.
- Fourth priority goes on general sale on a first come, first served basis.

9.5 Ticket availability and dates of sale will be available from the ticket office or on the club website.

9.6 For health and safety reasons all supporters using a wheelchair must be accompanied.

# APPENDIX 5: WHAT A FANS' ORGANISATION NEEDS

9.7 For all away matches it must be noted that the allocation of disabled tickets is at the discretion of the home side and therefore Partick Thistle Football Club cannot guarantee disabled tickets for all those requesting them.

9.8 In the event that demand exceeds supply for disabled away tickets, the priority will be the same as for general ticket allocations. Should there be insufficient tickets for first priority applicants then tickets will be issued on a first-come, first-served basis.

## 10. Equal opportunities

10.1 At Partick Thistle Football Club we respect and value the diversity that exists in our community and are committed to challenging attitudes that promote discrimination.

10.2 The club is dementia friendly and seeks to comply fully with the Equality Act 2010 by actively seeking ways to safeguard people who have a protected characteristic. We aim to ensure that no job applicant, employee, player, volunteer or customer receives less favourable treatment.

Those with protected characteristics can be found here www.gov.uk/discrimination-your-rights

This includes:

- Access to tickets and other products such as club merchandise.
- Ability to book corporate or other facilities.
- Ability to join membership schemes.
- The selection of candidates for employment or promotion.
- Pay and employment terms and conditions.
- Internal training and development activities.
- External education activities.
- Football development activities.
- Selection for representative teams.
- Appointments to honorary positions.

10.3 The club is an equal opportunities employer and has a Staff Equal Opportunities Policy, a copy of which is available on request from reception/HR Officer.

10.4 The club will not tolerate sexual or racial harassment or other discriminatory behaviour, whether physical or verbal, and will work to ensure that such behaviour is met with appropriate disciplinary action whenever and wherever it occurs.

10.5 The club is committed to confronting and eliminating discrimination of any individual with protected characteristics. The club wholeheartedly supports The Scottish Football Association in its commitment, through the Respect campaign, to develop a programme of ongoing training and education in order to promote the eradication of discrimination.

### 11. Environment policy

The club with its suppliers looks to be as environmentally-friendly as possible. Products used are resourced to have minimal effect on the environment and recycling of paper, glass, cans, plastics and cardboard are all recycled through a registered collector. To minimise our effect on the environment, power is always switched off when not required.

### 12. Data protection

12.1 In accordance with the requirements of the Data Protection Act 2018, the club will maintain the privacy and security of customer details held on record.

12.2 The club has an official website www.ptfc.co.uk and is responsible for ensuring data protection is in place in respect of any user data collected via the official site. If the club were to use a ticket agency to assist with the sale of match tickets then the agency is responsible for ensuring data protection is in place regarding details collected from the sale of tickets.

## Working Together Document

It is critical to the successful operation of the club and for community ownership to work that very quickly a Working Together document is put in place. Failure not to have this in place can lead to catastrophic consequences for the club and the owners, this more than anything embeds the principles of fan-owned not fan-run. It also ensures that everyone inside and outside the club understands the expectations of all concerned. A superb document has been produced by Stirling Albion many years after having major problems

# Appendix 5: What a Fans' Organisation Needs

not having one in operation. You can see it by using the link in the References section or by visiting www.safctrust.com

*Once again my deepest apologies to all the Albion fans for not having this in place when I left the club as it allowed the club to be run not by the owners for nine years.*

## What to Expect from a Working Together Agreement

The document explains the various legal terminologies used in the agreement and goes into details of who the document works for. It will set out what each party (club and supporters' group) has agreed to do. It will also establish how the board will be made up and managed as agreed by both parties.

The agreement will provide the details of what financial information is required by law and additional information that the club owners deem necessary to have reported to them. This may also look to the development of a short, medium and longer-term business plan and an agreement on when these aspects will be updated.

What is critical for this agreement to work is in establishing what Reserved Matters are accepted by the parties. These are important areas where the club board MUST consult with the owners on areas of key importance to them. It could be related to financial loans, heritage (name or colour changes) or fundamental football issues such as key votes on areas such as league reconstruction or other areas where for the democratic process to be working those fans can have a say on the matter. There will also be very specific conditions based on the percentage of votes by the fans (owners) that will be needed to change the ownership structure that is deemed to be in place.

The club owners have the right to adjust or amend the agreement if such an amendment has been requested and voted for by its members. This will have to be accepted by the club board. It is key to the successful operation of the agreement that confidentiality on many issues is established and here an agreement is reached between both parties as to what is confidential and what will remain confidential.

Reference will also be made to how the agreement will be used and how changes and challenges to it will be received and accepted by both parties. At the outset of the agreement it will be confirmed that the agreement is neither a partnership nor is either party acting as an agent for each other. Both parties cannot operate in concert – they must be independent. There will also be a legal definition of the agreement. If there is a failure of the agreement to deliver that its intended purpose (ie a working agreement between a club board and the club owners). The agreement will also look at the severance of the document.

This defines what happens if the agreement is held by any court or other competent authority to be invalid or unenforceable in whole or in part, this agreement shall continue to be valid as to its other provisions and the remainder of the affected provision. It also has to confirm that this is the only agreement in place on this matter, meaning no side letters or other adaptations will be allowed.

It will be clearly stated that the only parties to have any say on the agreement are those who have reviewed the documents and signed it on behalf of the two organisations. There will be an agreement to review the document: this states how often both parties consent to reviewing the document. This is probably best looked at every year or at the worst biannually. But it would be expected that there will be a timetable agreed as part of the schedule. What is also key to the effective operation of the agreement is having the acceptance of both parties as to how the agreement might be terminated, by who and when is this applicable. The document will have a space for the appropriate people to sign and a confirmation as to who is going to be signing on behalf of each organisation (Club and Fans' Organisation).

All the documentation will confirm what applicable law and what jurisdiction is applicable.

If it is for a Scottish club then it is governed by the laws of Scotland and it will indicate this in the appropriate section of the document, otherwise it will be the jurisdiction of where the club and fans' organisation is registered.

# APPENDIX 5: WHAT A FANS' ORGANISATION NEEDS

## Community Ownership Endnotes

A run-through of some of the experiences that I have had over the years. I have meeting notes for all of these and happily share the good the bad and the ugly of all this activity.

| | |
|---|---|
| 2002 | First failed attempt Clydebank FC |
| 2010 | Stirling Albion FC two-year campaign and two years running club |
| 2012–15 | Rangers; including set up of BuyRangers then Rangers First. Meetings with Dave King, Charles Green, Malcolm Murray |
| 2012–23 | Stenhousemuir consultation to club CIC conversion |
| 2012–14 | Dundee FC initial conversation about community ownership |
| 2012–15 | St Mirren working with Stuart Gilmour (owner); pathway to Gordon Scott/fan purchase |
| 2013 | Annan Athletic conversion to community ownership over a one-year period |
| 2014–23 | Kilmarnock FC Trust and club in conflict with Michael Johnston |
| 2014 | BuyHibs set up and development had 6,000 fans before the club created HSL to save Rod Petrie |
| 2014 | Dunfermline Athletic collapse; restructure working with administrator to deliver partial community ownership |
| 2014 | Heart of Midlothian collapse; restructure working with administrator, club, First Minister and nine fans' groups to adopt Foundation of Hearts model |
| 2014–23 | The Well Society working with club chairman to oust John Boyle, find alternative investor and then restructure |
| 2014–18 | Discussions with various clubs external to Scotland: Bath City, Drogheda United, Bury, Bradford City to name but a few |
| 2014/15 | BuyRangers then Rangers First development |
| 2014–23 | Working initial post collapse of Livingston FC and work continues to this day with the long-term objective of community ownership |
| 2014–18 | Various consultations: Berwick Rangers, Albion Rovers, Clachnacuddin, Forres |
| 2015 | Submitted the paper to the Scottish Government regarding my concept for a Fans Bank; finally developed and adopted in 2023 by the Scottish Government |
| 2016–23 | Stirling Albion: working with various parties behind the scenes to get rid of the unelected chair and board and get CO back to the club |

| | |
|---|---|
| 2019 | Morton called in by club CEO after another reorganisation wanted money to help Morton Together to fans' ownership. I gave free advice on behalf of the SFSA |
| 2017–22 | Delivered presentations in Belgium and in Germany on Community Ownership in Scotland |
| 2017–23 | Stirling Albion FC: Working with key business owners and trust members to remove the rogue chairman and re-establish community ownership at the club |
| 2019–23 | Partick Thistle: Thistle Forever set up with Colin Weir, leading to set up of The Jags Foundation and eventual conversion to community ownership |
| 2016–23 | Falkirk FC and the various fans' groups develop the successful pathway to community ownership, 2024 ongoing |
| 2015–23 | Berwick Rangers, Albion Rovers, Pollock FC, Giffnock Soccer |
| 2015–24 | East Fife – working on the proposals for fans to buy a 53 per cent share of the club |
| 2016–23 | Queen of the South – working with fans' groups on potential for co |
| 2023 | Malaga FC discussion and two meetings in Spain with international fans' groups re possibility of community ownership – presentations in Malaga and Marbella |
| 2023 | The Fans Bank – delivery of the concept that I created in 2013 and the paper that was presented to the Scottish Government in 2015 was finally launched with a £375,000 loan to Falkirk FC by the First Minister |
| 2023 | Albion Rovers FC – initial discussions re move to community ownership |
| 2024 | Partnership with Dundee University School of Business for further research into community ownership and presentation at European Co-operatives Convention June 2024. Football the perfect Co-operative and to play a senior role in further research developed with the University in association with the Scottish Government |

# References

## Articles

A22 Sports, website, URL: https://a22sports.com/en/competition/
Bannerman, Gordon, 'St Johnstone chairman Steve Brown says he will be last of family to hold reins at McDiarmid Park', *The Courier*, URL: https://www.thecourier.co.uk/fp/sport/football/st-johnstone/1158212/st-johnstone-steve-brown-family/
Blair, Alastair, 'For sale: where do Saints go from here...?', *The Potent Mix*, URL: https://www.thepotentmix.co.uk/post/for-sale-where-do-saints-go-from-here
BBC Sport, 'Kilmarnock: Fans group offers mediation with chairman', URL: https://www.bbc.co.uk/sport/football/22918055
BBC Sport, 'Petition calling for independent regulator in English football passes 100,000 signatures', URL: https://www.bbc.co.uk/sport/football/57144141
Celtic Wiki, The, 'Finance – Stocks & Shares', URL: http://www.thecelticwiki.com/page/Finance+-+Stocks+%26+Shares
Cole, Sean, 'Democratic Deficit' in *The Blizzard*, Issue 26, URL: https://theblizzard.co.uk/shop/issues/issue-twenty-six/
Conn, David, 'German model bangs the drum for club, country and the people's game', the *Guardian*, URL: http://www.guardian.co.uk/football/david-conn-inside-sport-blog/2012/dec/01/german-fan-owned-clubs-bundesliga
Conn, David, 'David Conn: Bury's begging bowl may not avert closure', *The Independent*, URL: https://www.independent.co.uk/sport/football/news-and-comment/david-conn-burys-begging-bowl-may-not-avert-closure-9161973.html#r3z-addoor
*Daily Record*, 'Buy Stirling Albion campaign starts *Stirling Observer* column', URL: https://www.dailyrecord.co.uk/sport/local-sport/buy-stirling-albion-campaign-starts-2749876
Dowding, Chris, 'Is Money Ruining "Our" Beautiful Game of Football?', Bleacher Report, URL: https://bleacherreport.com/articles/55533-is-money-ruining-our-beautiful-game-of-football
*El Observador*, 'Vientos de cambio en el fútbol: de hincha a socio', URL: https://www.elobservador.com.uy/nota/vientos-de-cambio-en-el-futbol-de-hincha-a-socio-2018429500
Herman, Ryan, 'Why did Ryan Reynolds and Rob McElhenney buy Wrexham? The full story of the National League club and the Hollywood owners', *FourFourTwo*, URL: https://www.fourfourtwo.com/features/wrexham-owners-ryan-reynolds-and-rob-mcelhenney-national-league
Hibernian FC Supporters Club, 'Future of Hibernian survey results', URL: https://hibsclub.co.uk/2014/09/26/future-hibernian-survey-results/
Hunter, Ross, 'Football fan bank launches with £350,000 loan to Falkirk FC supporters', *The National*, URL: https://www.thenational.scot/sport/23558652.football-fan-bank-launches-350-000-loan-falkirk-fc-supporters/
Jackson, Jamie, 'Premier League clubs can cut wages, Bundesliga's Christian Seifert say', the *Guardian*, URL: shttps://www.theguardian.com/football/2010/apr/04/premier-league-cut-wages-bundesliga
Juan, Don, 'Twitter exchange between Ewan Murray/Paul Goodwin', URL: https://www.

hmfckickback.co.uk/index.php?/topic/126220-twitter-exchange-between-ewan-murraypaul-goodwin/

Mutch, James, 'Plans for second Bury football fans groups merge vote', *Bury Times*, URL: https://www.burytimes.co.uk/sport/football/shakers/shakersupdates/23205365.plans-second-bury-football-fans-groups-merge-vote/

Neville, Gary, 'An Open Letter, Medium, URL: https://gary-neville.medium.com/an-open-letter-e5b4749fb50a

*Nutmeg*, Issue 6, URL: https://www.nutmegmagazine.co.uk/issue-6/

Partick Thistle Football Club, 'An Evening to Explore "The Good, The Bad and The Ugly" of Fan Ownership', URL: https://ptfc.co.uk/ptfc-news/an-evening-to-explore-the-good-the-bad-and-the-ugly-of-fan-ownership/

Planet Football, 'Ranking all 20 Premier League owners by their net worth', URL: https://www.planetfootball.com/quick-reads/premier-league-owners-net-worth-ranking-man-utd-city-newcastle

Roan, Dan, 'England "could face Euros ban" over regulator plan', BBC, URL: https://www.bbc.co.uk/sport/football/articles/c9wkjnvpy2k0#:~:text=Uefa%20has%20warned%20ministers%20that,government%20interference%22%20in%20the%20sport.

*Scotsman, The*, 'Hearts administration: BDO urged to consider fans ', URL: https://www.scotsman.com/sport/football/hearts/latest-hearts-news/hearts-administration-bdo-urged-to-consider-fans-1570002

'Supporters Direct Scotland contact Hibernian fans', URL: https://www.scotsman.com/sport/football/hibs/supporters-direct-scotland-contact-hibernian-fans-1528331

Scottish Government, 'Physical activity and sport', URL: http://www.scotland.gov.uk/Topics/ArtsCultureSport/Sport/football/WorkingGroupSupporterInvolvment

Scottish Greens, 'Greens set out plans to put fans in charge of football', URL: https://greens.scot/news/greens-set-out-plans-to-put-fans-in-charge-of-football

SFSA, 'SFSA Benchmark 2017 Survey Results Announced!', URL: https://scottishfsa.org/first-independent-evaluation-scottish-football/

SFSA, 'SFSA Members Audit Results', URL: https://scottishfsa.org/sfsa-members-audit-results/

SFSA, 'Supporter Ownership', URL: https://thefsa.org.uk/our-work/supporter-ownership/

Sked, Joel, 'A question not a statement: Why do some football clubs still treat Scottish fans with such contempt?', *Scotsman*, URL: https://www.scotsman.com/sport/sport-opinion/a-question-not-a-statement-why-do-some-football-clubs-still-treat-scottish-fans-with-such-contempt-3430373

Spiers, John, 'COG Update – 4th March 2014', URL: https://thekillietrust.wordpress.com/tag/paul-goodwin/

Symon, Ken, 'St Mirren plans Kibble charity tie-up to speed move to fan ownership', Insider, URL: https://www.insider.co.uk/news/st-mirren-plans-kibble-charity-21385765

UK Government and Parliament, 'Introduce an Independent Regulator for Football in England by December 2021', URL: https://petition.parliament.uk/petitions/584632

Waddell, Gordon, 'Fans fear financial meltdown but football troubleshooter Paul Goodwin believes cash crises can help transform our game', *Daily Record*, URL: https://www.dailyrecord.co.uk/sport/football/football-news/football-troubleshooter-paul-goodwin-pushes-1782254

Walker, Roberts, 'Gary Neville heads manifesto calling for reform of English football with independent regulator', TNT Sports, URL: https://www.tntsports.co.uk/football/gary-neville-heads-manifesto-calling-for-independent-regulation-in-english-football_sto7951529/story.shtml

## Videos

Falkirk TV, 'Falkirk FC Board & Management Q&A', URL: https://www.youtube.com/watch?v=Ebo93q9U4Lo

Michael Jackson FanSquare, 'Michael Jackson - Exeter City F. C. Speech (2002) [SUB ITA]', URL: https://www.youtube.com/watch?v=-KcmyDPK26Y

Telegraph, The, 'In full: Oliver Dowden says Government "will do whatever it takes" to stop European Super League', URL: https://www.youtube.com/watch?v=rXaFqGis8AI

## Documents

Draft Partick Thistle Club-Trust Agreement, URL: https://thejagsfoundation.co.uk/wp-content/uploads/2024/01/Draft-Club-Trust-Agreement-for-Consultation-2024.01.08.pdf

Football Governance, URL: https://publications.parliament.uk/pa/cm201012/cmselect/cmcumeds/792/792i.pdf

Football Governance Follow–Up, URL: https://publications.parliament.uk/pa/cm201213/cmselect/cmcumeds/509/509.pdf

Later Life in the United Kingdom 2019, Age UK, URL: https://www.ageuk.org.uk/globalassets/age-uk/documents/reports-and-publications/later_life_uk_factsheet.pdf

Ownership, Governance and Management, URL: https://dafc.co.uk/pdf/Ownership_Governance_and_Management_030415.pdf

Rebuilding Scottish Football: A Fan Led Review of the Game in Scotland, URL: https://scottishfsa.org/wp-content/uploads/2023/06/sfa-fan-led-review-2023-06-WEB.pdf

The Social and Community Value of Football, URL: https://www.efdn.org/wp-content/uploads/2016/08/The-Social-Value-of-Football-Final-Report.pdf

Working Together Agreement, URL: https://safctrust.com/wp-content/uploads/2023/01/Working-Together-Agreement-FINAL-Jan23.pdf

5 Way Agreement As Issued To All Parties For Signature PDF, URL: https://www.scribd.com/doc/192787924/179021754-164650989-5-Way-Agreement-as-Issued-to-All-Parties-for-Signature-PDF#

## Books

Hesse, Uli, *Tor! The Story of German Football*, Polaris, 2022
Goodwin Paul, *Back o the Net*, Luath Press, 2023
*Saving Scottish Football*, Tangent Books, 2012
Stefan Szymanski, *Money and Football: A Soccernomics Guide*, Bold Type Books, 2015

## TV and Film

*English Game, The* (2020)
*Men Who Changed Football, The* (2001)
*Our Club: The Fall and Rise of Pompey* (2019)
*Sunderland 'Til I Die* (2018–2024)
*Take Us Home: Leeds United* (2019–2020)
*Welcome to Wrexham* (2022)

# Some other books published by LUATH PRESS

## Back o the Net!
### Why We Love Scottish Football
Ed. Paul Goodwin & Donald C Stewart
ISBN: 978-1-80425-107-2 PBK £14.99

It doesn't matter where you are in the world or what stage you're at in life – you never forget when you first set eyes on your football club.

*Back o the Net!* is an ode to the unwavering love that every football fan has for their club, comprising voices from many different walks of life. The devoted, the long suffering, the hometown fans, the ones who didn't grow up living in the same town as their team, the winners and the losers. All with the same underlying tie – they are dedicated and devoted to the very end.

Whether it's in the back o our net or theirs, we'll always love our team.

*It helps if you've got an excellent band of contributors for a book like this and that's certainly the case with this Scottish treasure. There are heart-warming tales and brilliant anecdotes by the bucketload.* LATE TACKLE

*This book is a reminder for those who have stood and suffered, sat, and celebrated, argued, fought and struggled as well as kept coming back, that supporting is more than just a game. I can assure you – it is much more important than that!*—DONALD C STEWART, Ayr United

## We Are Scottish Football
Julie McNeill
with photography by Campbell Ramage
ISBN 978-1-80425-157-7 PBK £7.99

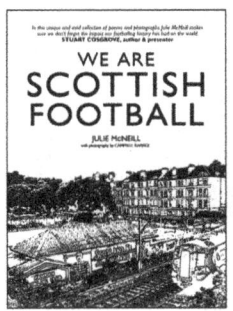

With a pen dipped in passion, McNeill explores the emotional landscape of football, bringing to life the highs and lows, triumphs and tribulations that define the beautiful game in Scotland. Her verses transport readers to the electric atmosphere of packed stadiums, where every cheer and roar reverberates through the pages.

With eloquence and insight, *We Are Scottish Football* stands as a poetic tribute, capturing the soul-stirring drama and unwavering devotion that make Scottish football an enduring and enchanting spectacle.

*A must read for any fan of football, history, poetry and Scotland.*—IAN MAXWELL, CEO SFA

## Scottish Football
### Requiem or Renaissance?
Henry McLeish
ISBN: 978-1-91214-759-5 PBK £9.99

Did I only dream about Archie Gemmill scoring one of the greatest goals ever in beating Holland 3-2 in the 1978 World Cup?

Did Jim Baxter really play 'keepie uppie' and torment the life out of the weary World Cup winners England in 1967?

Were Celtic really the first British team to win the European Cup?

Have we obsessives become untethered from reality?

Are we hanging on to a world real or imaginary, where football dominated our lives to such an extent, that it 'was more than a game', indeed 'more important than life itself'?

Has my natural childhood football environment and each of its overlapping parts – cultural, religious, identity, class, political, intellectual, psychological, sociological, philosophical and, sadly, tribal – created the conditions for distorted and highly selective lapses of memory and reality?

I don't think so.

In this personal and thought-provoking book, former footballer and First Minister Henry McLeish examines his own and his country's dysfunctional relationship with football. Read this book and rethink your own relationship with the beautiful game in the country that took it to the world.

*This is a thorough, fascinating and ultimately optimistic state of the Scottish game address from one of its wisest figures.*—ALAN PATTULLO, THE SCOTSMAN

## Stramash
### Tackling Scotland's Towns and Teams
Daniel Gray
ISBN: 978-1-91214-759-5 PBK £9.99

Fatigued by bloated big-game football and bored of samey big cities, Daniel Gray went in search of small town Scotland and its teams.

At the time when the Scottish club game is drifting towards its lowest ebb once more, *Stramash* singularly fails to wring its hands and address the state of the game, preferring instead to focus on Bobby Mann's waistline.

Part travelogue, part history and part mistakenly spilling ketchup on the face of a small child, *Stramash* takes an uplifting look at the country's nether regions.

Using the excuse of a match to visit places from Dumfries to Dingwall, Gray surveys Scotland's towns and teams in their present state.

*Stramash* accomplishes the feats of visiting Dumfries without mentioning Robert Burns, being positive about Cumbernauld and linking Elgin City to Lenin. It is a fond look at Scotland as you've never seen it before.

*There have been previous attempts by authors to explore the off-the-beaten paths of the Scottish football landscape, but Daniel Gray's volume is in another league.*—THE SCOTSMAN

*Truly splendid.*—ARTHUR MONTFORD

*A great read, because Gray doesn't write about just football, he uses football as an excuse to explore the histories of small towns in Scotland.*—THE SKINNY

## It's a Goal!
### A personal selection of significant goals and what they meant
Archie Macpherson
ISBN: 978-1-80425-139-3 PBK £11.99

## Should've Gone tae Specsavers, Ref!
Allan Morrison
Illustrated by Bob Dewar
ISBN: 9781912147595 PBK £7.99

The scoring of a goal in football unleashes emotions for the scorer, teammates, opponents and onlookers on terracing and living-room couches, that can play havoc with our anticipation of what constitutes an ordinary day.

Legendary commentator Archie Macpherson delves into the heart of the beautiful game, where the simple act of scoring a goal becomes a profound moment of human connection. From the roar of victory to the sting of defeat, Macpherson captures the essence of football's emotional rollercoaster through a curated personal selection of significant goals – some spectacular, some less-so, some not-at-all, but all significant – together with the fascinating backstory to each goal and the match in which it was scored.

With unparalleled insight and passion, Macpherson invites readers to experience the highs and lows of football, a game where so often a goal transcends the boundaries of the pitch to touch the hearts of fans worldwide.

*It's a Goal!* is a testament to the enduring power of football to unite, inspire and move us all – whoever our team, wherever we are.

*The voice and face of Scottish football... his iconic style, confidence and talent kept Archie at the forefront of sports broadcasting, and in Scottish living rooms, for decades.*—BBC ICONS OF FOOTBALL

Meet wisecracking referee 'Big Erchie' as he faces match-fixing, assault charges and the wrath of fans. *Should've Gone Tae Specsavers, Ref!* is about those people who hate football but go along to games to ruin them for everyone else – the referees!

*'Right, that's enough of your persistent fouling, my friend,'* Erchie said to the Aberdeen striker, *'You've got yerself a red card.'*

*'An' you know what ye can dae wi' yer card, ref. Ye can stick it where the sun don't shine.'*

*'Too late, son. There's hunners up there already!'* retorted Erchie. *'Aff!'*

Interweaving humour with a history of football in Scotland and featuring teams from Scotland's four divisions, this book is a must-read for every football fan.

**Details of these and other books published by Luath Press can be found at:**
**www.luath.co.uk**

# **Luath** Press Limited

*committed to publishing well written books worth reading*

LUATH PRESS takes its name from Robert Burns, whose little collie Luath (*Gael.*, swift or nimble) tripped up Jean Armour at a wedding and gave him the chance to speak to the woman who was to be his wife and the abiding love of his life. Burns called one of the 'Twa Dogs' Luath after Cuchullin's hunting dog in Ossian's *Fingal*. Luath Press was established in 1981 in the heart of Burns country, and is now based a few steps up the road from Burns' first lodgings on Edinburgh's Royal Mile. Luath offers you distinctive writing with a hint of unexpected pleasures.

Most bookshops in the UK, the US, Canada, Australia, New Zealand and parts of Europe, either carry our books in stock or can order them for you. To order direct from us, please send a £sterling cheque, postal order, international money order or your credit card details (number, address of cardholder and expiry date) to us at the address below. Please add post and packing as follows: UK – £1.00 per delivery address; overseas surface mail – £2.50 per delivery address; overseas airmail – £3.50 for the first book to each delivery address, plus £1.00 for each additional book by airmail to the same address. If your order is a gift, we will happily enclose your card or message at no extra charge.

**Luath** Press Limited
543/2 Castlehill
The Royal Mile
Edinburgh EH1 2ND
Scotland
Telephone: 0131 225 4326 (24 hours)
Email: sales@luath.co.uk
Website: www.luath.co.uk